PRAISE FOR CONDU MANAGEMENT

'A refreshingly enjoyable read, but more than that, a timely expert insight into why and how the financial sector has to change fundamentally the way it engages with politics and public goods. This change of outlook has implications far beyond financial markets – there are valuable lessons for policy-making at the highest level.'
Matthew Taylor, Chief Executive, RSA; Head of the Prime Minister's Employment Law Review; former Head of Number 10 Policy Unit

'A lively, interesting and very practical guide to understanding how regulators think, and getting on the front foot ahead of conduct risk. Using Dr Miles's techniques to "work risk-aware" makes good business sense, is highly engaging for all business people and is certainly a better basis for effective compliance than old fashioned box-ticking.'
Scott Wallace, Chief Risk Officer and Executive Director – Governance, Legal, Risk & Compliance, Martin Currie Investment Management Ltd; Committee member, Institute of Internal Auditors

'Many practitioners are at a loss how to deal with Conduct Risk, yet clearly it's a vital topic to understand, now that the threat of prosecution hangs daily over every senior manager. Roger Miles is one of the very few genuinely expert sources on what the science of "behavioural regulation" means for day-to-day business practice. This is a great opportunity to gather his insights, and enjoy his lively curiosity about where regulation comes from and will take us to next.'
Donald Macrae, Senior Consultant on Regulatory Reform, World Bank

'Dr Miles has important and timely lessons for the effective management of corporate risk, but this book goes well beyond a narrow risk focus and, with its application of and insights from behavioural science, will be of interest to students and practitioners of ethics, culture and conduct in

financial services and, indeed, more widely. I'd encourage all bankers, regulators and students to read this book, which balances well academic study with practical, real-world lessons and conclusions.'
Simon Thompson, Chief Executive, Chartered Banker Institute

'With the latest shocks to unsettle the predictable and rational world of deterministic and logical data driven assumptions analysis, culminating in our inability to foresee Brexit and the rise of Donald Trump, financial practitioners would be well advised to pick up, discuss and take note of the behavioural approaches outlined in Dr Miles's *Conduct Risk Management*. The tools in here will help practitioners to get themselves "match fit" for managing risk in a world where almost everything you thought you knew may turn out to be wrong.'
Dr David Hancock, Director, HM Government Cabinet Office – Infrastructure and Projects Authority; former Head of Risk, Transport for London

'Finally, a perceptive and knowledgeable view under the skin of what makes regulators and bankers tick and explains what really underpins management of Conduct Risk. Dr Miles brings behavioural frameworks and science sharply into current focus to help explain the uncomfortable, but critical truth of what motivates the actions that have undermined trust in financial services, not just since 2008, but since the origins of the industry. He shows us why strong controls, regulations and processes are just not enough, when human and personal conflicts drive decisions, and how human nature must be understood and managed to change culture in the industry. Only by applying these insights can the industry hope to raise standards of conduct enough to restore public confidence and support a return to sustained economic growth.'
Patrick Butler, Principal, Calitor Ltd and Regulatory Risk lead advisor, FINTECH Circle Innovate; architect of Barclays Compliance Career Academy at Cambridge University; investment banker and former Head of Compliance, Barclays, and Bank of America Merrill Lynch

'I was pleasantly surprised to read *Conduct Risk Management* much faster than anticipated – it's pacy and does a great job of telling the story in plain, easily understandable language. That story itself, about how politicians jumped on the "Nudge"/behavioural bandwagon, and how the financial sector has already written off billions of dollars in regulatory costs, is fascinating. So too is Dr Miles's response: his behavioural lens is of great interest as a productive way of engaging with these developments. The behavioural lens concept should be widely used, and in fields far beyond conduct risk management. It also makes me wonder how we might expect to see the spread of conduct risk management itself as an idea with value reaching far beyond the narrow realm of financial services. *Conduct Risk Management* makes a clear case for action, and for wide application of the behavioural lens, using financial market case examples. There's good supporting material too: the glossary is very well done, with easy to follow definitions and descriptions, and each chapter's themes clearly highlighted. This book should be required reading for every manager or aspiring manager in the financial services industry, and certainly wherever conduct regulation is already in force – starting with every financial service manager in the UK and Australia.'

Dave Franzetta, Principal, Designed Outcomes; former Chief Financial Officer, Prudential (US)

'We're in a new age of regulation, where enforcers are using behavioural science to compel firms to give "better answers" to questions about how they behave. This book does the industry a great service – it's very readable and with a lightness of touch on what can be a heavy subject. Roger Miles has a unique gift, not just of fine understanding of the complexities, but for telling the topic as an energetic story full of real-life, relatable examples. I wish all learning materials were this much fun to read!'

Judy Delaforce, Chief Executive, BP&E Global Ltd (Board governance and regulatory consultancy); former FSA and IMRO regulator

Conduct Risk Management

Using a behavioural approach
to protect your board and financial
services business

Roger Miles

First published in Great Britain and the United States in 2017 by Kogan Page Limited

2nd Floor, 45 Gee Street
London EC1V 3RS
United Kingdom
www.koganpage.com

c/o Martin P Hill Consulting
122 W 27th St, 10th Floor
New York NY 10001
USA

4737/23 Ansari Road
Daryaganj
New Delhi 110002
India

ISBN   978 0 7494 7861 2
E-ISBN 978 0 7494 7862 9

British Library Cataloguing-in-Publication Data

A CIP record for this book is available from the British Library.

Library of Congress Cataloging-in-Publication Data

CIP data is available.

Library of Congress Control Number: 2016048135

Typeset by Graphicraft Limited, Hong Kong
Print production managed by Jellyfish
Printed and bound by CPI Group (UK) Ltd, Croydon, CR0 4YY

CONTENTS

LIST OF FIGURES

LIST OF TABLES

ABOUT THE AUTHOR

Roger Miles is (formally) a Doctor of Risk, researching 'what actually happens' – that is, the contrary ways that humans often react to anyone who tries to change their behaviour. In commercial practice, he advises Boards on risk governance, introducing new tools that sharpen perception of risk and so build trust and protect value thanks to clearer decision-making. His recent research commissions include to analyse and benchmark 'grey areas' within conduct risk, for a consortium of leading banks, at Cambridge University. He has previously managed investor relations for some well-known corporate brands, lobbied internationally for financial sector interests, and run public risk communication initiatives for national government.

His publications include the *Behavioral Economics Guides* (LSE); serial commentaries on risk culture and conduct (Financial Times; Thomson Reuters; and Berkeley Research); and guidance notes on various forms of risk for professional practitioner groups (BBA, IOR and others). His study of the corrupting of senior risk managers in banks, 2007–9, published in *Operational Risk: New Frontiers Explored* (2012), accurately predicted the creation and behavioural agenda of the new regime of conduct regulators, starting with the FCA in 2013.

ACKNOWLEDGEMENTS

Thank you to...

... the private respondents (you know who you are) for allowing my impertinent questions, and for answering so frankly.

... kind fellow-travellers, for insight, war stories, strong coffee and general encouragement. Special thanks to Alain Samson, Brian Harte, Brooke Rogers, Carole Edrich, Chris Stears, Ellen Davis, Hans-Peter Guellich, Jan Hagen, Javier Marcos-Cuevas, Jonny Church, Judy Delaforce, Roger McCormick, Sally Wilks, Simon Hills and Trevor Jones. Any errors, misperceptions and other nonsenses are entirely my own, and no reflection whatever on your greater wisdom.

... my family, for three generations of love, inspiration – and patience.

To my family

Time for a fresh approach   01

Introduction and overview

Why take a fresh look at conduct risk?

If your cost of doing business suddenly rose by 400 per cent in one market, you would probably want to withdraw from that market.

Yet this is exactly what happened to regulatory costs, as the onset of the new 'conduct regime' of enforcement brought huge fines on financial service providers. This startling rate of change has propelled so-called conduct risk to the top of financial firms' list of concerns. At the core of this new regime, informing regulators how to control providers, lies a different, *behavioural* view of how business works.

The initiative to regulate firms' behaviour, rather than just their products, started in the United Kingdom and South Africa but has spread widely across the world. We have seen a rapid rise in the number of new behavioural regulatory agencies, complete with conduct enforcers and prosecutions. Where no such offences previously existed, conduct prosecutors now challenge financial service providers to show clear evidence of a customer-centric approach: you must prevent detriment to customers, and understand and respond to various hidden drivers of customer behaviour, including their cognitive biases. Given sweeping powers to intervene, prosecutors are levying massive fines and imprisoning business managers – as often for *not* taking precautions as for any active wrongdoing. Providers who design products, take commercial risks and sell any financial products must now do all these things with transparent good intent, or face severe personal consequences.

Against this setting, *Conduct Risk Management* provides new tools to help providers recognize, act on, and predict the impacts of conduct risk on their regulated business. These tools are not merely defensive; they also give managers better ways to protect and enhance the value of an enterprise. Realizing best value from this approach requires providers to see and work with risk in new ways, which this book presents.

Key themes and concepts – note

Each chapter in this book discusses a range of concepts from regulatory design, behavioural science and financial services practice – such as, already in this chapter, 'providers', 'conduct risk', 'behavioural' and 'customer-centric'. To help orientate the reader, key words and phrases are shortlisted in *themes and concepts* at the beginning of each chapter. A *glossary* at the back of the book offers brief explanations of key terms. If you wish to explore any of the concepts in more detail, there are also suggestions for *further reading*, with notes recommending why each item is worth a read.

Themes and concepts in this chapter

conduct risk – acceptable and expected conduct – Bayesian – behavioural/behaviour-based regulation – behavioural lens – behavioural risk – behavioural science – Black-Scholes – box-ticking – classical economics v behavioural economics – cognition of risk – cognitive biases (affect, loss-aversion, overconfidence) – command-and-control – common goods – cost-benefit analysis – customer-centric – decision science – derivatives – detrimental – drivers of customer behaviour – econometrics – 'Econs v Humans' debate – efficient frontier – enforcement self-regulation – gaming (of rules) – Gaussian copula – global financial crisis – legitimized – liquidity – micromorts – models-based – Newtonian (risk assumptions) – norming/normalized – operational risk – over-leveraging/over-gearing – personal liability – policy design – predictably irrational – (financial service) providers – proxy indicators – 'quants' – rational actor – rationality/irrational – 'real people' – regulatees – regulatory capture – 'relentlessly empirical' – risk appetite – risk mapping – risk perception – self-reporting – systems thinking – tracking of enforcements – 'what actually happens'

What this book is – and isn't

Along the way, it is necessary to see beyond many of the 'classical' structures and assumptions of risk management – including econometrics and various box-ticking tools of operational risk control – but, on every level, the resulting benefits are well worth the journey. This new, behaviour-centred approach does not merely support necessary compliance with the new regulatory regime; it also builds and defends value, improves an organization's agility in response to critical challenges, and vastly increases employees' sense of engagement with their work. It achieves this, not by requiring a complete change of behaviour, but by reconnecting with a set of human skills that many businesses simply don't realize they already possess. What these human skills are, and how to identify and use them, is a core concern of this book.

This is, then, no ordinary textbook on regulation and compliance – though it does, of course, cover key behavioural elements that conduct regulators want you to care about. Rather, *Conduct Risk Management* offers an unusual and, perhaps for some, unfamiliar route to understanding why and how conduct regulation came into existence. The back-stories of behavioural science and risk perception draw attention to both high-minded policy and low political motives behind the new regulatory agencies. These are not always the motives that we might have seen as obvious, or even desirable, in a public body but insight into them helps us to keep ahead of the regulator's agenda. By getting to know some of the behavioural basics summarized in this book, the reader may quickly gain the level of insight that the regulators themselves apply, in what is a new and rapidly developing field of human research.

What this book is, and isn't, for

Yes, it is…
   … an easy introductory guide to 'good behaviour' under conduct regulation, in plain language (as far as that's possible); introducing real, everyday identifiers of good conduct; explaining where conduct regulators get their ideas from, to get you closer to understanding their point of view;

▶

seeing what 'customer-centric' means in practice; sharing practitioners' own anecdotes about what is and isn't 'good'; a *complement* (but not a substitute) for a professional compliance programme and framework.

No, it isn't...

... a technical compliance manual or framework; legal advice; or an academic text.

Nor am I about to tell you to replace your common sense and intuition with a load of checklists. Conduct regulators don't want to publish checklists either – for good reasons (see Chapter 7).

Instead, they (and you) will get on best when firms self-start their own initiatives to promote good behaviour. *That's* a road this book can help you along.

An era-defining change

The back-story of the conduct regulator's agenda includes – again perhaps a surprise for many – some 300-year old science. As is so often the way with truly ground-breaking discoveries, an important finding by a scientist early in the Age of Enlightenment lay largely unnoticed until mid-20th-century researchers began to recognize its value. (The story of Daniel Bernoulli's 1738 discovery of 'moral expectation', and why this matters to conduct risk managers, appears in Chapter 2.) From that point onwards, and after a series of Nobel Prize-winning advances from the 1970s onwards, the new science of behavioural economics started to become important not only to our public understanding of human life, but also as a regular item in the policy design toolkits of public servants everywhere, not to mention a favoured tool for ambitious politicians with agendas to promote.

For the reader new to the topic, this book also offers a short grounding in the core principles and discoveries in the field of behavioural economics (BE) itself. The behavioural science of human decision-making is a deeply engaging topic in its own right, answering as it does many versions of the often-raised question, 'Why do people behave as they do?' (or indeed 'Why do people insist on doing the opposite of what we thought they would do?'). The primary concern here is how and why that science has become a point of reference for so many of the world's modern legislators. All the same, it is intriguing and – frankly – fun to find out just how far the new knowledge can be applied more widely, with many implications for the way we live our lives from day to day.

In fact, if one had to isolate the single most significant change in how humanity understands itself, and in how we seek to shape society in the modern world, BE would have a strong claim to be that change. The new insight that BE represents is the product of a debate that is as old as humankind: the tension between logic (aka 'science') and intuition (aka 'emotion'). Because for thousands of years the activity we called 'science' was seen as rooted in extreme rationality – with a mission to explain logically how the world works – it is almost as if we forgot that human beings are also *irrational* animals who have always used intuition to help us avoid harm. Even now, it is still barely more than a decade since the research establishment itself accepted the challenge of this new science as a healthy and useful antidote to some of the old methods, with their assumptions that many saw as failing.

We are now, for example, more sceptical that statistics alone can represent a true picture of all that is happening. We seek to know more about the underlying 'vibe' of human behaviour, our emotional and intuitive take on 'what actually happens'.

The advance of behavioural science was given a further, massive push forward when the events of 2008 suggested that classical economic science seemed to have failed to foresee the onset of a global financial crisis. The tools of the old science, notably econometric analyses and risk mapping, seemed not to capture reality as most people experience it – complete with the behavioural dimension of hopes and fears, affect and biases, overconfidence and risk-aversion. For many people behavioural science explains better, and with greater empathy and understanding, what went wrong. It also shows us, more clearly than classical economics does, how to avoid repeating similar mistakes in future.

Not that anyone need be anxious that we are about to embark on some form of dry lecture tour: quite the opposite. In fact, almost all of humankind lives with this topic of debate as an everyday presence in our lives, whether or not we choose to notice it. The tension between the rational and emotional parts of human nature has been a focal topic, not just for new academic scientists, but throughout much of the history of the creative arts, and more recently, plenty of popular culture too. Where would we be, as a civilization, without popular stories driven by the clash between reason and intuition, logic and emotion? For a start, try to imagine *Star Trek* without the tension between Spock and Kirk; or Bertie Wooster without Jeeves; or *Poirot* without, well, Poirot.

Back in the field of behavioural regulation, the new rules may look to many people in the financial world like some kind of advancing juggernaut, bearing down on practitioners who are simply trying to do their best and make an honest living. Yet, as will become clear in the course of this book, strangely and sometimes in unintended ways, behaviour-based rules are also doing us all a favour, once we are open to seeing this. By opening a window onto human behaviour in general, the conduct regime offers us all the opportunity of reconnecting with a type of insight that we were in danger of losing, at the start of the 21st century, after 10,000 years of human civilization. *Conduct Risk Management* takes up this opportunity in its approach, inviting anyone who is willing to celebrate the benefits (including improved business value and profits) that the new method of insight offers. Besides being a primer in the mechanics of the new risk, this is an invitation to participate, to retune our perception to some ways of seeing that it seemed we were in danger of forgetting, after centuries stuck in a command-and-control, machine-intelligent age.

The focus of this book

At the core of this book is a new mode of regulation that has begun to permanently change the control landscape of the financial services sector. Although the new regime is very young, its sources of information in the fields of risk cognition and decision science date back more than two generations – in some cases, far longer. By investing a little time in getting to know these sources, it is perfectly possible to catch up with and even (say it quietly) overtake the level of understanding that the regulators themselves apply.

That said, it is also important and useful for good practice to note key points of the very short, though fast-moving, history of the regulation itself. Conduct regulation in the financial sector arrived effectively in 2013, with the creation and launch of the UK's Financial Conduct Authority, whose principles have since been widely adopted around the world. Within the first five years of its existence, conduct regulation has cost financial providers globally some US $300bn[1], much of this paid in fines to national exchequers. When a new policy initiative produces such spectacular cash returns, it is hardly surprising that the new mode of regulation has attracted the sudden and intense interest of revenue-seeking governments around the world. Behavioural regulation promises politicians a rare triple win: a tax-free way to reduce public deficits; the ratings-boosting bonus of prosecuting named senior financiers who appeared to have 'got away with it'; and that ultimate prize, electoral appeal. For a national government in any country where financial markets are active, these triple attractions are hard to resist.

On the surface, the sheer level of revenues from new enforcements vastly overshadows both the cost and personal liability element of exposure for offences under all previous regimes. Yet behind the big headline figures, a subtler narrative has begun to emerge. We are witnessing the evolution of a new breed of enforcer. Behaviourally savvy, the new type of prosecutor is more interested in how people interact than in how legalistic points specify the mechanics of contracts for transactions. Perhaps most distinctively, the new species of enforcer is a global citizen, willing to travel anywhere on the planet to inject their behaviourally informed insights into financial reform programmes in any country where a national government is striving to transform a discredited control regime.

Conduct Risk Management sheds light on the significance of these developments, as conduct regulators begin to approach the ideal and distinct possibility of globally synchronizing the control regime for behavioural risk. This book identifies major drivers of the current, furious rate of development in conduct regulators' initiatives around the world, and points to where these will lead financial practice, and markets, in the near future.

Major driving forces: overview

Unexpectedly for some, the adoption of a conduct risk framework is not just a regulatory aftershock from the financial crisis of 2008, although this event played a strong part in catalysing the regime change. Rather, the new behavioural focus draws together several separate but long-standing trends in the commercial practices of financial markets, public governance, consumer campaigning and science. Later in the book, there will be a more detailed look back over key formative influences, a look sideways at where we stand now, and a look forward to predict, with some confidence based on a topical research, what practitioners need to watch out for.

For many conventional risk specialists, that word 'behavioural' still jars, as an aspect of risk analysis that apparently fails to pay its dues to actuarial or audit studies. For professionals who have grown up and qualified to regard risk as a phenomenon definable by Gaussian copula, micromorts, cost-benefit analysis and efficient frontiers, the notion of risk engagement as purely a product of human behaviour – of brain-wiring and social habits – may seem deeply suspect; an existential challenge, even. To the dedicated quant, behavioural risk may look suspiciously like a new Darwinian threat to a way of life that, pre-2008, had been peacefully untroubled, insulated from experiential realities and safely bounded by econometric data.

This suspicion among the old guard is probably not alleviated by the newcomers' own behaviour. It is not uncommon for behavioural scientists to regard themselves as the rock-n-roll innovators in their community, who rather enjoy using their new tools as sharp objects to prod traditionalists' sensibilities. And why not? Lately the 'BE' camp seems to be having almost indecent amounts of fun as they rush about knocking over stacks of old economic and regulatory assumptions. Their behaviour rather recalls the early, heady days of the dot-com boom: these days one can find more and more groups of behavioural economists gathering, in online forums and in the pubs and coffee bars of the world's financial centres. The more often they meet, the more the stories that they share gain currency, with a mood that's self-aware, confident and iconoclastic[2].

Certainly, if you meet a behavioural specialist in person, it is often apparent how BE is capable of exciting something approaching a passion of devotion among its many new followers. For its fast-growing band of devotees, their 'BE' is a hot new fashion. Try joining them at the bar at any industry-wide event, and you could meet behavioural specialists from rival institutions swapping jokes and anecdotes about local cases they've found of the 'Econs versus Humans' debate in action. It can feel almost like alternative comedy night as the (often predictable) targets of cynical jokes roll out: the historic failures of Command-and-Control, of models-based systems thinking, of the Rational Actor Paradigm, and of many other now-obsolete sacred cows from the 20th century. (Example: How many classical economists does it take to change a light bulb? – None; if the bulb needed to change, market forces would have taken care of it.)

Under siege from these new exotica of behavioural science, Compliance and Risk traditionalists might be forgiven for wishing it would all go away, in favour of a return to the relatively cosy quant-based certainties of credit default probability and Value-at-Risk. But if your research involved listening to the debate among these traditionalists, as this author does, you would find little cause for comfort. There are still senior bank risk practitioners who cling to some distinctly reactionary defensive views. Recent research among bank chief risk officers produced some risk dialogue gems (see box).

Stuck in the past?

Opinions of (a few remaining) unreconstructed risk officers:

- 'Conduct risk training? Oh yes, we've sheep-dipped everyone already.'
- 'If we really had to deal with wilful blindness and information asymmetry, no bank would be in business.'
- 'De-biasing – what on earth's that?'

Fortunately for the future of the sector, not to mention any chance to rehabilitate its social function, such views are now in the minority. The advent of conduct risk has removed once and for all any chance of a retreat to the old numerical certainties. With the genie of behavioural science now out of the bottle, the regulator has found a magically gifted new friend whose powers include a global reach and popular appeal, and who, knowing their own talents, does not plan to stop for a rest any time soon.

The following chapters will provide a global view of the origins of conduct risk to understand where the new regulation will go next. For many, the value of this understanding will lie in seeing what work needs to be done to put the new approach profitably into practice in their own institutions because, surprisingly for some, where good behaviour replaces the old patterns of opportunistic selling, it is also good for business.

What needed fixing and why: a brief preview

Although a mode of regulation based on human behaviour at first feels unfamiliar and uncertain, it can help to see conduct risk as simply the natural outcome of a sequence of past circumstances. It is the product of a set of preconditions that, over a generation, have drawn together certain previously scattered forces. Real-world developments are now being mirrored by a change in the way that analysts have come first to study, then to make sense of, those preceding events. Almost a decade later in the mid-2010s, from out of the massive sea of research literature examining causes and consequences of the crash of 2008, a set of salient new explanations has finally risen to the surface, pointing our attention towards an alternative set of causal factors that offer a clearer and less convoluted explanation of what went wrong.

It is now clear, for example, that the roots of market failure lay not just in the stresses that were obviously present in trading conditions during 2007–8. While it is now received wisdom that the crisis flashpoint was a failure of liquidity (itself occurring on top of widespread over-leveraging among major institutions), there are better insights to be gained by considering the thought-processes that prevailed in the period before the credit crunch. These deeper conditions – including cognitive biases, regulatory capture, a range of fragile human assumptions based on 'systems thinking', and a range of destructive but embedded behaviours – now deserve a closer look than they were given at the time.

Reviewing this period using the new outlook that this book offers, the behavioural lens, it is now a simpler matter to explore and dispel the old false assumptions. As we now know from behavioural studies, people's responses are 'predictably irrational' when you try to impose a new risk control[3]. In the past, initiatives for risk control were driven almost entirely by a rationale based on cost-benefit analysis. This approach proved catastrophically blind to human behavioural consequences, or in plainer language, 'what actually happens' (WAH). By contrast, WAH is the *starting* point for behavioural economists' 'relentlessly empirical' quest for new truths[4].

This will be explored in more detail in the course of the book. For now, here is a foretaste of some of those destructive, behaviour-blind preconditions.

Over the two decades before 2008, providers' head offices had systematically stripped risk decisions away from local front-line managers and passed them to centralized regional offices. Making this disconnection worse, senior management then separated debt instruments from the original debtors, and in many cases even from the underlying secured assets, bundling each and interpolating layers of derivatives contracts.

Similarly harmful systems-based practices were introduced on the risk reporting front. Providers became accustomed to self-certifying compliance, basing their risk decisions on assurances calibrated by proxy indicators of performance – mainly based on measures of movements of money. The same assurance processes also relied on control designs often premised on box-tick compliance statements, a structure flawed by its method of forcing every respondent to self-report, with a tick, the declaration 'yes, I'm compliant', when the underlying reality, the WAH, is inevitably more nuanced. For a determined few (and possibly a wider many, in the more frequently abused product lines), by 2008 a more complex gaming of risk reporting had also become normalized, as a routine feature of their working lives.

Even where risks taken were purely commercial, and not the regulator's call, some harmful patterns of behaviour had become legitimized, then embedded without question. Notably, many financial products were – and many remain even now – designed on the basis of available funding, rather than developed to respond to a newly identified consumer need. In similar fashion, many poor decisions on risk appetite could be made to vanish, so diffusing personal responsibility, by simply aggregating the separate risk reports from various line businesses into one group-level consolidated report.

How behavioural science took on outmoded regulatory design

The research/roots of conduct risk

As so often in political history, the prevalence of abuses suggested that something clearly had to change and, by 2010, it did. While financial providers had busied themselves with their creative reporting activities, over in the public policy space there were early stirrings of change in how a modern regulator could resist practitioners' vested interests and begin to challenge the sector's heavily defended assumptions. Although the necessary change in scientific understanding had started pre-2008, sadly at the flashpoint of the crisis the science was not quite advanced enough to overturn financiers' incumbent rationales. At first, the market crisis rolled on unrestrained by any behavioural critique. Until shortly after the crash, the consensus on how to do regulation, and whether behavioural insights mattered at all, worked broadly as follows. Regulators, and indeed governments and their advisors in most countries, adhered to three then-fashionable principles of regulatory design.

The first was that, because regulators inevitably have weaker resources than the industries they seek to control, each regulator must co-opt its regulatees' resources to gather risk information:

the so-called enforcement self-regulation model. Despite national governments' near-universal acceptance of this control model, academic analysts had warned for many years about the danger of 'regulatory capture' that it presented.

Also back in 2008, many governments were equally wedded to another long-standing but lazy premise of regulatory design: systems thinking[5]. This approach to drafting new rules accepted without question a form of rationale first set out in Isaac Newton's laws of physics: that when you apply a force for change, the object you are leaning on will react by moving accordingly and predictably. In every-day life that object might be, for example, a physical challenge such as a car with a flat tyre that needs to be jacked up for changing. In regulated finance, the object is more likely to be a trading floor full of badly behaved salesmen whose excesses need restraining. Yet, for all the differences between those two situations, the logic of control used to be apparently the same. Fans of the 'Newtonian' approach to rule design included most of the world's civil servants, commercially employed economists, and all of the financial sector's 'risk architects'. This massive, influential, and largely self-regarding constituency was united in the belief that every human being makes decisions by logically evaluating the options and then acting in its own self-interest. The Newtonians had developed an elaborate research jargon around this assumption, labelling us all as 'resource maximizers', or 'rational actors' – that is, saying that each of us will always look for whichever option will produce the best (most lucrative, most materially com-fortable) result for ourselves[6]. To prop up this argument, all the above professions relied on econometrics; that is, numbers that set out a historic account of how a financial contract had performed. There were, of course, two enormous and (in hindsight) obvious flaws in this conceptual approach. Firstly, that people are often irrational and, secondly, that the tracking of financial contracts is not a very good way to approach the measurement of human values and qualities. Yet before 2008, neither of these major objections seemed to have intruded into policymakers' comfortably rational view of the world.

Meanwhile, over in the compliance space, corporate officers had systems-based denial formats of their own. When compiling risk reports, business managers tended to opt for a version of reality which appeared to reduce any scope for doubt: questions that demanded a binary choice of a 'yes' or 'no' tick in a box. The outcome of this control design framework was to deter anyone who might have wanted to take a qualitative, let alone perception-based, view of risk.

These are just some of the weaknesses in how regulations were designed, back then. At this point, some readers might be thinking that, surely, hadn't 'decision science' been offering an alternative point of view since at least the 1970s? In reality again, although other viewpoints were indeed available, these were far from the mainstream for most people in the financial sector, and were little acknowledged even by financial risk experts. One might even say that any financial providers who *did* know about these research fields were keeping quiet about it – perhaps they saw this knowledge as having a danger-ously disruptive potential of its own. True, there were some pockets of behavioural enlightenment in the financial sector pre-2008: credit card providers had realized that Bayesian Inference (first hypothesized in 1760) was rather useful for marketing purposes; and the Black-Scholes formula (published in 1973) had helped the world's derivatives traders to locate expected price points. But these were not exactly mainstream popularizations of behavioural insight – that would require a new force for change. That force duly arrived in the summer of 2008, in the form of two events.

One was the global crash in financial markets. (More precisely, what occurred was a failure of liquidity, leading to a seizing up of credit, in turn triggering the collapse of numerous institutions that had overextended their credit and/or over-geared financing of their own activities.) Commercial responses to this sequence of events were, at least with hindsight, rational enough and included liquidations, capital raising, de-gearing, and the divesting of 'toxic assets' and 'bad banking' activities. Later on, traders' bonuses would be withheld, consumer services would be protected against the 'casino'-scale hazards created by investment bankers and the public purse would rescue some institutions. In several countries, voters even ejected their gov-ernments, blaming them for failing to regulate to prevent the disaster. Yet in many places, including the countries where governments had fallen, financial firms seemed simply to keep going – leaving many ordinary citizens, and demoted politicians, to conclude that corrupt financiers had 'got away with it'. At a practical level, this may appear to remain true to this day. For most in the industry though, it has become clear that something in the background conditions began to change then, and has now changed irrevocably.

The nature of that change was not at first apparent. Such was the scale and shock of events unfolding in financial markets that many people did not, for a while, notice another quieter but possibly more profound event: the reshaping of how we understand human risk perception. This was because another significant happening of 2008 – at least among public policy and rule-makers – was the publication of a little anthology of behavioural insights, called *Nudge*[7]. Initially this was seen as just another popular science book to read over the summer holidays. Yet the summer break also created the big break for the little book, when UK political leader David Cameron packed it in his holiday suitcase. As Cameron's fortunes rose, so did those of *Nudge*: less than two years later, he was elected Prime Minister. Did *Nudge* help secure this promotion? Tempting to think that it played a significant part, as *Nudge* sparked into life a political fascination for behaviour-based regulatory design that continues to this day and which is now reshaping the landscape of financial regulation all around the world, after the British example. Less than a decade later, the new behavioural mode of regulation has begun to bite financial providers in all kinds of sensitive places they hadn't previously noticed.

What had just happened? How did a set of left-field social theories come to disrupt half a century of market orthodoxy? The plain answer is that, while the markets were busy having their crisis, a small but determined (and frankly, controversy-loving) group of behavioural scientists had found that mainstream media commentators enjoyed running with this new story provided by the scientists' work. To be sure, there is a simple, tabloid-news fascination in the idea at the heart of behavioural science: not the point that human beings are irrational, but that the new science can foresee how patterns of irrational behaviour will play out. News editors saw how they could use this new foresight to predict how a person in any given setting will go ahead and do the 'wrong' thing. In popular culture, the idea that all of us humans are 'predictably irrational' animals began to take hold of the public imagination and would not let it go.

Going mainstream

As behavioural science eased itself into the mainstream of public consciousness, some researchers and commentators began to suggest that this might offer an alternative, and more popularly credible, explanation of what had just happened with the financial crash. It might even explain in plain language why all those financiers had got their sums wrong. Certainly, the explanations offered by behavioural science seemed both simpler and more intuitively familiar than the old jargon of economics – common sense, even, after all those opaque experts seeking to explain away what was obviously still a crisis. Behavioural science seemed to have a homely quality, with its concern to explain what most people think of as 'human nature', that appealed hugely to the general public. And when the public embraces a new way of thinking, canny politicians will follow. In any case, the political classes had been casting around for some plausible new form of risk control to replace the models that the financial markets had just expensively shattered.

From the behavioural researcher's point of view it is tempting to apply the wisdom of hindsight, to mark this tipping point in public awareness as occurring when Professor Colin Camerer issued his challenge-cum-insult to the classical economic establishment, in 2003, with a lecture called *The Challenge to Economics: Understanding real people*. In truth, for most of the non-expert 'real people' living outside the academic bubble (and including world leaders) it is more likely that the act of reading one of those politically challenging little BE books, such as *Nudge*, or *Predictably Irrational*, *Misbehaving*, or *Thinking, Fast and Slow*, was their moment of conversion (see **Recommended reading** at the end of this book). More than any previous piece of behavioural research, even including the three Nobel prizes already won in the field, it was *Nudge* that opened ordinary people's eyes to a new vision of how human beings really make decisions: to 'what actually happens' in our heads and in our daily lives, beyond the reach of wrongly applied Newtonian assumptions. Since its appearance, booksellers have reserved shelf space for many more BE titles.

And this is where several motives for the surge of behavioural regulation, including conduct risk rules, begin to become clear.

Suddenly the new science of BE was able to explain the mistakes of global institutions, not just with complex algebra, but by showing us something half-familiar, if half-forgotten from our own evolutionary past. In an intuitive flash, it let us quickly grasp how a predatory board resembles a gang of troublemaking teenagers lurking by the school gate. By rediscovering certain human factors, the science reassured us all that it is acceptable and helpful to talk about such things in the context of regulating how businesses behave, changing the remit of risk management in ways far more fundamental than BE's first exponents ever expected. After a few trial behaviour-driven policy initiatives for government started to succeed, the potential for BE to 'fix misbehaviour' in financial services became apparent. There followed vigorous political support for the first of the new financial regulators, launched in the United Kingdom in 2013, with the announcement of a behaviour-led agenda[8].

Is something else happening?

However, we should not delude ourselves as to why politicians take on new regulatory ideas. More than 20 years of empirical research and three decades of practical experience, both in financial markets and in the business of corporate affairs, has led me to a certain point of opinion. Politicians always get excited by new regulatory initiatives – which they often refer to at the time as 'clampdowns' – just after some old form of regulation has failed. The event of a regulatory failure is, of course, an event of political embarrassment. Indeed, the history of regulation in every sphere of enterprise is a cyclical sequence of failures followed by a political reflex of rule-making. Each successive set of new rules is usually to some extent expedient: that is, it seeks to overcome public anger and exonerate political leaders from blame attaching to the failure that has just happened.

For any of the national governments stuck on the back foot after the last financial crisis, the new behavioural approach seemed to deliver all that was needed, solving several of the toughest problems then facing public risk control. It equipped prosecutors to indict any person in the industry who simply appeared as if they were behaving badly; and it placated the many voters who suspected that anyone who works in financial markets is immoral. It also worked – spectacularly quickly. Rather than waiting 12 months for regulatees to produce risk reports based on self-regarding and backward-looking econometric indicators, a prosecutor could indict them in person for detrimental conduct. Best of all, one didn't have to set out prescriptive standards of behaviour. The regulator also did not need to spell out too precisely what constitutes bad behaviour. In this respect, modern conduct regulators abide by an old principle from the US Supreme Court, where a judge famously refused to specify a legal definition of hard-core pornography, on the basis that 'I know it when I see it'[9].

Besides these political expedients, the new regulation brings larger prizes in the form of strategic policy alliances. Conduct regulators relish their freedom to make strategic alliances with regulatory agencies in other fields, for the common good; after all, doesn't *every* regulator want its regulatees to behave better? Hence the much-discussed prospect of the new regulators 'hunting in packs' (see Chapter 6), with treaties and alliances between analogous regulators across different jurisdictions, or between dissimilar regulators within the same jurisdiction. Thus, the mortgage regulators of the Netherlands and the United Kingdom cooperated on a report in 2014; the announcement of an intra-UK alliance between competition and financial regulators in 2015; and the adoption of UK-style behavioural regulatory principles by the Australian financial regulator in 2016[10].

Best of all, finally, a behavioural regulator presents itself as valuing the interests of the customer above all other concerns: how the customer experiences a transaction becomes the paramount measure of 'acceptable and expected conduct'. And so, at a stroke, by this regulatory alchemy the industry is required to turn its view of compliance inside-out – or more accurately, outside-in, seeking external independent assurance. This overturns a long history of introspection and self-certification.

Given this sea change in the premise of regulation, every practitioner might be feeling the need for an informed outlook on how conduct rules come to be made, and where regulators are heading next. If so, read on.

Chapter structure

The following chapters will examine the origins of the new regulatory approach before moving on to consider the international spread, current and future compliance hotspots, and longer-term outlook for behavioural regulation.

Chapter 2 reviews the roots of behavioural science, from obscure origins among 18th-century mathematicians, through genre-defining experiments from the 1970s onwards, to its mainstream influence in present-day public policymaking. Along the way, it will define, and highlight the differences between, some key terms that newcomers often confuse: behavioural science, behavioural risk, conduct regulation and conduct risk.

Chapter 3 focuses on the dawn of modern financial conduct regulation, highlighting how market failures around 2008 exposed weaknesses in econometric models and assumptions, sparking the need for change in control designs. It traces the political genesis of the world's first financial sector behavioural regulator, the UK's FCA, looking at how its agenda has developed and changed since launching in 2013.

The success of the FCA and other prosecutors has driven a global expansion of behavioural regulatory principles. **Chapter 4** raises some of the unanswered questions to give the practitioner a clearer view of the dilemmas that regulators themselves grapple with as they seek to exert control. It compares and critiques the assumptions that underlie different approaches to regulatory design; and looks at how financial conduct regulators have struggled to overcome the large inherent problems that face rule-makers in general, and financial control agencies in particular. Finally it shows how, having overcome many of these obstacles, financial conduct regulators are looking to the future with renewed confidence in their own capacity to catch wrongdoers.

Taking its cue from that point, **Chapter 5** considers where misconduct comes from in organizations, undermining their value to society. It highlights nine particular factors driving misbehaviour, as identified by research, and suggests that the new regulators' approach by focusing on behaviour takes a better point of entry to tackle these abuses.

Chapter 6 questions whether conduct regulators are sticking to the principles of behavioural science, as they mount their prosecutions, or if political populist motives are intruding to compromise their 'regulatory enterprise'. Drawing on new research, it predicts the next trends in conduct enforcement, and welcomes the advent of a 'global taxonomy' that draws parallels between the many conduct regulators now operating around the world.

Because the new conduct regime affects every practitioner, everyone wants to know 'what "good behaviour" looks like'. **Chapter 7** answers this need, and notes why regulators remain unwilling to produce their own standards for this, or endorse others' standards. It reviews a range of good and bad behaviours – in particular the 'games of compliance' that the regulator is keen to stamp out – and identifies good practices and behaviour patterns that regulators will approve.

Chapter 8 introduces a new tool for keeping ahead of every behavioural regulator's expectations, and alerting you to the changes in public concerns and political agendas that inform them: the *behavioural lens*. The behavioural lens helps predict and prevent conduct risk exposure. It looks beyond the conventional, operational risk view to provide a fresh initiative for firms wishing to improve their grasp of behavioural hazards. The technique is easily learned, and Chapters 8 and 9 provide context and worked examples to help the reader to embed it in their own organization.

Chapter 9 applies the behavioural lens to a range of current conduct risk dilemmas ('grey areas') and by extension, wider risk governance concerns. Using the lens to examine conduct risk from three different points of view, including the board, helps to open up discussions among senior managers, and among staff generally. This then makes way for effective new internal initiatives to reduce conduct costs and build enterprise value.

Finally **Chapter 10** recaps the key learning points; offers a forward view of conduct regulators' upcoming points of concern; and provides some key points of advice for keeping ahead of developments. Equipped with the behavioural lens, practitioners can foresee the regulators' future preoccupations and avoid the expense of prosecution 'hot spots'. This in turn enables anyone whose business involves making risk-based decisions, to reduce strain on capital (and shareholders' patience), to serve customers' interests without detriment, and to anticipate in a more risk-aware way future market needs and expectations.

Conduct risk: the hottest topic?

The creation of the UK's conduct regulatory regime set off a tidal wave of articles and introductions to the subject. Some of these have proved more constructive and objective than others; many had too obviously a self-serving eye on sectional interests, notably for consulting, legal or audit service support. *Conduct Risk Management* takes a distinctively different, and by intent more independently valuable approach from what's gone before. This approach offers distinctive value as the regulatory regime enters its second phase of global growth.

This book uniquely applies a behavioural critique to regulatory design, which others have not covered, and explores the origins of regulators' increase in reach, whether through inter-agency alliances; personal prosecutions under 'SMR'; or globally common ideas such as bias-correction.

It is also unafraid to raise for further debate certain questions which conventional analyses find inconvenient because they lack easy formalized answers. For example: How do the regulators' private concerns differ from public statements made? How far do regulators themselves really understand how to apply behavioural economic principles, and to map behavioural risk generic concerns onto specific conduct risk offences? Does behavioural regulation have a long-term future? What patterns and outcomes of 'expected behaviour' are now becoming discernible? Finally, the most often asked question of all: in future, what will 'good' look like?

Notes

1 See *Conduct Costs Project* at conductcosts.ccpresearchfoundation.com
2 Eg 'Behavioural Boozenomics' social group at meetup.com/London-behavioural-comms-monthly-informal-drinks
3 Ariely, Dan (2008) *Predictably Irrational*, Harper
4 Thaler, Richard (2015) *Misbehaving: The making of Behavioural Economics*, Penguin

5 Seddon, John (2008) *Systems thinking in the public sector*, Triarchy

6 Becker, Gary S (1976) *The economic approach to human behaviour*, Chicago

7 Sunstein, Cass and Thaler, Richard (2009) *Nudge: Improving decisions about health, wealth and happiness*, Penguin

8 Financial Conduct Authority, UK, 2013 and 2014 *Risk Outlooks*, at fca.org.uk

9 Ruling in the case of *Jacobellis v Ohio*, 1964

10 Miles, R (2015) *The conduct regulators' agenda*, Berkeley Research Group

Behavioural science sets regulators thinking...

Introduction

After the 'crash of 2008', many analysts and economists were, reasonably enough, anxious that their conventional risk metrics had failed to predict what happened. The wider public, regulators and government were at least as concerned that the edifice of public risk protection appeared to have suffered a catastrophic failure. Old systems had failed and new answers were needed.

With the benefit of hindsight, it became clear that we had been relying on the wrong indicators. While markets had been busy with conventional compliance and risk management, checking basis point risk, yield curves, efficient frontiers, and weighted rates of return, a routine hazard had gone unnoticed: liquidity.

To put it another way: Financial providers had been so preoccupied trading with each other that no one had paused to consider what would happen if there was simply, one day, a collective failure of nerve. The risk of a liquidity freeze may not have featured in economists' models – despite its global economic consequences – yet we now know that it fits a pattern of human activity that was already quite familiar to another kind of risk analyst: the human behaviour specialist. Collective retreat is a 'group mind' or 'crowd effect'. So much so, that most people intuitively know about it. If you can remember ever driving on the motorway, among a close group of cars, when everyone suddenly slowed down at the same time for no apparent reason, that's the same effect: a precautionary gut-response, akin to the invisible restraining force that will prevent you leaning too far over a cliff to admire the view.

Themes and concepts in this chapter

accepted and expected behaviour – behavioural risk – classical economics – constructed preferences – delayed harm – denied agency – detriment to customers – dynamic sensing of risk – econometric risk measures/models – economic benefit – generalizability – 'good behaviour' components – group mind/crowd effect – hindsight – imposing – indicators – the 'in-group' – input measure v outcome – liquidity freeze – monitoring of behaviour v products – Murphy's Law – 'normal people' – norms (current) – point of reference – pro-social – rational actor – reason v intuition – response effects – risk culture – risk equity/inequity – risk metrics – social cues – social proof – the Streisand Effect – System I/ System II thinking – what 'good behaviour' looks like – 'what actually happens'

A new resource for regulators

Where econometric risk measures had failed, clearly other forms of risk-detection were needed, and into this conceptual space stepped a group of scientists who had already been hard at work, since the 1970s, on shaping a more advanced understanding of human nature and its response to risk. The challenge to commercial risk officers – as also to government and financial regulators – was to redefine the measurement of risk, removing it from an over-reliance on classical economics and towards a greater inclusion of 'what actually happens': how real people behave, often regardless of what any rules or economic models say they should be doing. This area of research is loosely known as behavioural risk, and within five years of the 2008 crisis was adapted by financial regulators as the basis of what is now known as conduct risk.

The first head of the UK's conduct regulatory agency spoke often about his train of thought in addressing the challenge:

'The first instinct of modern governance is nearly always to reach for numbers in assessing risk... partly because there's pressure on boards to base strategy on scientific measures of risk. [But] there's a danger that analysis replaces judgement, rather than supports it.'[1]

He went on to say that conduct risk is an element of a broader review of 'risk culture'. The money-rich environment of financial markets presents particular ethical hazards for practitioners; specifically it 'creates a greater [than usual] test of moral resolve... [which] has the capacity to weaken the 'honesty norm' in its workforce.'[2]

The regulator's proposed cure for these problems was a simple but radical change: a surge in transparency; entirely new, behavioural risk reporting; and direct personal responsibility, including personal liability, among all managers from the board downwards.

For many managers, the third of these changes came as the hardest blow: the law would now hold them personally liable for any misconduct. The FCA's new Statements of Responsibility require every senior manager to 'satisfy regulators that [he/she] took reasonable steps to prevent contravention'[3]; and holds each manager under suspicion until they can prove their innocence. (In their original draft form the statements held managers guilty until proven innocent; this 'presumption of guilt' reversed an age-old principle of English Common Law that a citizen is innocent until proven guilty.) Either way, practitioners had every right to be nervous.

As the incoming regulator in 2013, the FCA's approach echoes a Judge's conclusion on a banking scandal 20 years ago, that 'Management teams have a duty to understand fully the businesses they manage'[4]. The industry's perception of regulatory risk is undergoing a fundamental change to adapt to this approach, although many practitioners have yet to realize quite how fundamental the change is. It is not a matter of relabelling old compliance processes. Some entirely new techniques and insights are required.

Looking afresh at the human factor

For a long time, economists' risk models had relied on a very old assumption: that any 'economic actor' in a market has a simple motivation: to maximize economic benefit to themselves – usually meaning, making as much money as possible. This view was technically known as the Rational Actor Paradigm. This assumption collapsed, along with much else, in the summer of 2008. To understand the new regulator's motives, it is helpful to drill into some of the economic thinking that informs them.

As human beings, in general we do not make fully rational decisions. We lean on emotions, such as: 'How do I feel about this? Does this offer make me angry?' We have biases, such as: 'What's the quickest way to sort this out, so I can go home? Can't you just tell me the least I need to know?' We get distracted. We ignore many pieces of information – some of which matter, actually. We forget things; often we just don't know what we want in the first place. Rational-assuming, classical economics didn't manage to get any traction over these everyday human frailties.

An economist's 'rational model' implies that people given the same set of input information for a decision will always decide on the same outcome. In practice, real life simply isn't like that. Whether you call it the 'what actually happens' effect, Murphy's Law, or whatever, there's a simple underlying point: people are too complex, too inconsistent, too emotional, and too contrary, for their behaviour to be defined or controlled by logic-based models.

Murphy's Law

'If anything can go wrong, it will.'

If 2008 saw the crux of economists' problems being revealed to the world, it also marked a turning point, because that year also saw a leap forward in public understanding of how risk is conceived.

Behavioural economics' experimenters had in fact been toiling away since the 1930s, and the seeds of the new science had been sown in the 1730s (see following section). Their work began to hit mainstream public consciousness, and public policy-making, after the publication of a book called *Nudge*[5], and its championing by US President Barack Obama and (shortly to be) UK Prime Minister David Cameron.

How to model what real people do

Modern behavioural economics writes a dramatic new chapter in a centuries-old battle of ideas. This battle – between Reason and Intuition – had started with the ancient Greeks, although pre-2008 most people assumed that it started in the era we call the Enlightenment, in the 17th and 18th centuries. It is true that the modern version of the contest was set up by two of that age's cultural heavyweights. In the blue corner was Sir Isaac Newton, explaining the world in terms of action and reaction, causes and consequences. In the red corner was William Blake, who saw the world as a subtler formula of practical challenges and emotional values: 'Without contraries there is no progression: Attraction and repulsion, reason and energy, love and hate, are necessary to human existence.' Not for Blake the simple explanation that we do things because we 'need' to.

Now, when Blake said 'You never know what is enough unless you know what is more than enough', without realizing it he was echoing the work of a man now regarded as the world's first behavioural economist: Daniel Bernoulli (also a contemporary of Newton's)[6]. Bernoulli, a maths professor, had been working to model 'rational expectations' in business contracts when he noticed a curious thing, which he invented a new name for: 'moral expectation'. Being a mathematician, he summed it up with numbers, like this: 'If I play the lottery and win 10,000 ducats, I can't be ten times happier than if I win 1,000 ducats.' He had hit on a rich vein of thinking – so rich, in fact, that it took scientists another 200 years to work out why it is so significant (see box).

Bernoulli, underrated ancestor of the new science

Bernoulli's theory eventually became the basis for Prospect Theory[7], a cornerstone of modern behavioural economics.

The history of scientific discoveries is full of these long pauses, while everyone else catches up with what a discovery actually meant. Another maths-genius contemporary of Bernoulli, Rev Thomas Bayes, in around 1750 devised a theorem of probabilities that was ignored until it was suddenly found to be a vital way to model risk for credit card providers in the 1990s. John Nash, inventor of Game Theory, same story: no reaction for 30 years, then suddenly a Nobel Prize, global fame, and an Oscar-winning role for Russell Crowe.

Fast forward to the early 2000s, to another great iconoclast, Professor Colin Camerer, lecturing at Caltech, Pasadena. Camerer's lecture title[8] is a calculated insult to every classical economist on the planet: 'The behavioural challenge to economics: Understanding normal people'. The professor proceeds, efficiently, to rip into every major assumption that economic modellers have been relying on.

A case in point: To build their old models, classical economists needed to assume that human decision-making is informed by 'complete preferences', 'separation of belief and value', 'self-interest' and 'invariance' of process. Real people, says Camerer, don't work like that: for example, we 'construct' our preferences, often relying on the opinions of people around us. Humans are social animals, often relying on social cues (that is, what other people say and do) to inform decisions. It's not that you economists are wrong, he says; you're just carrying too much old baggage – your academic discipline has blinkered you to new and better forms of understanding. From now on, we behavioural economists have a duty to 'remind [classical] economists how little is truly known about the basic facts needed to shape policy... to complete [economic] theory by specifying... psychological regularities.'[9]

Punchy stuff, and all quite irritating to classical economists – that is, until the crash of 2008 proved his point quite spectacularly.

Behavioural economics in its modern form had been around since the 1970s, but nobody had given much thought to using it on banks. Suddenly this new science opened a window onto how all kinds of non-rational factors influence how we make decisions. True, we may deliberate carefully and rationally ('System II' thinking[10]). Or, we may use trial-and-error. Or we may just make a snap decision, based on 'what feels right' ('System I' thinking[11]). Then again, we dislike uncertainty, even where this leads us to make a bad snap decision; we 'frame' our choices, tuning into or out of various sources of information that may or may not relate directly to the decision, that may just be what's available, or what 'everyone's talking about'. All of which much better explains 'what actually happens' – and why pathfinder manuals such as *The Behavioral Economics Guides*[12] now get downloaded by the thousand.

Fast forward again to the present, when all of this has serious implications, looking ahead, for financial firms wanting to find the measurable components of 'good behaviour'. Because if you have been used to selling a product based on pure economic rationale – that it is the lowest-priced, say – that is no longer a good defence in the eyes of a behavioural regulator. There are new questions now. Does the product suit the customer's life circumstances? Can we reasonably expect the customer to be able to afford, for example, to pay their premium over a period of 20 years? Is the customer still contented with the state of their long-term purchase, years later?

In the plainest terms, then, the test of best practice, or acceptable conduct risk, relies on customers perceiving that they have bought a product that they genuinely need, at a fair and competitive price, and without any coercion. Only one of those tests (price) depends on an economics-based rating, and even then, the customers' view is coloured by their personal perception of what constitutes good value.

What, then, are the most relevant behavioural indicators: that is, what 'readings' of behaviour, or lines of enquiry, will yield the results that will best persuade the regulator not to send you to prison, at least this year?

Causes, effects, reliable predictors and unreliable indicators

The question of 'generalizability' is a big part of the new challenge of how to report on behavioural risk. The regulator has handed financial practitioners the urgent task of identifying which measures of behaviour are reliable. And reliability, as any research student knows, comes in several parts.

To truly represent what it's reporting on, a measure has to be consistent (you can repeat it and get the same result) and third-party verifiable (another observer would note the same conclusion, so it's not just you saying it). When it comes to behaviour, that's hard, mainly because our 'readings' of other people's actions are subjective.

There's another false trail of measurement that behavioural scientists are well aware of. It is all too easy to measure the wrong part of what's happening. A classic behavioural 'wrong indicator' is to measure the effort someone is putting in ('input measure'), rather than the result that their effort is producing ('outcome'). In fact, this is a favourite trick in public sector programmes: a minister or mandarin will announce that a social problem has been the subject of 'a multi-million pound intervention programme', without telling us what if anything the programme achieved. Or a government agency will announce the hiring of many new staff to help tackle some other social problem; but again remains coy about real progress in alleviating the problem.

This brings us to the question of causes and effects, which preoccupies risk analysts a lot. Was Crisis Event B caused by Earlier Event A, or were they just two events that happened to occur in sequence? Is it fair to measure Event A as a contributing factor to Event B, if we can't prove a connection? To say, for example, that 'it rained, so I got wet', ignores many other plausible outcomes and interventions (starting with: 'but I'd brought an umbrella, so I didn't get wet'; and: 'so I stayed indoors until it stopped raining'). Serious risk analysts[13] will always reject the lazy logic that infers that a crisis is 'caused' by a single factor; they will talk carefully in terms of 'prior events', 'associated factors' and 'preconditions'. Catastrophes are usually the final outcome of multiple stressor factors converging over a long time, triggered perhaps by an event that in itself is relatively minor[14]. There are hundreds of historic examples of this pattern. Some stand out for the sheer banality of the trigger event, such as the aircraft that crashed after overloading with champagne for its own launch party (see box).

A fatal champagne party

The story of airship R101's demise is as banal as it is tragic. In October 1930, the UK's Air Minister insisted that, for 'public policy reasons' (ie political expediency), airship R101 must set off on its maiden international flight, despite bad weather conditions, with him on board along with a (heavy) extra load of cases of champagne for his party. It was already known that the airframe had serious problems maintaining lift, and a tendency for the gas buoyancy bags to rupture. The combination of design faults, bad weather, the Minister's obstinacy, and his champagne, soon brought the airship hurtling to the ground, killing 48 of the 54 people on board.

How are we to be sure that a factor *causes* something, in the murky realm of human behaviour? More than this, how do we avoid the problem that people who are being measured, know they are being measured, and will adjust their behaviour accordingly? Behavioural research, and research with live respondents in general, is plagued with 'response effects', where the interviewee 'says what they think the researcher wants to hear'. This can produce tragic outcomes, as when opinion polls' failure to capture the public mood at election time gives doomed leaders false hope. Another, more harmful effect is to generate 'games of compliance', where regulated practitioners falsify the reporting of risk[15]. These effects are explored, together with other forms of compliance gaming, later in this book.

Cultural indicators

When approaching risk culture, it can be helpful to ask the obvious questions – because often nobody has asked them recently. A major failing of classical, econometric risk management was its assumption that people are rational. It therefore makes sense to probe some areas of irrational, yet still 'common sense' human experience. Some example lines of probe question, based on behavioural regulators' (FCA) concerns, are suggested here[16].

Product design quality/process

- How *unfamiliar* is the customer with the product?
- Test how well a real customer actually understands any explanations you offer: Where in your explanation are the 'hotspots' of mis-understanding? How will you fix these?
- Keep alert for any new sources of external critique of your products and services, especially complaints handling (such as: reports from Ombudsmen; consumer groups; angry customers clustering in social media groups).

Distribution channels

- How do customers *perceive their choice* of product?
- What organized sales-side biases skew that choice? (eg commission structures, trained-in 'acceptable' levels of aggression)
- How well do the salespeople understand the product? (Have you ever audited this independently?)

Oversight

- At both product level and board level, can you show objective assurance that risk controls/governance are working?
- How do you show customers that you are not *alarming* them, in any of the ways that behavioural science usually registers this? For example, by imposing:
  - *delayed harm* (short-term advantage outweighed by long-term cost or tie-in);
  - *denied agency* (preventing customer's control).
- How can you prove to the regulator, and customers, that your assurances about risk controls are real, and not 'performative'[17] or 'response effects'[18]?

Reputation risk

- Are you aware of any gaps between customers' expectations of good service and what you actually do? How do you check what are the current 'norms'?

- Even when your staff are not selling to them, do customers see staff behaviour as acceptable?

Fairness

- Is the customers' view of risk and return based on a clear understanding, not just of economic return but of:

  - wellbeing and fairness (personal 'risk equity')?

  - fair charging for service (not hidden or extortionate)?

  - fair balance of risk (not 'rewarding failure', or privileging an 'in-group' at the expense of ordinary people).

- Do customers see their purchases as doing something genuinely useful, or self-serving by the provider (pro-social or antisocial)?

The cognitive challenge: dynamic risk-sensing

Where previous financial regulation had focused on products and markets, the new approach centred uncompromisingly on people; in particular, the customer experience and whether this involved any 'detriment'.

This requires a change of emphasis – indeed a change of direction – in firms' monitoring of their activities. Whether you are a regulator or a regulatee, if you want to monitor *behaviour* as opposed to *products*, there are a few points about the nature of behaviour that need to be taken into account. While the latter parts of this book will explore behavioural effects in more detail, for now we will focus on the most challenging characteristic: that behaviour is dynamic. What does this mean, and what does it imply for would-be behavioural controllers?

As humans, we are essentially social animals; we often live and thrive in groups. We use these wider groups to help make sense of our own life. When we are seeking to explain what some new experience means to us, we look to other people's experiences. If I am thinking about buying a new coat, or a new car, I look around at what other people are wearing, or driving, as I make up my mind. But here's an important point about that process of social sense-making: the range of possible coats, or cars, that I fancy buying will to a great extent depend on what other people I know wear, and drive. Makers of coats, cars, and indeed everything else, will seek to persuade me through advertising, social media and so on, that 'people like me' are wearing, or driving, their product. The process of looking around for comfort about those people like me is the essence of social proof. And here is where, for a new regulator in particular, things get difficult.

While the regulatory urge to control behaviour is quite under-standable, as a practical challenge it becomes harder the more closely you consider it. This is because our behaviour is constantly changing, with age, with the activities we are doing and the people we are seeing, as new influences come into our lives and old ones leave. So, for example, the car I drove when I was 18 years old, and hanging out with other 18-year-olds, was not at all the same car that I aspire to as a fiftysomething father of three. Come to that, the car I actually drive, as a practically minded fiftysomething family man and behav-ioural analyst, is not necessarily the car that I'd aspire to drive if I did not have my current personal or professional arrangements. Then again, even if my life were different, and I wanted to behave like an unencumbered playboy, would I actually want to be seen driving some of the cars that are marketed to that demographic? The extraordinary success of programmes such as *Top Gear*, or indeed the whole media industry directed at wannabe buyers of cars, homes, clothes, food or whatever, shows just how much of our time we like to spend engaging with social proof – casting around for other people's opinions and experiences of 'what worked' for them.

As this shows, as a consumer nobody is a fixed point of reference. Our needs are constantly changing, in response to at least four factors. (There are of course many more subcategories, and a whole marketing industry to debate endlessly the topics of consumer category boundaries, demographics, and so on.)

Reference points that inform our changes of outlook

- Age
- Home and family situation
- Work colleagues and employer organization
- (Chosen) social life

First of the four, we change our outlook as we *age*. As with the car example above, the stuff we like and want in our lives at 18 is not the stuff we like at 30, 50, 70. This is clearly true of financial product consumers: at even the most basic level of product need, the school leaver's priorities (simple banking, student loan) are evidently different from the middle-aged family's (mortgage, savings), and different again from the retiree's (pension). These are of course oversimplified examples, just to make a basic point.

Extending that point, we also change our outlook, behaviour and needs according to our *home and family setting*. Young children will tend to care rather more about favourite toys than their future career; what's 'cool' to teenagers suddenly becomes a lot less so as they become young adults; when setting up home with a significant other, priorities often change again, and so on. As another example, it has been said that the difference between parents and everyone else is as significant as the difference between genders – albeit that in the modern age notions of 'family unit', as with notions of gender, are often somewhat more fluid.

The next point of changing influence is *who we work with*. Again as a child the answer is straightforward enough: our view of what's normal behaviour is strongly influenced by school classmates, who these days are also often the first reference in social media space; and to some extent by teachers. Later, in the employment marketplace, we will tend to seek work that as far as possible reflects our view of ourselves and our skills and talents; on arrival in a job one of the first things we generally do is look around to see how other employees behave, and adjust our own behaviour accordingly. Again somewhat obviously, people who want to work as librarians are unlikely to have the same outlook on life as people who want to work as

Eurobond traders. On arrival at work, the librarians are likely to behave quite differently from the traders – in tolerance for noise levels, for a start. But there's one final factor that may make the behaviour of the librarians and the traders more similar than their career choices might suggest.

That final factor is *social life*. It is perfectly possible that the librarians and the dealers might find themselves attending, say, the same pub quiz, the same sports club, the same gig; or even the same charity parachute jump. This is because what we choose to do in our leisure time does not necessarily take the same behavioural pattern as our work time. To some extent, it is not dependent on our age or family/home setting either: plenty of families have one or more members who engage in dangerous sports, for example, even though the presumption (not least by sponsors) is that this is an activity preferred by footloose teenagers and young adults.

The point of all four factors is that they shape, throughout our lives, our view of what is *accepted* and *expected* behaviour in each setting. As we age, and as the people we interact with in our family/home, work and social lives change, so our own views change in response. How and why we need to deal with this in a regulated commercial setting forms the core of the second half of this book.

Conclusion

Now that the regulator has made it vital for firms to track their behaviour, providers need to pre-empt the wrong kind of regulatory attention. But assessing behaviour is not the same as internal auditing: you cannot objectively observe yourself, any more than you can plausibly declare yourself to have 'perfect ethics', or assess your own behavioural biases. You cannot even objectively assess the behaviour of your team – because they are already biased by being *your* team; whether you hired, or joined them, your own outlook is partly a function of their collective view. As an assessor of potentially risky behaviour, you also cannot directly question people's behaviour (theirs, or indeed your own) without creating response effects (the way people tend to offer the answer that they think is expected by the questioner).

All in all, then, when it comes to behaviour in general, and conduct risk in particular, we need to find a new approach to measuring risks and setting tolerances.

A number of new activities and forms of indicator are necessary. They include buying in independent, external studies of attitudes and behaviour; and noting carefully any gaps that these reveal, between your public claims of good behaviour (especially by optimistic senior managers) and customers' real experiences. Self-certification of good behaviour was never credible, on common-sense grounds. Looking ahead, we should expect conduct regulators to reward firms who present well-researched, truly objective studies of how their employees behave. There will be welcome recognition, and potentially massive savings in compliance budgets, for firms who get this right. But while the definition of 'what good behaviour looks like', in a technical conduct-risk sense, remains undecided, it is up to practitioners to take the initiative; the rest of this book offers one such initiative for keeping the regulator content.

Notes

1 Martin Wheatley, Chief Executive of the FCA, *Speech to ResPublica Vocational Banking conference*, London, 27 June 2015

2 Ibid

3 Ibid

4 From the English Law Lords' ruling on the Leeson affair, 1995. (See Chapter 8); see also www.telegraph.co.uk/finance/newsbysector/ banksandfinance/11427501/Barings-the-collapse-that-erased-232-years-of-history.html

5 Sunstein and Thaler (2008)

6 Bernoulli, D (1738) *Exposition of a New Theory on the Measurement of Risk (Specimen Theoriae Novae de Mensura Sortis)*, St Petersburg Imperial Academy

7 Kahneman and Tversky (1979)

8 Camerer, Colin, at econpapers.repec.org/article/fipfedbcp/ y_3a2003_3ai_3ajun_3an_3a48_3ax_3a1.htm

9 From Camerer, C *The Behavioral Challenge to Economics: Understanding normal people*, Caltech, Pasadena, 4 June 2003

10 Kahneman, Daniel (2011) *Thinking, Fast and Slow* model: System I is the fast intuitive, 'snap-decision' mental approach to decision-making; System II takes time while it evaluates the pros and cons.

11 Kahneman, ibid

12 At www.behavioraleconomics.com

13 Whose ranks notably don't include tabloid journalists

14 See Thomson Reuters infographic, July 2015: *What Just Happened?*

15 Bevan, Gwyn and Hood, Christopher (2006) *What's Measured Is What Matters*, Public Administration, 84 (3)

16 Using the FCA's initial five Conduct pillars (*Risk Outlook 2014*) as a starting point.

17 This is essentially just behavioural science jargon for 'looking busy, but doing no real work of any value'.

18 See note on 'knowing you're being measured', above. 'Response effects' is just a social science jargon phrase for 'doing what the questioner seems to want me to do'. In a famous experiment by Stanley Milgram (1974), many respondents were willing to electrocute people, without question, because 'the Professor expected us to'.

The onset of financial conduct regulation 03

Introduction: a real-world shock

The arrival of a crisis has been described as a form of 'abrupt and brutal audit' of your corporate defences[1]. So it happened in late summer of 2008, when after a year of increasing uncertainty in financial markets, several big banks found themselves unable to sustain liquidity – that is, other banks were no longer willing to trade with them, believing them unable to pay their trading debts. The problem with a liquidity squeeze is that it soon becomes a self-fulfilling prediction, as more and more players in a market decide to withdraw from trading, so that everything slows down and eventually stops. At that point, the prices that traders previously regarded as 'normal' in a market will go into free fall, as no one has the confidence to bid optimistically. So often, rising markets have been driven by optimism alone. Loss of confidence brings loss of value; two anxieties then feed off one another as the market spirals down.

The people charged with regulating markets can have a tough job even when those markets are steady or rising; when a market drops suddenly, the assumption that most regulators have to make, that their controls help to maintain markets in a steady state, starts to look thin. Indeed, the assumption fails. It is a sadly common feature of regulatory design in many sectors that the controls are so arranged as to function optimally when the activities being controlled are running smoothly; although the regulator may itself impose 'stress-testing' on market participants, curiously the stress tests do not apply to the regulator's own framing of regulations.

Themes and concepts in this chapter

abuses – apportioned responsibility – behavioural lens – benchmarks – black-letter law – business culture – capital adequacy – client assets – cognitive bias – conduct costs – conflicts of interest – confusion marketing – corporate social responsibility (CSR) – delusional – drivers of risk – due skill and care – enforcement against inaction – external trust – fair outcomes – financial capability – framing – information asymmetry – inherent risks – joined-up (risk management) – knowledge certainty – liquidity squeeze – mental accounting – optimism bias – overconfidence – over-extrapolating – patterns of demand – preferences and beliefs – present bias – principles-based v outcomes-based regulation – product lifecycle – projection bias – reference-dependence – regret – regulatory design – risk appetite – risk governance – rules-of-thumb – Senior Managers Regime (SMR) – Skilled Persons Review (Section 166 notice) – social influences – stakeholders – steady-state assumption – stress tests/stress-testing – three lines of defence – 'tone at the top' fallacy – treating customers fairly ('TCF') initiative – unfairness – unrealistic expectations – volatility – watchdogs – weak/failed assumptions – yield

The new control challenges

In this historic context, and the control design context of weak assumptions about steady-state markets, when the world's markets actually did fail comprehensively in 2008, regulators and their political masters found themselves facing a number of challenges. In particular, they faced a sharp rise in public distrust – of politicians, regulators and financial markets – and a pressing demand for a change of regulatory landscape. In the politicians' own jargon: regulation needed a new narrative. Market failure had exposed as fallacy many of the assumptions that regulators and market-makers had relied upon. Among these, that financial indicators (such as asset prices, yields and volatility) give a thorough picture of the mood of a market; that the greater the volume of data available, the better the quality of decisions that traders will make; and that the ethical quality of a business is mainly determined by the 'tone at the top' – the announcements and signals that a board gives out to the world. Within five years after the crash, the new science of behavioural economics had disproved all these assumptions and more.

All of which raised one main question in everybody's minds: What was it that most needed changing to stop such a meltdown from recurring and to keep savings safe, markets moving and homeowners soundly in their houses? Chapters 4 to 6 will explore in more detail the underlying theories of regulation, behavioural economics and the political machinations that combined to create a new UK 'behavioural financial regulator' – an initiative shortly copied by other countries around the world. For the present, this chapter will consider the more straightforward genesis of the new regulator in terms of how it came to be founded, and the practical steps then taken to address the main abuses seen.

The 'invention' of conduct risk: wider antecedents

The term that is now used to embrace controls over all areas of ethical behaviour and fair treatment of customers is conduct regulation. This became the catch-all phrase following the launch of a new regulator whose name announced that it was explicitly tasked with controlling behaviour, the Financial Conduct Authority (FCA), in 2013. However, the notion of desirable and required conduct, and the need for a regulatory steer towards this, had existed long before.

Many fields of professional, commercial and public-sector practice have had conduct requirements for ages. Lawyers and doctors, for example, swear to uphold good conduct as a condition of receiving their professional licences. Military personnel may be dismissed for the summary offence of 'conduct unbecoming an officer'. Yet while many of the subgroups of financial service practitioners had their own Codes of Conduct, often directing how to behave in relation to certain types of customers or their professional peers, there was no overarching set of defined practices that constituted good conduct generally.

What *had* existed was a series of initiatives sponsored by earlier regulators, to direct practitioners towards greater awareness of the impact that their activities ultimately made on customers. This is an oddly counterintuitive thing to have to do, one would have thought: Why would any customer service industry need to be told how to serve its customers? Most industries survive *only* by maintaining a keen awareness of how best to serve customers; indeed, history is littered with examples of big commercial names who had failed because they had not managed to change with the times and accommodate new patterns of customer demand.

It is clear that as a sector, financial services had managed to a great extent to avoid such direct commercial pressures on its continued existence. Some of the reasons for this are more fully explored in Chapter 5, but for now it is enough to note that, over many generations, service providers had generally succeeded in shamelessly taking advantage of the anxiety and ignorance that many consumers felt when having to deal with money matters. Over preceding centuries the classical model of financial marketing had been: engineer a product by identifying a source of funds; package the product in the provider's livery; then push it towards customers. This process rarely if ever involved any reference to customers' real-world needs or concerns (other than the simple needs to save or to make a purchase).

Direct antecedents: 'TCF' and friends

Twelve years before the FCA, and indeed seven years before the financial crash, an earlier regulator (the Financial Services Authority, FSA) set off a train of thought by publishing a discussion paper provocatively called *Treating customers fairly after point of sale*[2]. By treating customers fairly, the regulator floated the radical notion that perhaps everyone might be persuaded to behave better in provision of products, if we could only get away from our mindless following of ever more prescriptive rules. Indeed, a well-behaved market might be expected to need significantly fewer rules, since everyone would have an intuitive sense of what good behaviour consists of. Helpfully, the FSA proposed some core notions of what 'fairness' should mean, and some circumstances in which 'unfairness' might be seen to have occurred. These included customers being fuddled by providers' jargon and 'confusion marketing'; having unrealistic expectations raised; lack of information as a long-term product ran its course; and poor handling of complaints[3].

Meanwhile, the FSA continued to reflect on its own role in trying to make things better, generically, for consumers. Because of providers' history of taking advantage of (and indeed creating) customer confusion, by 2004 the regulator had begun to consider promoting steps to give customers a clearer view of what to expect, and to be able to compare the service they were getting with the service they might receive if they shopped around a bit. The premise of the study[4] is itself, again, revealing: that while many customers might be receiving poor service but were unaware of it, many more were aware that the service was poor but did not think it was worth shopping around, since providers are 'all the same' – meaning, all as bad as each other.

The same study proposed a new way for the regulator to look at products, as having a 'lifecycle'. Product lifecycles ran from inception (design and governance) through target marketing and promotion, sales and advice, and on into after-sales and complaints handling. In judging whether customers were treated fairly throughout the lifecycle, the regulator proposed to use a set of principles, or more precisely a 'principles-based approach' towards determining 'what is fair in each particular set of circumstances'. Following a wider principle of law – later also adopted into behavioural economics – he acknowledged that there is a low practical limit to the range of circumstances that fixed rules should attempt to address. In a policy adhered to by every financial regulator since, he also refused to be drawn to issue a 'definition of fairness'. Despite nearly every provider asking the FSA then, and still asking the FCA and others now, there was, and remains, no single core authoritative statement of 'what good behaviour looks like'.

But the FSA was making a thoughtful point of jurisprudence, and about human nature. Fixed rule systems, of course, offer great comfort to a compliance specialist or lawyer; their so-called black-letter law is much easier to apply, and more defensible than a personal value judgement. (This topic is so important to understanding behavioural regulation that it will get a whole chapter to itself: the limitations of fixed rule systems, as an inherent problem of regulation, are further discussed in Chapter 4.)

For now, we can simply note that rules fail for a range of reasons, most often because they are inflexible and unrealistically rational. That is, since fixed rules cannot adapt to accommodate rapid change as an unforeseen situation arises, or they may just appear pointless when narrowly applied regardless of wider circumstances, many rules can fall quickly into public contempt. We are all familiar with situations where public bodies appear 'out of touch' or 'not getting it'. It is to the FSA's credit that they attempted to tackle this core conceptual problem of regulatory design, nearly a decade before it was better resolved by a new regulator (FCA) adopting the behavioural approach that was later to become politically fashionable.

Besides setting out a general requirement to treat customers fairly, the original FSA principles called for integrity, good information, fair and clear communication, not to mislead, and to exercise care when giving judgement-based consumer advice. The principles were shortly converted into a set of customer outcomes that the regulator expected to see: the advent of outcomes-focused regulation that was, in turn, to morph into conduct risk when the new regulator took over. The original (FSA era) outcomes were, in summary:

- customers observably confident that the provider valued fair dealing;
- products designed and targeted only against clear consumer need;
- a flow of good information maintained;
- advice given appropriately and sensitively;
- product performance honesty presented;
- ease of making complaints or switching products.

Critically for the future of what was to become conduct regulation, the FSA suggested that this initiative aspired to encourage providers to realign their business objectives towards indicators of good customer care, and away from mere profitability. More, it dared to ask for firms' 'behaviour... to change to adjust to this shift in emphasis'[5].

A conduct-specific regulator

There was, of course, a strong clue in the title given to the new regulator: it was to be an authority overseeing financial providers' *conduct*. In view of all that had gone before – see the preceding section – at its statutory launch in April 2013, the Financial Conduct Authority (FCA) had some strong pre-existing material to draw on. The FCA set out to maintain three standing (statutory) duties, beneath the over-arching aim to make markets function well: protection of consumers; the integrity of the UK financial system; and effective competition.

The FCA lost no time in honing the definitions and scope of those whose interests it defended, and whose activities it would control. For example, there was a newly clear demarcation between simple retail (high street) customers, retail investors and wholesale product users. The regulator also republished its predecessor's principles, but now extended these to 21: a set of 11 Principles for Business and a further 10 Supervision Principles. It is worth being familiar with these, not only because (as they are brief) they are quite easy to remember, but because they inform so many of the regulator's initiatives and publications – including, for our purposes here, all conduct-related initiatives.

FCA Principles for Business (summarized)

A firm must[6]:

1 Conduct its business with integrity.

2 Conduct its business with due skill, care and diligence.

3 Organize and control its affairs reasonably and effectively, with adequate risk management systems.

4 Maintain prudent, adequate financial resources.

5 Observe proper standards of market conduct.

6 Pay due regard to customers' interests and treat customers fairly.

7 Pay due regard to clients' information needs, communicating with clients in a way that is fair, clear and not misleading.

8 Manage conflicts of interest fairly, between itself, any customer, and other clients.

9 To sustain customer trust, ensure the suitability of advice and discretionary decisions for any customer who is entitled to rely upon its judgement.

10 Arrange adequate protection for client assets when responsible for them.

11 Relate to regulators in an open and cooperative way, appropriately disclosing anything of which the regulator would reasonably expect notice.

FCA Supervision Principles (summarized)

1 Ensure fair outcomes for consumers and markets.

2 Be forward-looking, pre-empting potential risks before any serious impact.

3 Focus on big issues; the causes of problems with significant impact on FCA objectives.

4 Take a judgement-based approach, looking to achieve the right outcomes.

5 Ensure firms act in the right spirit, to consider customer and market impact, not just compliance.

6 Examine how business models and culture affect consumer and market outcomes; how the way that a firm makes money drives its risk-taking.

7 Emphasize individual accountability, holding senior managers personally responsible.

8 Be robust when things go wrong – ensuring problems are fixed, consumers protected and compensated, poor behaviour (and its causes) rectified.

9 Communicate openly so that everyone understands the issues they face.

10 Have a joined-up approach, making messages consistent between the various regulators.

One of several striking features of the new regulator has been its readiness to prosecute firms for *failing* to adhere to the principles – that is, many have been fined for the *non-event* of creating a control. This suggests that it is useful to review the original principles for the way in which, in the years since 2013, we have observed the regulator applying them in practice.

The conduct link to operational risk

The FCA also appreciated from the outset that much of the pre-existing work done by firms to control their people and processes could be retrofitted into the new 'conduct space'. During its first year of operations the regulator developed through a series of *Conduct Risk Outlook* papers an approach that explicitly links its supervision role with various extant operational control layers. These are summarized here:

- The regulator proactively checks a firm's business model and strategy setting, to identify potential risks to customers or market integrity.

- It also examines each firm's culture, since this both reflects and conditions how every single employee feels able to behave. Culture sets the tone as to which behaviours a firm promotes and rewards.

- The regulator will find out whether a firm's front-line business processes, from product design through to complaint handling, are designed to give customers what they need and expect.

- The firm will need to show how its systems and controls have been made and are effective to identify and deal with conduct risks (and to prevent money laundering).

- The regulator will watch closely to see how the firm's risk governance (board and committees) ensures that everyone implements customer and market-focused values (see Chapter 9).

The way that the new regulator spelled out these points also echoed its underlying faith in an existing approach to the control of operational risks called Three Lines of Defence (see box, for any reader unfamiliar with these conventions).

The Three Lines of Defence approach

The first defensive line is operational management; these are the managers in the day-to-day running of the business, who maintain internal controls that identify, assess, manage and mitigate risks. Their involvement in managing risk is effective because they are often the ones who can see what is actually happening, at the sharp end of the business.

▶

> The second line is the dedicated specialists in risk and compliance, whose job it is to help the first-line 'risk owners' to see how their local risk-taking sits in the context of the wider organization, providing them with frameworks and goals, helping to develop generic control processes, giving alerts of topical issues, and setting the organization's overall risk appetite. Job functions within the second line of defence may include financial control, security, quality checking and risk management.
>
> The third line is internal audit, who report to senior management and/or the committees responsible for corporate audit, board and risk governance.

The FCA's 'drivers' of conduct risk

The FCA set out its behavioural stall with good intentions, over a range of publications including annual *Risk Outlooks* and occasional *Economics of Intervention* papers[7], citing significant research sources in support of its model of the causes of 'bad behaviour'. These sources are noted here, not because the FCA's view of causation is authoritative, but because it is helpful to understand the scope (and indeed limitations) of this particular regulator's approach. Later in this book, in Chapters 7, 8 and 9, a behavioural lens approach is introduced. This is a complementary approach that is easy to introduce at all levels of an organization, as it is highly intuitive and does not require specialist risk management insight. The behavioural lens is well grounded in a range of significant and pre-existing behavioural science findings that regulators, notably in the United Kingdom, Australia and South Africa, are continuing to explore. For now, this book presents this knowledge lightly, to provide both a more straightforward and more thorough way to address the often deeply ingrained factors in a firm that produce poor behaviour.

As the first FCA *Risk Outlook* proposed, the whole range of risks that the regulator supervised could be divided into three groups of three key drivers. Among financial markets and their participants, we find inherent risks that arise when people interact to buy and sell: information asymmetries (when one party knows more than the other); biases, rules-of-thumb and mental shortcuts (ways that people's brains lead them to make non-rational choices); and levels of financial capability (such as simple lack of access, or lack of 'literacy'). Then there are the risks arising at the business end, from structures and conduct: how firms handle conflicts of interest; their overall culture and the incentives that reinforce this; and overarching each firm, the market structures that may themselves induce 'expedient' bad behaviour. Finally, every provider trades within an environment that conditions what risk-taking is acceptable: this may be shaped mainly by market economics, or technology, or policy and regulation – or in practice an often-tangled combination of all three.

A simple and much-quoted example in the FCA's literature has been information asymmetry (see box).

Information asymmetry – exploiting ignorance

The buyer of a product (typically a retail consumer) is at a disadvantage to the salesperson, who in the past has tended to have more information not just about the product but about how truly competitive it is – or not. It is easy enough to see how a cautious consumer may buy something that is a poor fit for their needs, or is merely unnecessary, or poor value.

With the coming of social media, especially product comparison websites, some of the old ignorance and 'confusion marketing' is being dispelled.

Old mis-selling habits die hard in the financial sector, as the regulator sees it. Remember, this is the industry that had to be reminded at regular intervals to 'know your customer' and to 'treat customers fairly', as if the default position was perhaps to ignore, or condescend to, the consumer. Too often perhaps, this was the case.

Biases driving conduct problems

Seeing this, and as well as addressing the structural factors that provoke poor behaviour at the provider end, the new regulator wanted to start a revolution in thinking about human behaviour at point of sale. By forcing the industry to acknowledge openly how both sellers and buyers are prone to weaknesses of human nature, the regulator opened up what is perhaps the world's first authentic dialogue with financial providers about what it means to a human animal, alive in the unnatural environment of a financial market.

Compiling a shortlist of biases was no small feat for the regulator: the list of possible biases to include stretches into several hundred[8], and the literature of behavioural scientific research involves multiple overlaps and competing schools of thought (each with its own preferred jargon, of course! – this is academia, after all). In the end, the FCA settled on highlighting just 10 biases, seen as the most critical factors[9]; although even these had multiple aspects and names, in several cases. Again, the bias list was sorted into three categories for ease of reference.

Bias types

- Preferences
- Beliefs
- Decision 'helpers'

The first of the three bias categories, preferences, highlighted how each consumer comes to a purchase with pre-existing ideas about what he or she wants. The three preference biases chosen to represent this were present bias (as where a buyer wants a quick purchase, never mind the longer-term consequences); reference dependence (such as underestimating gains and having an undue fear of losses); and emotion/regret (as when making a 'gut' decision to buy, then regretting it).

In the second bias group, beliefs, are people's internal images of risk – as far as they are concerned, this is how the future *ought* to turn out for them. Many people are overconfident, either that things will work out for the best, or about their own skills in making a judgement call. People also over-extrapolate – they take a long view based on a short one; for example, that if house prices are rising this month, this must mean that they will keep rising, which makes it 'worth' taking out a huge mortgage. Related to that is projection bias, the idea that the future will be 'more of the same', without allowing for the inevitable changes in our lives.

The third bias group specifically concerns how we handle decision-making. For example, without consciously thinking about it, we often engage in mental accounting; although in reality all the money in our bank account is the same, we subconsciously label 'bits' of it as set aside for some particular purpose (such as to spend in the New Year's sales, or on a holiday). Problems arise when we don't stop to consider that, for instance, money borrowed on a credit card is costing us far more than the interest we might receive on the same amount in a savings account. Framing and limited attention describe ways that we fixate on how product information is presented (framed), and switch off when we find there is 'too much information'. Another thing we do, when faced with a wall of information, is resort to using rules of thumb – we use an over-simple decision strategy, such as: faced with three options, ignore the first and last ones, and concentrating on the middle one. Finally, the regulator highlighted how much we are swayed by what other people say and do, our social influences. One form of social influence is a persuasive salesperson who is simply charming; people buy from people who they like, suspending logical judgement.

The Senior Managers Regime: principles, plus a pointy stick

The most contentious – but also true – point that the FCA brought forward among all this was to put the financial sector on notice that it would no longer accept them profiting from consumer biases. In plain terms, firms could no longer exploit human weakness. More than this, the whole effort of providers' product design, targeting, marketing and sales should start to acknowledge openly the existence, types and impacts of biases. At first, this seemed a tall order; and it remains a work in progress across the sector. But before long, the regulator had a further plan to bring firms into engagement with this agenda: a newly direct approach to enforcement, which stripped away the corporate front that firms had always used to defend their positions, and instead held each individual manager to account. In its latest and most explicit form, this regulatory approach became the Senior Managers Regime, or SMR.

Under SMR, each firm now has to publish to the regulator a clear guide to which manager is responsible for each aspect of running the business and of protecting customers' interests. This entails apportioned responsibility, meaning a clear dividing up of roles so that various questions that the regulator might have must get a clear answer from one person only – the principle of 'the buck stops', preventing blame-shifting. While senior managers must, in any case, file regular formal reports that they are 'fit and proper' persons (that is, not dodgy), and also 'skilled and competent' in knowing their business, these requirements and more now fall under a certification regime. This essentially means that the regulator holds on file, and can challenge at any point, each individual manager's formal assurance that he or she is up to the job – and that he or she knows, and oversees directly, the risks that are reported on.

Where this has the potential to become personally painful is the regulator's broad powers to place any suspected manager on trial, at first through commercial scrutiny under civil law, then potentially as a defendant in a criminal case. In other countries where the FCA model of behaviour control has been admired, there are plans to bring immediate criminal prosecutions where managers are already facing civil action for regulatory offences.

Initially senior managers expressed alarm at the regulator's implied assumption that everyone had something to hide[10]. However, in the spring of 2016 the first round of senior manager certification at first passed without incident; except that the regulator let it be known that all certified claims (of skill and competence) might be subject to further proof. The UK regulator's chosen tool for this is to require a compulsory Skilled Persons Review (known to compliance people as a 'Section 166', s-166 [report on] or s-166a [appointment of], after the paragraph in the legislation[11] that gives the regulator this investigative power).

A final feature of the new control design worth mentioning initially, as this will be further considered later, is that the regulator can also prosecute individual managers for *not* taking action – as when failing to install any system to provide early warning of excessive sales activity (potential mis-selling). Another real example has been the prosecution of managers who failed to take proactive steps to fix a technical systems error that repeatedly compromised trading activity.

After the crisis, further crises

Having reviewed, in summary, the arrival and agenda of the first financial regulator, it might be tempting at this point to imagine that everything got steadily better from this point onwards; that market confidence and integrity improved, and that good behaviour became normalized within the sector. In fact, as any UK-resident reader may be aware, the opposite happened. A series of misconduct scandals continued, each of which, while not as catastrophic as the major crash of 2008, nevertheless strengthened in the public mind the perception that far from being contrite for past damage done, the sector was blithely continuing with (corrupt) business as usual. Although behind the scenes, the impact of the new conduct regulation on the perpetrators was near-fatal, with fines severely damaging the balance sheets of a number of major brands, in the short term it appeared – appears, perhaps? – that the central lesson of conduct risk has not yet been internalized by the industry. Time will tell.

As noted soon after by a Parliamentary Commission on Banking Standards: after the financial crisis, we experienced a separate, conduct crisis. After 2008, regulators' and politicians' first instincts were to inject new capital into the banking system, to reawaken liquidity. Also, to reform structures so as to, for example, divide off 'casino' banking from consumer accounts, protecting retail customers from further disaster. On their own terms, these reforms succeeded, but from many observers' point of view these initiatives were still facing the wrong way, failing to address a bigger missing piece: trust and confidence, which were still deep in deficit. Regulators had talked about behaviour but had still looked to financial measures of control, to balance sheet stability. It was still possible for a bank to appear profitable, yet be hiding an underlying culture of misconduct such as opportunistic selling, or a careless approach to client money. At least until SMR began to take effect midway through 2016, pockets of individual bad behaviour persisted.

And what damage they caused! In each year following the global crash, it seemed that a new wave of scandals broke: banks were continuing to allow, or condone, or at least not prevent, aggressive commercialism. Traders tampered with the reference points used by global markets (including LIBOR, the interbank offering benchmark which can affect mortgage pricing; and foreign exchange trade benchmarks). Branch staff continued to mis-sell unnecessary insurance contracts (PPI, supposedly a scheme for consumer protection). International subsidiaries continued laundering money on behalf of corrupt regimes, helped by banks' sales staff, helped in turn by local advisors in countries including Mexico and Panama.

Yet the consequences, for banks in particular, were beginning to pile up. Misconduct had ceased to be a cost-free route to profit; fines were swelling to become very much more than a 'friction cost of business'[12]. The regulatory costs of misconduct rose to a point where they could hurt a bank's most treasured resource, its capital adequacy. Under previous regimes of control, like many commercial organizations, financial firms had regarded costs of regulation as falling broadly into two categories: cash (needed to settle fines, rearrange the furniture following a dismissal, and crank up some fresh marketing); and routine cost of capital (meaning the share price taking a hit, or a rise in the cost of raising money on the interbank market). Suddenly a third, much larger category of regulatory risk cost was emerging: a threat to existential survival (what if conduct costs overwhelmed the balance sheet, laying the bank open to a hostile takeover?).

Not coincidentally, as these later crises of confidence unfolded, the Bank of England in its role as guardian of 'prudence' in the banking system started to run its own stress tests to see what effect 'conduct costs' were having on capital adequacy. The Bank looked back over three years and forward over five, and opined that the new 'misconduct costs' had cost British banks *every penny of capital that they had raised* during those three years – that's £30bn. In other words, *all* of the banks' hard-won new support from their backers had been expended straight away, used to pay off fines to the regulator, to pay compensation to various mistreated customers, and to pay for the withdrawal of their own inappropriate products from the market, at the regulator's insistence. Worse, the Bank of England projected that UK-regulated banks would have to stump up a further £40bn during the next five years, to complete the project and settle for past misdemeanours. Going forward, on a purely technical point, banks now take potential conduct-related losses into account and include these sums in their published statements of capital adequacy[13].

Grasping the 'conduct problem': here's a fresh approach

That shift in corporate reporting, to set a figure on expected conduct-related losses, was simply the hard leading edge of a deeper change in attitudes towards acceptable and expected behaviour – the analysis of which lies at the heart of this book, in particular with the techniques detailed in Chapters 8 and 9. The key to making lasting change among cynical practitioners is the extent to which they can be encouraged to internalize a sense of good behaviour. As a specialist in behavioural risk, I have been asked many, many times – on average at least once at every event where I'm speaking on conduct risk – to offer a simple prescription or 'silver bullet' in answer to the question 'What does 'good behaviour' look like?' The managers asking this question are usually, at an apparent level, sincere about wanting to do the right thing; but under the surface, more often than not, there is always the old idea that a plain prescription of 'good' items will allow everyone to tick off these items and get on with business as usual. When it comes to resourcing regulatory compliance, many firms' instincts remain to go with a cost-benefit analysis, to 'play to the measure'. As one CRO has elegantly put it, the challenge to firms' culture is 'to be clear whether conduct really matters to us, or whether we make it matter because we have been asked to make it matter'[14].

Late, but perhaps not too late to turn the industry's cynical attitude around, a Parliamentary Commission of enquiry in 2012 heard how one of the industry's leading figures had changed his own priorities following the LIBOR scandal. Asked by the commission why his own study of financial firms' governance just three years earlier[15] had failed to detect the conduct crisis that was even then in progress, Sir David Walker acknowledged that his focus then had been to prevent banks from taking undue risks. He accepted that his bank governance report had aimed first to ensure that banks protected their own capacity to provide sound credit, rather than to pay attention to what the wider population might regard as acceptable behaviour[16]. This was rather like saying that 'we simply didn't realize that the poor ethical conduct of banks would turn out to be a problem in its own right'[17]. Walker also conceded that banks' boards' emphasis on 'risk appetite' and returns to shareholders had been 'set in a vacuum' that paid too little regard to 'wider social externalities'.

There are several tough, designed-in problems when it comes to dealing with entrenched bad behaviour in large organizations (explored in Chapter 5). A significant one is the way that aggregated reporting (adding all subsidiary performance figures into a single 'bottom line' total) and limited liability (that public companies don't need to settle debts greater than the total value of their shares) make it easy for directors to feel that they need not acknowledge that misconduct is happening. Behavioural regulation addresses this by incentivizing firms, through conduct prosecution costs, to take into account the interests of all stakeholders – not just their shareholders and the regulators, but the public at large, including of course retail customers and also public interest advocates such as politicians, news and social media, and consumer watchdog groups.

The same (2012) Parliamentary Commission found that a culture of permitted misconduct may persist in a firm, and could contaminate others across a market in such a way that no market participant would call time on it. This acknowledged an effect that had been widely known about in private, and in academic studies of financial practitioners[18], for years beforehand: that misbehaviour has been often perversely sustained by a belief that 'we can't be the first to stop, it's making too much money for everybody', and that 'I'll miss out on my sales targets if I don't make the numbers (by continuing to mis-sell)'.

Revealing the costs of 'lawful but awful' conduct

Thus, even after the launch of behavioural regulation, there still persisted in the minds of practitioners a delusional and inward-facing view of how to calibrate 'acceptable behaviour'. The sense was that any activity that was technically legal, or not explicitly forbidden, must be the same thing as acceptable. This clearly failed to address a different question raised by public opinion and the new generation of behavioural regulators: It may be legal, but is it right? Within banks, for example, although Chief Risk Officers were nominally tasked with keeping an eye on acceptable conduct, in practice many were rewarded by board-approved incentives to focus only on reducing the cost of regulatory capital to their employer[19]. It would have taken a CRO or compliance head with an unusually high level of independent thinking and authority within the firm, to have questioned the prevailing view of acceptable conduct – a casual approach to corporate misbehaviour that criminologists memorably describe as 'lawful but awful'[20]. As one study of this points out, when regulators concentrate exclusively on what is 'officially defined' as crime, they overlook a larger threat of corporate conduct that is 'within the letter of the law' but has 'multiple adverse social consequences'.[21]

The regulator realized that breaking down this attitude would require more than just loading on more laws: the key was to hold senior managers, and managers in general, directly and personally responsible in law for the effects of their behaviour and decisions. And the best way to get their attention – apart from ramping up obvious personal threats such as the prospect of going to prison – was to hit managers where they would feel the pain, in their business budgets. So conduct risk entered a second phase immediately after its behavioural science-backed launch: a steep rise in the level of fines and other costs levied against misbehavers. UK banks had to find more than £30bn to resolve the damage caused by PPI mis-selling; in the United States, mis-selling of mortgage-backed securities triggered similar costs.

As 'conduct costs' mounted, analysts have begun to study them[22], for the benefit of the industry's wider understanding of the risk, with startling findings. Assuming, with good reason, that these costs should be taken to include any form of expense relating to fallout from a conduct prosecution, analysts began to include not just the original misconduct fines, but also restitution and compensation payments to wronged customers, future conduct cost provisions in firms' annual accounts, and the costs of clear-up such as hiring new staff to replace discredited (or banned) leavers.

One analyst team found, on that basis, that up to June 2015, the 16 largest US and UK financial firms had collectively had to pay out £205bn in conduct-related costs (fines, restitution, reorganization, and so on). To put that figure in some kind of context, that's in the same league as the entire annual national economic output (GDP) of a medium-sized nation such as Denmark, Singapore or South Africa[23] – and all money wasted for the sake of not taking care of conduct.

At the highest level, then, seeing these enormous total sums for the first time, financial firms' boards have begun to take serious notice of the need for more robust principles and practices of good behaviour. To inform their view of what to do, besides asking behavioural analysts such as this author, they are gathering new kinds of evidence, assembling non-financial indicators that give a clearer focus on a different type of concern. Two key indicators, not previously given priority, are levels of external trust in their organization; and levels of knowledge certainty in relation to board competence.

It is slightly alarming to note that the latter scale, knowledge certainty, was a new arrival on the analytical landscape as recently as 2016. As far back as 1995, a British judge had given a famous opinion on the directors of Barings Securities, following their corporate collapse at the hands of (heavily incentivized) rogue trader Nick Leeson; directors were clearly instructed from then on to 'know your business' – that is, nobody should ever hold office in a financial firm unless they understood how the firm's business worked, in practice. And by extension, anyone who did not understand their business was a fair target for prosecution. Now, this principle has been extended through conduct rules, and SMR in particular, to ask the much more telling questions: How sure are directors in their knowledge of their business, and the regulations that govern it? How do they *know* that they know what they're doing – that is, that they're not being over-optimistic (or delusional) about their own capacity to manage things? And how do *we* (the public interest, represented by the regulator) know that they know what they're doing?

Looking ahead

Following regulators' own industry-wide review in 2015[24], enforcers began to take account of how firms ranked in a notional table of offenders, ranking their levels of past contribution and future exposure to costs of misconduct. Going forward, firms' thorough 'disclosure of costs arising from misconduct' is considered as 'a way of incentivizing improved ethical behaviour'. In the past, financial firms had limited their reporting and calibrating of 'ethical activity' to the narrow and often self-selecting context of reporting on their own corporate social responsibility (CSR)[25]. From now on, they should expect to have their costs of misconduct published by analysts and regulators – a very public 'naughty list' league table of misconduct incidents and enforcements. The past practice of aggregating away misconduct incidents (that is, burying them deep at the back of the annual report, and losing their line-item cost in a larger total figure for compliance expenses) is now under threat.

Firms at first objected to this, citing the fair concern that if the regulator refuses to publish a clear standard for 'what good looks like', they may be unfairly exposed to the whim of a regulator who may happen to dislike their judgement calls in so-called grey areas (conduct decision points not covered by conventional regulation or law). A recent analysis project[26] has been working with banks to set out standards to scope the grey areas. Strikingly, this research context proposes a new, behaviourally aware meaning for the term 'standard': a conduct standard means the latest right behaviour as *socially defined* – that is, what ordinary people accept and expect (see Chapter 8). This approach to definition respects the regulator's intentions to reflect how customers see the world, and what they want. What constitutes the 'right' behaviour may change, sometimes rapidly, in an area where people are genuinely unsure what correct behaviour is, because people's perceptions and expectations change. New scrutiny has already brought to light various abuses that used to pass unchallenged: for example, how banks used to deal with hard-pressed small business borrowers (see Chapter 9).

In fact, public expectations have already changed powerfully in recent years with the advent of social media. People have become more ready to question and to criticize. This is good for democracy and governance, although the social media revolution of course also brings online its own forms of antisocial activity. We may also expect people's views and needs to continue to change rapidly as, for example, the new generation of challenger banks gains traction in the market and shakes up the old providers.

Where this chapter has traced the practical debut of conduct regulation in the real world, and its regrouping following something of a false start, the following chapter steps back to consider the underlying obstacles that all regulators face and which, also being regulators themselves, conduct enforcers still struggle to overcome.

Notes

1 Lagadec, Patrick (1993) *Preventing Chaos in a Crisis*, McGraw-Hill
2 FSA Discussion Paper DP7, 2001
3 Extracted from FSA's *Progress report on TCF*, June 2002
4 FSA, *Progress report on TCF*, July 2004
5 FSA, *Principles-based regulation, focusing on the outcomes that matter*, April 2007, s1.2
6 Precis of FCA's *Principles for Business*, 2013
7 Available at fca.org.uk
8 See, for example, extended expert lists in the *Behavioral Economics Guide* (LSE, 2016); and popular lists such as *The Art of Thinking Clearly* (Dobelli); and *You Are Not So Smart* (McRaney)
9 FCA, *Occasional Paper 1*, 2014, available at fca.org.uk
10 The so-called 'reverse burden of proof' discussed in Chapter 6
11 The Financial Services and Markets Act 2000 (FSMA to its friends)
12 See Miles, R (2012) *From Compliance to Coping*, King's College London

13 As required by Prudential Regulatory Authority, Supervisory Statement 31/15

14 Ramtri, V (2015) Monograph: *C-Tunes: How to keep up with Conduct in a post-crisis world*

15 Walker, D (2009) *A Review of Corporate Governance in UK Banks and Other Financial Industry Entities*

16 Walker, D, Written evidence to the Parliamentary Committee on Banking Standards, November 2012

17 McCormick, R, Cambridge University/Conduct Costs Project lecture, *The Cost of Trust Gone Wrong*, February 2016

18 For example, Miles, R in *Operational Risk: New Frontiers Explored*, 2012; and McCormick, R, ibid

19 Miles, R (2012) *From Compliance to Coping*

20 Passas, N (2005) Lawful but awful: Legal corporate crimes, control fraud and criminology, *Journal of Socio-Economics*, **34** (6)

21 Passas, ibid

22 Notably the Conduct Costs Project (LSE/Cambridge), and the 'Corlytics' conduct/OpRisk analysis team at University College Dublin

23 IMF World Economic Outlook data for comparative period (year 2015) at contemporary exchange rates. US dollar GDP figures: Denmark 295bn (£201bn), Singapore 293bn (£200bn), South Africa 313bn (£214bn)

24 The Fair and Effective Markets Review, sponsored by the Bank of England, HM Treasury and the FCA

25 Published standards for reporting corporate social responsibility, such as the Global Reporting Initiative's Sustainability Reporting Guidelines ('GRI')

26 The Conduct Risks benchmarking project, CRISP, managed by CCP at Cambridge Judge Business School

Why regulators had to change direction

04

Introduction

The challenge of creating rules that work

Where Chapter 3 set out the recent history of how conduct regulators began to act on their new agenda by taking action in the specific context of financial services post-crash, this chapter will pull back the focus to look at wider problems facing all regulators. Where many manuals on conduct risk approach their advice from 'downstream' (how to comply defensively, using checklists), this book tackles the topic from 'upstream': to develop an intelligent understanding of how regulators themselves think about problem-solving. This approach will prepare the reader to get the best value out of the behavioural lens approach in the second half of the book.

There is one simple and vital question that starts us down this path. It's a question that continues to fascinate me, even after many years of analysing human behaviour in groups and organizations: Why do rules fail?

Because, quite clearly, rules often do not succeed in achieving what they set out to do. If you doubt that, try this quick test of 'what actually happens' (see box):

A quick 'rules fail' observation

Out in your street, take a quick look around you. I'm willing to bet that within five minutes you will see one or more of the following:

- a driver, making a mobile phone call while driving;
- a pedestrian running across a crossing even though the traffic lights are against them;
- a vehicle, missing its licence plate;
- a person putting recyclables into a landfill waste bag.

And so it goes: casual rule-breaking is all around us. Not just in the street, of course, but in the workplace too, and in many places where we go. What does this say about rules and about how people relate to rules?

Themes and concepts in this chapter

audit ritual/ritual compliance – behavioural lens – binary v scalar view of compliance – careless regulatees – catastrophe-driven regulation – citizen mobilization – cognitive gap – collapse of public trust – collective (virtual) consciousness – command-and-control – communication errors (encoding, transmission, reception, decoding) – 'comply or explain' – data fallacy – death of deference – de-biasing – de-risking – derivatives – econometrics – enforcement self-regulation – expert bias/'the expert problem' – fantasy documents – Freedom of Information laws – gaming of rules – 'heads on spikes' – hysteresis – juniorization – legitimacy – Newtonian rationale – open government – origin of regulations – performative – post-rationalizing – predictably irrational – propensity to comply – proxies/proxy indicators – rational actor – 'rear-view' regulation – regulatory capital – regulatory capture – relativistic risk-view – risk-aware working – routine nonconformity – satisficing – self-regulating – social contract – social licence – speech perception – spotlight effect (bias) – systems thinking – transparency – 'what actually happens' test – why rules fail

Typically, committees of rule-makers design rules as forms of control, to try to stop people from doing something dangerous or antisocial, or to get them to be more careful and pro-social. For rules to succeed, everyone affected by them has to respect them, and be prepared to modify their own behaviour to accommodate what the rule has asked of them. That's the (very) broad theory.

Yet people's relationship with rules has been changing during the past generation. In the most general terms – and of course there are many exceptions – it used to be true that most people were content to live with the idea that laws and regulations serve a purpose. Thanks to that prevailing attitude, rule-makers were in turn content to adopt a command-and-control style of governance and government, also known as systems thinking. Under this approach, lawmakers and rule-writers believed (mistakenly) that ordinary people are fully rational and will obey a rule either 'because they know what's good for them' (aka 'mother knows best') or because 'it is the rational thing to do'. These assumptions ignore the fact, obvious to behavioural science and shortly to become clear to us here, that people do not react rationally, especially when formally instructed to do so.

Predictably irrational stuff happens, all the time

Delightfully, the general public may sometimes respond to an instruction in a completely contrary way. This can be amusing to other people in general, occasionally terrifying and often teeth-gnashingly frustrating for the institutions that are trying to manage the situation. In the age of social media, where a mildly subversive 'buzz' is highly valued, we should expect this to occur more and more often. There are many, many, real-world instances of contrary, anti-institutional popular responses; from a very long list, three favourite examples (see box):

When 'what actually happens', happened

- In January 1984 the BBC banned airplay of the song 'Relax', by the band Frankie Goes to Hollywood, on the (correct, as it happens) grounds that the song is about sadomasochistic sex and therefore unsuitable for

▶

airplay on public service radio. The song then went straight to Number 1 in the music charts, going on to become one of the highest-grossing singles of all time, and soundtrack to the popular comedy, *Zoolander*.

- During the latter 1990s, the Enlightened Tobacco Company enjoyed commercial success, and avoided health hazard labelling restrictions, marketing a brand called Death Cigarettes. (To misquote another brand, the appeal of the Death product proposition was that it 'does exactly what it says on the packet'.)

- In 2016, the British Government held a competition for the public to create and vote for a name for its prestigious new polar research vessel. One of the competition's organizers, 'as a joke', added to the list of choices the name 'Boaty McBoatface'. This name then became the runaway winner of the competition, gathering more votes than all other options put together. As the internet commented, 'a typical British reaction to being asked to name something'.

This phenomenon has various names, including contrariness, cussedness, and bloody-mindedness. It is also informally referred to as the 'Streisand Effect', after the notorious example of the Hollywood star whose attempts to ban internet pictures of her home resulted in the pictures being widely reposted. Whatever we call it, as the judge once said, we know it when we see it.

There is, sadly, a more serious underlying point about the capacity of authorities to control hazards to the public. In the modern age we have seen a collapse in public trust in many of the institutions of government and commerce, together with a questioning of earlier control assumptions about who has a right to rule over us, and a rise in mobilization of citizens' interests – this has been called 'the death of deference'. Many political analysts see this change as a good thing, as a fresh wind of public critique blows through fusty old state institutions, bringing the fresh air of transparency and accountability[1]. On one hand, it is good that ordinary citizens are finding a stronger voice: this can lead to big positive shifts in public engagement with government, such as the coming of democracy to Eastern Europe in the 1990s, or to Myanmar in 2015. Social media assists this by making open discussion and criticism, and demands for openness in government, more immediate. Many governments have responded positively to this, passing Freedom of Information laws, for example.

As with any human endeavour, there's a darker side. Social media release into public spaces a sustained, loud and open style of criticism of legitimately elected governments and regulators. Over time, this creates a misleading impression that *all* holders of public office are self-seeking and incompetent, and deters good people from running for public office.

Partly thanks to the rise of collectively shared knowledge through the internet, partly due to the perceived 'blunders of governments'[2] and corporations' 'callous' rollout of mass job cuts, more and more of us as 'normal people' are taking a relativistic view of the commands that laws and rules seek to impose. There is a creeping sense that governments and employers have broken their social contract with ordinary people, and that therefore no allegiance is owed. The behavioural lens will explore and shed light on such links – for example, it explicitly connects anxiety, perceived fairness, and social licence (individuals' tolerance of a particular institution).

As soon as a person acts on the impulse to 'opt out' of a rule that they see as irrelevant to their own life, the force of all other rules begins to diminish; compliance becomes a matter of personal judgement. One prominent theory of risk and human behaviour[3] suggests that 21st-century citizens are less united into social groups, and more like islands of individual judgement, with each person making up her or his own mind about whether or not a particular rule applies to them. Yet there is also a counter-trend: against this background of society fragmenting towards us all judging risks for ourselves, there is the rise of collective consciousness by sharing of opinions through social media as we become more connected than ever before, through virtual spaces. On balance, we should try to think of greater public transparency as a positive development for good governance, including the good management of risk in general and conduct in particular.

Through my risk workshops, engaging with many hundreds of people across the years, from top managers to general staff to junior students, I have found that there are a few easy warm-up questions that quickly get everyone on-side with the point that we *all* break rules, sometimes knowingly or deliberately, sometimes carelessly or ignorantly. As seen above, out in the street there are countless examples of knowing-plus-careless rule-breaking all around us. So here is another very short question set I use to make the point personal to each person at the workshop:

The taxi test

1 Have you taken a taxi recently? Yes / No

2 If so, did you wear a seat belt? Yes / No

3 For 100 per cent of the journey? Yes / No

(This is not, of course, a real test – just a rather basic opinion poll.)

The standard answers tend to be:

1. Yes, 2. No, 3. No; or…

1. Yes, 2. Yes, 3. No.

(If you answered 1. No; or 1. Yes, 2. Yes, and 3. Yes: that's fine, I respect you, of course.)

If you gave either of the standard sets of answers, as more than 50 per cent of almost every one of my workshop groups does, then you're a rule-breaker.

It's that simple. The law in many countries requires you as a passenger to wear a seat belt in a taxi. Yet in the real world, more people don't comply, than do. Why is this?

In the workshop sessions, we often go on to take a snap view of the composition of the belt/no-belt groups. Over the years, we have observed that the group of compulsive taxi-seat-belt-wearers includes specific subgroups such as financial compliance officers, recently qualified drivers, and parents of young children. The not-bothered-with-seat-belts groups include (often) high-status men in their 50s, single twentysomethings of any gender, and off-duty police officers. Again, why is that so, and could we have predicted that?

The behavioural lens approach answers these questions, along with many more serious questions related to governing risk, encouraging good conduct and preventing misbehaviour. All will become clear as we explore how to put the behavioural lens into practice, over the course of the next few chapters.

First, though, it may be helpful to explain some of this with the story of when I first encountered what is now known as behavioural science.

Starting to understand the 'regulatory problem'

Back in the 1990s, I had the good fortune to meet an academic whose work on social acceptance of laws is admired by many, including me (if at first from afar). Dick Ruimschotel was, and is, a distinguished professor of law, psychology and philosophy at the two leading Dutch universities, and later also Harvard. Like many properly clever people, he has the wonderful knack of summarizing and explaining big social problems in everyday terms. As we sat in his office at Erasmus that day, his explanation of why rules fail sounded just right; it also fitted neatly with much of what I'd already learned studying linguistics. It is worth unpacking a bit of the linguistics background, as this helps to focus one's understanding of what Dick explained to me, and our collective appreciation of what regulators must try to achieve – whether or not the regulators themselves fully appreciate this.

Linguistics analysts are fascinated by (along with a load of other fascinating things) why a person listening to a speech *hears* a meaning that's different from what the speaker intended. Or, to put that more directly: What you hear me saying isn't the same as what I thought I was saying. This is one of life's enduring challenges, familiar to us all. One of the most popular British comedy sketches ever, 'Four Candles' by the late Ronnie Barker[4], plays brilliantly on this challenge, as a customer and a shopkeeper wrestle to understand a shopping list whose every item has two, three, or even four possible meanings.

There are all too many real-world anecdotes about misunderstood instructions, some with tragic consequences (see box).

Not what I meant I said

In the trenches of the First World War, a French army unit was coming under heavy attack. With limited time to summon help, their commanding officer telegraphed a hasty note, in French, to the nearest British command post: *'La France demande qu'on nous fait secours'* ('France requests you rescue us'). Not being a French speaker, the hard-pressed Brit commander disliked his allies' 'demand' that the English put their own lives at risk to save a failing French mission, and refused to help. The French soldiers were massacred. The tragedy was all down to simple misunderstanding of that one pleading French word, *'demande'* – which properly translated into English of course means 'requests' (and not 'demands').

The science of linguistics, then, explores the reasons why communication breaks down between someone speaking and someone listening. Let's try to stuff the whole of linguistic science into one brief sentence here. Communication breakdowns may occur at various stages: encoding (choosing what words to speak), transmission (such as speaking against a lot of background noise), reception (hearing clearly) and decoding (making sense of what was just said).

There is a good reason why it is worth unpacking that simple example of how perception works: by applying this kind of analysis to the everyday acts of speaking and listening, we begin to think more critically about the way that instructions are given and received, or rules issued and obeyed (or disobeyed).

Now let's go back to the conference in Rotterdam with Dr Ruimschotel all those years ago. He showed me a new way he had devised to think about how people engage with laws and rules. This method greatly helps to explain why each person responds in their own way to an instruction. Called the Table of Eleven[5] (T11), it is still being used by lawmakers in Holland and around the world. T11 invites us to consider the propensity to comply, which each person brings with them.

Take the example of a government proposing a new law: at one extreme, some citizens will often support anything that their government does, either because of their own ideological support for the ruling party, or from a naïve fatalistic sense that 'government knows best what's good for us'. At the other extreme, there will always be some citizens who reject whatever any government proposes, either again on ideological grounds (because 'we didn't vote for them') or on principle ('we're anarchists/survivalists, etc'), or also commonly – remembering Boaty McBoatface – that 'we resent the State telling us what choices to make in our lives'. In between these extreme poles of the T11, comes a scale of nine other groups, including for example those who distrust government but are willing to be persuaded to change their behaviour for the common good; those who would intuitively disobey the new law if they were unaware of it, but would obey it once made aware, and so on.

The T11 approach has enjoyed considerable success, starting with the Dutch Justice Ministry ('Justitie'), who saw it as an effective way to test how draft laws would be received by the public, and later also to repeal old statute laws which nobody was bothering to obey. By using the T11 tool to question, as it were, the extent to which the public holds the law itself in disrepute, Justitie found they could improve the social legitimacy or social licence of the whole body of law – that is, they could induce the public into more law-abiding behaviour, and build a common perception that the government was not wasting citizens' time making trivial and irrelevant laws.

Regulators' 'inherent problems' (1): Well-meaning experts

These two experiences set the scene for us to consider the size of the uphill task that all regulators face. Luckily for the professional analyst, this is such a vexed topic that it has kept political scientists happily busy for decades, if not centuries. Luckily for the reader here, all this background research has produced a few commonly agreed points of understanding, which are shared here.

As a starting point for your new understanding of the politics of rule-making, imagine you wanted to find out how far the average person's quality of life has improved thanks to better framing of the law and regulations in the modern world – because, of course, it has improved… hasn't it? You might take a long view of human history over two or three millennia, and see the story of humankind as a steady progress of improvement to the quality of the average person's life. Certainly, laws and regulations have achieved plenty for society: longer life expectancy; the curbing of violent and antisocial behaviour; standards that support trading and safety worldwide; improvements in human rights and equality of opportunity; protection of the environment; better working practices, public health, and so on. All of which might make you feel slightly smug, perhaps, about living in the modern age.

Mainstream history, then, tempts us to think of our orderly present-day society as a relatively safe, if dullish end to centuries of major turmoil. Although a few regional threats persist, the modern world we live in is more at peace than it has ever been for any sustained period of history. Partly thanks to modern technology, which provides more direct and collective social contact, medical science, collective wisdom making for better laws, law enforcement and good governments, we have largely succeeded in seeing our common humanity. This has calmed many of the earlier extremes of human behaviour and has helped to install orderly, democratic civil society around the world. This is perhaps one of humanity's proudest achievements.

But wait a minute…

There is, of course, an alternative view of human progress. Throughout history, stuff has gone wrong. Often really, really badly wrong. In the struggle to make responsible use of our resources, and in new fields of human endeavour, and in the way we bring in new technologies, as human custodians of the world we have failed repeatedly, and often catastrophically, to keep control and to get the job done. In a way, it is good that as humans we take risks and allow for failures, because that helps us to grow in civilization; we couldn't put an astronaut on the moon without risking, and occasionally losing, the lives of earlier astronauts. Each time there is a failure, we follow it by tightening up our control systems, creating new rules and safeguards.

So then, consider this: all regulation is produced as a consequence of failure, as a reflex after the event of a catastrophe.

From catastrophe to regulation – quick example

Modern European environmental law is known as the Seveso Directives. Here's why.

The law was introduced in response to a catastrophe at a chemical factory in Seveso, northern Italy, in 1975. A huge leak of toxic dioxins from the factory had led to the emergency admission of 1,600 local people to hospital, the abortion of 26 unborn babies and the death of more than 80,000 farm animals.

Now consider how that thought plays through one challenge in particular: how best to regulate financial markets. Regulations are rather like old-fashioned history books, laying out an orthodox version of how the world works, or ought to work: they set out sequences of conclusions and instructions. (By regulations, let's take this to include laws, policy documents, compliance manuals and professional practice handbooks, for the sake of argument.) All of these are produced by and for the people who are qualified and paid as professionals to work with such expert forms of rule-making. Such people include regulators and regulated professionals, all of whom have a legitimate, if vested, interest in reinforcing their own rule-based view of how the world works.

So consider this too: systems of rules can also fail, just like those human endeavours and technologies that we looked at a moment ago. There are common, and in fact quite foreseeable, reasons why rules fail. Broadly speaking, they fail because they don't manage to gain any real traction over the behaviour of the people they are seeking to control. *That* tends to happen because the people who design risk controls (policymakers, regulators, boards, risk managers and others) themselves fail either to understand or acknowledge an important gap in popular understanding (a cognitive gap, or dissonance). *That* gap lies between a designed system of control, which is usually idealistic, and the messy reality – what real people do in the world outside product engineering and policy think-tanks. Even though it is vital to acknowledge the gap, many rule-makers, rules, and risk control systems ignore or deny it. Keeping this all in plain terms: rules tend not to be drafted with any insight into how ordinary people respond when someone in authority tells them to change the way they behave. Not that this stops the drafting experts from toiling away energetically to bring us new rules, of course.

Meanwhile, most of the regulated people are not themselves experts in regulation, nor do they wish to be, even if they hold professional licences. The ranks of so-called careless regulatees can include sales teams, customers and line managers. These regulatees are not on the policymaking side of the fence; they just want to get on with their work. Yet experts in policy, including regulators, routinely ignore their own 'spotlight bias' – they overlook the fact that their 'expert' interventions can appear as naïve and irrelevant to the regulatees as the layman may appear to the experts.

Overcoming the 'expert problem' in rule-making

We, of course, want the people who frame regulations to have expert knowledge of the field they are overseeing. The experts are therefore typically qualified lawyers, career regulators, policy analysts or professional (legal) drafters. All have a more or less direct career incentive to focus on framing the rule so as to deal with what they see as the central aspect of a problem, but not so much the wider issue as the general public sees it. Thus, financial regulators in the past were interested in product descriptions; customers meanwhile saw the problem more in terms of dislike of having to deal with financial advisors at all. At least until the arrival of behavioural thinking, financial rules were created in this 'inside-out' fashion, with the focus on the provider's processes rather than the customer's needs and experiences. Again, there are many examples from parallel fields of regulated activity.

Expert bias let loose in the world: three examples

Come here, get murdered

In the 1990s, senior police advisors wanted to increase engagement with local communities in a bid to improve the 'clear-up rate' for crime (catching the perpetrator and securing a conviction). They hit on the bright idea of posting witness appeal notices around the scene of major crimes. The expert advisors predicted – correctly on one narrow point, as it happens – that doing this would generate more public offers of support and information. What the experts failed to consider was the effect of posting large notices in the middle of communities, in effect advertising that 'People Get Killed Here'. Although the witness appeal notices work, they also massively raise levels of public anxiety. (Were the experts right to suggest posting the signs? Is heightened fear a price worth paying for more favourable police statistics?)

Just a technical fault

One summer evening in 1989 on the River Thames in the middle of London, a commercial dredger rammed and sank a large pleasure boat-load of passengers, in full view of astonished passers-by. Accident investigators at first ascribed mass fatalities to 'navigational oversights'. Only after grieving relatives forced a second enquiry did plainer, sadly familiar factors emerge: drunken crew and forged safety compliance papers. (How often do experts frame an event, or a risk, in expert terms that alienate others who have a legitimate concern about it?)

I'm a professional, you're not. Oh, maybe you are though

For more than 150 years the engineering profession was fragmented, because its earliest founding fathers refused to give membership to anyone who developed an 'unorthodox' technology. From the 1850s onwards, as each new field of applied technology emerged (including some really important ones, like harnessing electrical energy), members of the existing professional bodies barred the new pioneers from joining their precious institution. Unable to ally professionally with mechanical engineers, the electrical engineers set up their own professional body, and so on – at one point into more than 80 separate institutions.

That last example, from the engineering profession, is not simply a Victorian tale of expert governance gone mad: huge domains of professional skill can be artificially divided in this way. For most of its history, the English legal profession demanded separation of advocates [barristers] from client handlers [solicitors/attorneys]. Actuaries get very sniffy about being described as accountants. Surgeons hate being called 'doctor'. And so on. Why is it that experts insulate themselves in professional silos? Perhaps a behavioural approach can help to overcome this.

This type of 'not seeing the wood for the trees' is a common problem among regulatory elites who often have little or no direct experience of what is actually happening at local level. Rules are always out of step with the changing practices of the real world.

Then there's the psychological problem of expert bias. Experts are human, too, and are prey to the human weaknesses of being over-eager to help, or sometimes to show off, by exaggerating their expertise. This may be a misguided attempt to try to 'help' someone, or to save face, or perhaps to impress a courtroom full of expectant jurors and lawyers. This type of vanity exacts a high price – usually on others – in the form of false convictions, false acquittals, or sometimes mistrials when the expert deception is discovered. The trouble is, it can be hard for a non-expert (even a trial judge) to know when an expert has overreached; expert bias hides itself well.

Finally, the expert approach tends to rely on a data fallacy. Experts like to think of statistical data as somehow more significant than qualitative human experiences. When policymakers cite expert research to justify new regulations, they tend to quote numbers to confirm that the problem exists, and the assumption that they must take action. Of course, it is unsettling to consider the alternative view of numbers: that no statistic can ever present an absolute truth. Any reported number is simply what one observer (or sensor) noted at a certain point in time. Observers make mistakes and have biases of their own. Research designs can be misconceived; irrelevant factors may be measured – and with hindsight, often have been, as when financial regulation failed to detect the onset of a liquidity crisis in 2008. Even when data is gathered by mechanical sensors and information systems, these may malfunction, or may be wrongly tasked, or show the system's human operators signals they cannot comprehend – the key factor in a significant number of 'pilot error' air disasters. People in general, and especially regulators, want to believe that numerical data are simply true. Yet the uncomfortable truth is that statistics are only ever one way of noting how things look, usually to somebody else, and that the numbers may anyway have been assembled for some purpose other than our reason for looking at them.

Let's draw a couple of summary points from the early part of this chapter, and introduce a light scattering of behavioural economics jargon at the same time.

Rule-makers too often persist in wanting to think of people as rational actors. They assume, for example, that a well-meant regulatory intervention will be recognized as such, and so attract spontaneous support from regulatees. Unfortunately for policymakers, real people are not Newtonian in their thinking. Bless us, we're biased, emotional and irrational. Where the regulator would like to believe we're all rationally minded good citizens like *Star Trek's* Mr Spock, more likely we were all busy voting for Boaty McBoatface. As part of this Newtonian/Spockish view of the world, the rule-makers also subscribe to systems thinking. This takes many forms, and includes many fallacies, most commonly command-and-control ('you'll just do as I say') and econometrics ('numbers are truths'). Such formulations have been beloved of political scientists in the past because they present a, well, politically scientific view of how people think and act. But, once again – real people don't, necessarily.

The first part of this chapter has considered the difficulties that regulators have with their own expertise, and with unhelpful assumptions about the willingness of regulatees to respond positively to rules. The rest of the chapter considers some of the practical, structural (or 'designed-in') challenges that the regulator also has to wrestle with; how these affect the likely behaviour of regulated groups; and how regulators' own approach is beginning to change to overcome these problems.

Regulators' 'inherent problems' (2): Facing backwards

This has historically been a massive point of structural weakness, yet it is surprisingly easy to explain in a very few words. Essentially, regulators have often been 'out of step' with what is happening in real time in the markets, for one simple reason: they are looking backwards.

Until the advent of conduct regulation, which keenly demands future improvements in behaviour, financial regulation was mostly about reviewing and responding to past events. Regulators would review, for example, the previous year's trading figures as supplied by a regulated firm, and from that view develop an opinion on whether or not to intervene against the firm.

This was memorably described by one of my research respondents, a seasoned Finance Director in an international investment bank, as 'like trying to drive your car using only the rear-view mirror'. Clearly not properly sentient behaviour, and not a situation you would think anyone would want to persist with, owing to a high risk of frontal collision. Is it better to try to cope by justifying past failures, or by looking ahead and adapting to oncoming change? Enough said.

Regulators' 'inherent problems' (3): Lack of resources

No regulator ever has enough resources to be able to control everything that's going on in their regulated field. Regulators therefore have to make up the resource shortfall in various ways that we will now consider.

To put it another way, a regulator has to live with the annoying fact that the people they are trying to regulate have far superior resources. To overcome this basic skew, regulators have to co-opt the resources of the sector they oversee, typically by compelling, sometimes with threats, regulatees to disclose their management, risk and financial information. But the regulator doesn't have control of how the information is produced, which means (among other things) that the sector has some leeway to present the information as it pleases. Even though a regulator can magnify its apparent presence by exacting 'symbolic' (ie large) penalties, a real imbalance of power remains. Of course, unscrupulous regulatees know and may attempt to exploit this.

How regulators' own models have changed to cope

In case you had ever wondered how regulators themselves describe the models of regulation they use (what do you mean, you hadn't?) here is a brief history of the last quarter-century of regulatory models. It is worth knowing, on the basis of understanding the regulator's point of view, getting to know how your regulator thinks – the value of getting in behind, as actors put it, 'What's my motivation here?'.

As part of the deregulatory 'Big Bang' in financial services in the 1990s, the British government required various professional market practitioner groups to set up self-regulating bodies. This the professionals did happily – what's not to like about certifying your own competence? – but it came as no great surprise to anyone when subsequently self-regulation was found to have harboured a colourful range of abuses. By 2001, the original principal self-regulator, the Securities and Investments Board (SIB) and others were folded into a new body, the Financial Services Authority (FSA), signalling a change of regulatory regime. The FSA subscribed to a newly fashionable approach called enforcement self-regulation, made politically acceptable by being recommended by regulatory scholars at the time[6]. This in essence still relied on firms cooperating to report risk and other data to the regulator, but made explicit the idea that any stand-offish behaviour would be regarded as suspicious: one of the FSA's mantras was 'Comply or explain'.

The enforcement self-regulation model has some positive features, which have largely survived to be imported into the post-FSA era of conduct regulation (FCA). It is worth knowing about these.

First, enforcement self-regulation sets out to gain the cooperation of regulatees by tasking individual firms with producing standards and negotiating these standards with the state. This makes the state (meaning the regulator) well placed to require firms to formally accept and abide by their 'privately written rules'. The firms have to support these rules because they produced them, and do so not only collectively through their trade associations but also at an individual level because each firm relies on this commitment to maintain its trading licence, which the regulator grants. The regulator retains the right to rewrite the rules.

Next, the regulator's resources are greatly eased by transferring onto practitioners many of the critical but labour-intensive aspects of control, such as collating transaction data and explaining product design.

Finally, by mandating firms to have their own internal compliance inspectors, the regulator (in theory) places itself closer to potential wrong-doers; the in-house compliance people are arguably better versed in the firm's 'subject-matter', and so for example can make a more expert impression when demanding reports than could an external regulatory case officer. The firm's internal officers' nearness to the source of the activity to be controlled also makes the control system more efficient and responsive to change.

In a nutshell, this is the regulatory principle of 'leveraging internal control capacity'[7]. And it's all wonderful in theory, of course.

Regulators' 'inherent problems' (4): Asymmetry of engagement

For all this to work in practice, however, requires 'symmetry of incentives to comply'[8] – that is, internal incentives (to comply) must be aligned with external incentives (to do business and make a profit). Where these are not aligned, it is tempting for regulatees to do something else, such as 'ritual' compliance[9], which may involve for example producing lots of paperwork as a substitute for actually changing any behaviour; or minimal compliance ('satisficing'), doing only just enough to pass inspection, and no more. Other forms of performative response include producing 'fantasy documents'[10] and the 'gaming' of compliance reporting targets[11].

One bind for the regulator, then, is that the regulator's own credibility and legitimacy are hostage to the quality of information provided by the regulated firm. Another related one is that intervening aggressively against a firm may provoke a hostile response – known to regulatory science researchers by various names which might feel familiar: a 'culture of minimal compliance', 'routine non-conformity', 'interpretive flexibility', and so on.

We should also keep in mind that firms see themselves as having completely different aims than regulators. Firms are happy to publish well-meaning statements of support for the regulator, but it is by no means clear that a statement will be acted upon. This is supported by an enormous stack of research literature on the difference between formal and informal organizations. In a nutshell, the formal organization is what someone's business card says their job is, what the firm says in its annual report and its sales literature, and so on. The informal organization is simply 'what actually happens'. As one highly regarded observer puts it, once a firm has published its 'organizational script' or official version of what it is going to do, 'it is not necessarily the case that [this] will be complied with or co-operated with'[12].

Regulators' 'inherent problems' (5): Regulatees' bargain-seeking

Research also offers a fascinating glimpse of the problem of 'regulatory capture'. This is where, in essence, regulated firms, either singly or grouping together, approach the regulator and argue that as everyone agrees that this whole compliance thing is really rather hard work, and a bit of a drain on resources, why don't we all strike a deal that saves face for everyone?

Regulatory research is full of case studies of such 'cosy local agreements'. In case you think this only happens in banana republics, think again. In 2008 – admittedly before the crash revealed the extent of corporate corruption – a respected study suggested that regulatory capture may be a normal state in many financial markets: 'There are intractable constraints whereby powerful [firms can] undermine and circumvent regulatory process. Enforcement initiatives that appear brazen on their surface [become] blunted over time through

accommodation and a disjuncture between intention and practice...
[because of] essential power differences between regulator and
regulated'[13].

At the most basic level, it is clear that regulators and financial firms
have divergent ideas about what 'risk management' means: for the
regulator, it is about public protection, for the firm, profit opportunity.
Commercial employees tend to decouple requests for compliance
from the reality of getting on with their moneymaking work. All of
which makes for fairly dispiriting reading, you might think.

But at this point we can climb back in the history helicopter and
take a fast tour through the changes of regulatory outlook that bring us
right up to date with the future-facing agenda of the conduct regulators.

Table 4.1 summarizes key themes and the changing regulatory
landscape around conduct risk. These themes are expanded in this
section.

In the regulatory climate pre-2008, commercial practitioners
tended to regard risk as something separable from underlying assets.
For example, a mortgage was not seen as necessarily attached to the
physical house that it was contracted for; the mortgage contract
could be resold, repackaged and made subject to other, derivative
pricing arrangements – often without the consent or knowledge of
the householder who had taken out the original mortgage. As seen
earlier in the chapter, institutions were only too happy to certify their
own compliance, and in some cases to game their reporting of risk
(see Chapter 7), such as by 'massaging' the declared figure for regulatory
capital or by under-reporting customer complaints. When originating
products, they also liked to create and market packages that tapped
into any current availability of wholesale funds, rather than anything
that responded to an identified customer need. Wholesale and retail
operations coexisted within complex corporate ownership structures,
so that responsibility for problems could be diffused; local mistakes
could be quietly diluted and smoothed away through aggregated
reporting of group-level results; blame and accountability could be
similarly diffused through multiple layers of management.

Meanwhile during this era, regulators maintained old and unhelpful
traditions, which we could summarize as systems thinking. These
traditions included the ideas that a suitable focus for a regulator is to

Table 4.1 Regulators adapting to overcome 'inherent problems'

	Pre-2008	Now	Looking ahead
Commercial practices	• Removing risk decisions from the front line • Separating debt from debtor/asset; virtualizing money • Self-certifying compliance, gaming of risk reports • Supply-driven products • Diffuse responsibility, opaque structures	• Further virtualizing money • De-gearing and divesting • 'Audit rituals' • Supply-driven products • Early challengers • 'Still getting away with it'	• Enforcement shocks for non-financial brands • Major disruptors; commoditized v premium; demand-led products • Further market shocks, eg mortgage market correction(s) • Risk-aware working; licensed mistake-making? • Personal responsibility burden degrades quality of management/ applicants?
Theories of behaviour and regulation	• Systems thinking • Enforcement self-regulation and 'light touch' • Binary compliance • BE in business, but not in regulation • 'Treating Customers Fairly'	• 'TCF+' • Behavioural regulation, human factors acknowledged • Scalar compliance • 'Regulatory tsunami' • 'Heads on spikes'? • Regulatory alliances, 'hunting in packs'	• Global standards; behavioural approach dominant • Regulatory imports between sectors, jurisdictions • Personal accountability • De-biasing?

scrutinize financial products and businesses, on their own terms; that regulated groups respond rationally to instructions; that customers review information to make rational choices; and that measuring how money moves around tells us all we need to know about behaviour (econometric proxies). As seen earlier, the political vogue for 'light touch', enforcement self-regulation appeared to be vindicated by a six-year continuous rise in financial markets between 2002 and 2008[14]. Compliance reports at this time, as ever previously, relied on simplistic binary question designs ('Are compliant, yes or no?'), leaving no room for nuance about varying states of readiness. Although there was some awareness of behavioural economics, this was largely held within businesses, rather than by the regulator: derivatives traders might use value calculations based on Black-Scholes or Nash; marketing departments applied Bayesian algorithms to analyse the habits of credit card customers. The regulator reminded banks about 'Treating Customers Fairly' ('TCF'), but that was the extent of its intervention on behavioural grounds.

Now, of course, some (but by no means all) of those old tenets have been thrown out. With the dawn of amalgamated regulators who focus on conduct, financial prudence, and competition, firms have responded commercially as we might expect. Providers have been jettisoning 'undesirable' customers and business lines, in a wide-spread policy of de-risking – which arguably drives bad practices further underground. For many conventional providers, it is business as usual, creating supply-driven products, going through the motions of compliance (such as the 'audit ritual'), and at least initially avoiding the attention of the new regulators. But this overhang period of denial (hysteresis) is unlikely to last, as both challenger providers and new regulators press harder for change, through new markets and new controls, respectively.

Since the reforms of 2013, the regulators' power has seemed to be growing – though not without a few false starts along the way[15]. The broad premise of behavioural regulation has been floated and accepted, with many providers interpreting it as a familiar idea dressed in new clothes; as 'TCF+'. Although some of the human factors of the new approach are certainly familiar, under the general heading of 'customer outcomes', many more of these factors need to be found in the field of cognitive psychology, which financial providers had not previously been required to explore. The regulator now asks providers to observe directly how their people behave, especially around points of sale, and to think in relative, rather than absolute, terms about states of preparedness and acceptable behaviour.

The previously unthinkable notion of scalar compliance is now beginning to be understood: the idea that in the past a simple 'yes' to the compliance question was often a lie, which needs replacing with a more truthful 'here's how far we have progressed towards achieving it'.

Conclusion: The way ahead

Looking to the future, we may expect to see regulators moving beyond the familiar pattern of enforcement actions against providers of financial products. There are many businesses that sell financial products but that don't consider themselves financial providers, such as car makers and house builders, who offer loans; manufacturers and retailers who offer credit cards. In the future, any business that offers any kind of financial service should prepare to get a visit from the regulator. For the unprepared, there might be a nasty surprise, in the form of a misconduct prosecution for customer detriment. The twin drivers of new technology and a larger youthful audience will present older providers with a tipping point when customers desert old business models for new: the much-feared 'Uber Moment'[16]. As with other consumer markets that disruptors have turned over, new providers will offer buyers a smoother, more demand-led experience, and markets will divide sharply between commoditized (that is, cheapest possible) and premium (pay more, get more service).

The sheer amount of credit in many nations' economies may be expected to come home to roost in various forms – some of which may already have happened between my writing and your reading this: a house price collapse, a national default on sovereign debt, or a consumer credit squeeze, to name just three possible forms. As providers will have to adjust to accommodate these shocks, so will regulators. Amid all this macro-scale hazard, we must hope that providers and regulators have by then taught one another to be more tolerant of genuine mistakes – by promoting a constructive approach to risk-aware working, as explored in the second half of this book, better outcomes are possible for both sides. In the shorter term, however, the opposite seems likely, as tougher personal controls on senior managers have already provoked some contrary and unwanted responses, such as shortening of contracts, poorer quality applicants, and 'juniorization'[17].

For the regulators themselves, the outlook remains bright for the coming decade. The behavioural view is likely to dominate the regulatory debate, at least for as long as conduct enforcement remains a big and popular money-spinner for national treasuries. Regulators will continue, and accelerate, programmes of sharing expertise and staff between each other, nationally and internationally. The first shock of high-profile enforcements against individual senior managers may be expected to give way to a more sustained and, some may say, considered regulatory programme of genuine attempts to work with providers to design bias out of their marketing and sales systems; any attempt to create standard de-biasing initiatives across the sector will fail, however – for reasons that will become clear in the latter part of this book.

While the earliest focus of the original conduct regulator, the FCA, might seem to many to have been more about aggressive punishments and fines, than about positive incentives to good behaviour – more 'stick' than 'carrot', as some have said – there is an encouraging underlying trend to greater engagement between regulator and regulatee, which is useful to consider. In 2015, the FCA made this change in emphasis explicit, pledging to be in future 'encouraging more than scolding', but this remains hanging in the air. Meanwhile, there remains a high probability of sustained rounds of personal prosecutions under the Senior Managers Regime, so we should consider what this apparently contradictory situation invites us to do in practice.

For as long as regulators stay reluctant to produce their own 'best practice' guidelines, or to endorse those produced by firms, most practitioners agree that our best collective course is to tease out the question of 'what "good" looks like'. Absent of specific guidance from the regulator, the industry needs to continue to find its own way to devise and present best practice guidance. To that end, Chapter 7 offers some robust answers, proven by research among regulators and practitioners; meanwhile, some further light can be shed on the topic of where bad behaviour comes from, and how conduct regulators are appearing, like spring flowers, all around the world.

We have seen how conduct regulators face structural and systemic problems including regulatees' (partly predictable) human contrariness; communication gaps; overconfident experts; post-rationalizing to disown past failures; resource stretch; lack of traction; and susceptibility to 'capture' by regulatee groups. By targeting regulatee senior managers personally, and by hugely increasing penalties, the new wave of conduct regulators is addressing some of these challenges. The tougher conceptual challenge of reconceiving compliance from a binary (yes-or-no) to a scalar (nuanced and truthful) form of reporting remains very much a work in progress.

Notes

1   For example, *The Guardian* editorial, Hasten the death of deference in the civil service, 9 October 2012, at www.theguardian.com/society/2012/oct/09/hasten-death-deference-civil-service

2   Many catalogued in King, A and Crewe, I (2013) *The Blunders of Our Governments*, Oneworld, London

3   Beck, U (1992) *Risk Society: Towards a New Modernity*, Sage, London/Frankfurt

4   Simply YouTube search 'four candles'

5   See, for example, www.sam.gov.lv/images/modules/items/PDF/item_618_NL_The_table_of_Eleven.pdf

6   For example, Ayres, I and Braithwaite, J (1992) *Responsive Regulation: Transcending the Deregulation Debate*, Oxford University Press

7   Miles, R (2012) *From Compliance to Coping*, KCL at kclpure.kcl.ac.uk/portal/en/theses/from-compliance-to-coping(e2634d8e-1682-4790-8110-405b0ed2b359).html

8   Miles, ibid

9   Power, M (2005) Organizational Responses to Risk: The risk of the Chief Risk Officer in *Organizational Encounters with Risk*, Cambridge University Press

10   Clarke, L (1999) *Mission Improbable: Using Fantasy Documents to Tame Disaster*, University of Chicago Press

11   So-called 'Goodhart's Law', aka 'What's measured is what matters', 'teaching to the test', etc

12   Hutter, B (2005) *Ways of Seeing: Understandings of risk in organizational setting*, London School of Economics

13   Williams, J, Out of place and out of line: Positioning the Police in the Regulation of Financial Markets, *Law & Policy*, July 2008, 30 (3), pp 306–35

14 See, for example, FTSE Index history at a.citywirecontent.co.uk/
images/2012/04/10/581123-System__Resources__Image-644414.gif

15 Such as the Treasury minister's removal of the first head of the FCA;
and the regulator's abandoning of a planned review of risk culture in
banks (both in 2015–16)

16 See *The Guardian*, 25 November 2015, Banking facing 'Uber moment',
at www.theguardian.com/business/2015/nov/25/banking-facing-uber-
moment-says-former-barclays-boss

17 See Reuters, Bankers jostle to be junior as accountability rules kick in,
7 March 2016, at uk.reuters.com/article/uk-britain-banks-regulations-
idUKKCN0W808V

The roots of misconduct

05

Introduction: mission creep and research comfort

Since its first introduction into UK markets in 2013, conduct-based regulation has been subject to 'mission creep' (political expansion of purpose) and also to global expansion in scope and application. It is no exaggeration to say that this new mode of regulation has become a political gold rush, with new regulators in many other jurisdictions around the world making haste to adopt and expand on the principles first set out by the UK's Financial Conduct Authority. There are a number of political drivers for this development, which this chapter will explore.

This chapter also considers a range of systemic drivers of 'bad behaviour' risks confronting the new generation of conduct regulators, challenging them to prove to a sceptical public that financial practitioners have not been allowed to 'get away with it' after the crashes and bail-outs of the late 2000s.

Themes and concepts in this chapter

abstraction – behavioural view – biteback – calibrating 'normal' – cognitive bias – the credit crunch – formal v informal organizations – granular regulation – lack of concerted challenge – limit of agency – macro 'bad behaviour' factors – 'mission creep' – predictive power – projection bias – rational non-compliers/rational calculators – regulatory arbitrage/ jurisdiction-hopping – regulatory assumptions – 'regulatory dance' – resource asymmetry – social purpose/socially useful – 'tone at the top' fallacy – tribe/tribal network culture – 'what actually happens'

Challenges to financial providers' orthodoxy of 'too big to fail'

The events of 2008 encouraged many behavioural researchers to focus explicitly on issues of financial provider misconduct. The resulting research findings begin to offer both some welcome comfort for compliance and risk teams within the sector, and an indication of the future shape of regulatory policy that could shape better forms of control over 'bad behaviour'.

Regulators for a long time withheld any published definition of what good behaviour looks like, instead declaring an intention to compel providers to reflect on this and to produce their own standards. Researchers have now begun to step up to this challenge, some seeking to define 'good behaviour' benchmarks[1], others transforming the industry's own understanding of how to judge acceptable conduct[2]. These and other initiatives are now extending general knowledge of the origins of 'bad behaviour' in institutional settings and paving the way to develop new tools to prevent it.

These latest behavioural research studies explicitly confirm, in various ways, that forms of bad behaviour arise wherever there is a clear set of preconditions in place. In combination they advance the 'predictive power' to analyse the onset of conduct threats, and to put in place better interventions to deal with them pre-emptively. In plain terms, the new research helps providers to see far more clearly when and where bad behaviour can arise in an organization, and so to stop it before it takes root. The new research insights offer welcome relief to all those corporate officers whose main concern is the subset of bad behaviour known as conduct risk, and who continue to face an explosion in compliance resource budgets, fines and costs of reputational fallout.

The most controversial finding among the new, finance-specific behavioural research projects, which upset the preconceptions of numerous regulators, was the destruction of the orthodoxy of 'tone at the top'[3]. This idea, previously very popular among regulators, suggested that the behaviour and statements emanating from the board would be a good starting point, and continuing indicator, for determining how well an organization is committed to embedding good behaviour and mitigating conduct risk. Following publication of research results validated by a massive international study, it emerged that 'tone at the top' simply gives no valid indication whatever of the organization's probity overall. It was not the effective indicator that regulators wanted it to be, or had assumed it to be. The same research, together with other conduct analysis projects, pointed to other more reliable sets of indicators able to predict exposure to conduct risk. However, these indicators were not in the places that regulators (or practitioners) had assumed they would be; later in this book (Chapters 8 and 9) these indicators will be revealed in more detail and presented in a form ready for practical use.

When bold new research shatters old beliefs

Truly useful new research findings have a way of shattering the vested interests and assumptions of those in power, as many a scientist down the centuries has found out, often the hard way. As you may recall, Galileo was kept under house arrest for a decade in the 1630s for daring to suggest that the earth revolves around the sun. After Lavoisier explained to the world the chemistry of how we breathe, he was guillotined by French Revolutionaries for his efforts.

While new behavioural research findings may not have brought quite these levels of cosmic significance, nevertheless they have helped to tilt the human-factor axis of the compliance world. Strikingly, although the new behavioural insights have arrived from discrete research programmes from several different continents, their conclusions are consistent in building a new picture of where bad behaviour comes from, and how to identify and prevent it. The new insights began to, and have continued to, upset a stack of comfortable preconceptions held by compliance people, policymakers and indeed regulators themselves. To understand their full significance, though, it helps to have a bit of context.

Conduct cost shocks and 'social value' questions

The arrival of conduct risk in global markets brought traumas of enforcement for many financial brands, including major international firms. Within its first three years, the conduct 'regulatory project' has generated multimillion dollar/pound costs of fines, remediation payments and reorganization costs.

By any measure, this scale of costs is a big step up from previous regulatory regimes, where incremental change had always appeared to be the norm. Under earlier regulators, new rules were frequently market-tested by the industry in GSVR form (see box below) – that is, industry groups would introduce their own Code of Practice designed to deflect public criticism.

Pain-free floating of new regulations the GSVR way

GSVRs are 'government sponsored voluntary regulations', often in the shape of industry codes of practice, supervised by regulators. Industry lobby groups frequently introduce codes of practice as a defensive move when they're in trouble for bad behaviour towards certain customers. The industry's preferred code is backed by the regulator's threat to extend powers of prosecution for non-compliance, or the formal adoption of the code into law at a later point if the industry fails to mend its ways.

We have lived through many such codes, for example for bank service to customers, for mortgage selling, for credit card charges, and to protect small businesses against lenders' over-hasty foreclosure. This had all seemed to work, more or less, at least in theory and for as long as financial providers were perceived not to be actively working against the public interest. That all changed following the events of 2008, when even central bankers started to question the extent to which commercial banking had lost its 'social purpose' (see box).

The social purpose of finance: a change of tune

Senior regulators including Bank of England Governor, Mark Carney, have raised the profile of a debate about the societal value of banking, challenging banks to show that they are aware they must be 'socially useful'[4]. It is no longer sufficient to invest only in economic capital; one must now consider social capital; to stop markets 'devouring social capital', firms must acknowledge their wider social responsibilities[5].

This is in marked contrast to a previous Governor of the Bank of England, speaking 80 years earlier, who was notably less pro-social. Governor Montague Norman told his audience that banking had a duty to 'protect itself in every possible way, both by combination and legislation. Debts must be collected, mortgages foreclosed as rapidly as possible. When, through process of law, the common people lose their homes, they will become more docile and more easily governed through the strong arm of the government.'[6]

Despite the global suffering caused by the credit crunch, it took more than five years for the regulatory change of mood to be felt directly at the business end. Researching risky behaviour in financial markets, this author has had frequent informal debriefs with conduct risk leaders in institutions of all sizes, hearing their frank reactions to the latest developments, particularly in matters of regulation and enforcement.

A word here about those informal briefings and research sources: given the right controlled setting and safeguards, informal briefings offer insights that can be just as valid, and valuable, as pre-structured research. In particular, 'war stories' about recent experiences often present unvarnished truths. In the right research hands, these war stories (or in the academic jargon, 'sense-making narratives of risk') have strong explanatory power and are, indeed, one of the pleasures of doing research in this field of human behaviour. It is also why as an analyst I approach many behavioural investigations from the dark side – that is, talking to creative compliers about 'what actually happens' rather than making assumptions about how things *should* be working.

With this technique, rather than starting with formal rule structures and then looking for non-compliance as the exception, we start from the premise that spontaneous and full compliance are in fact rarer events, only occurring when people perceive that they have no alternative. In reality, as opposed to in their reports of compliance, most people comply incompletely – sometimes not at all – and then seek to explain away this behaviour, both to themselves and to others. Real world events continue to suggest that this 'what actually happens', listening approach has greater explanatory power than econometric models-based alternatives.

Shortly after the start of the new regime of conduct-related enforcements, my research sources began to acknowledge the impact of the new regulator, saying things like: 'The new regulation is real now', and 'We can't, any more, take the view that we'll just "pay off the fine" and carry on.' One chief risk officer described to me how conduct risk has had 'a seismic impact on the landscape' of corporate risk: 'Our biggest concern now is something we never expected we'd have to engage with from a compliance point of view. It's not so much the direct cost of enforcement actions – big though that is – no, it's the cost of reputation risk that our conduct creates, that's looming far larger.'

Previously, reputation risk had been the domain of people working in consumer affairs, corporate social responsibility (CSR), corporate branding and investor relations. The speed at which conduct risk moved front-and-centre for compliance people, during 2013–16, told the sector all they needed to know about resetting its conduct control priorities. A first step in doing so was, and is still, to understand where good and bad behaviour generally comes from.

Origins of misbehaviour (1): Formal v informal groups

To understand how patterns of misbehaviour arise and become ingrained in regulated organizations, it is necessary first to adjust normal preconceptions about who's controlling whom in the three-way 'regulatory dance'[7] between government, industry and regulator. (There is a theoretical framework that helps to explain how organized groups of people try to make an impact on other organized groups of people: the theory of Agency – see box: Why don't people behave even worse? below. It offers a surprisingly helpful insight into how analogous effects operate in financial markets.)

A key real-world point that this helps us to understand is where power lies in organizations. In plain terms, it answers a question that seems simple but isn't: 'Who's really in charge here?'

While there is the initially obvious answer, of course, that 'The boss is in charge' (meaning the CEO or head of operating company), that answer may not be true in practical reality. Conventional control and governance systems publish a formally drawn up hierarchy of corporate control based on job titles and responsibilities. According to this view, the CEO must be in charge, and so must the Chairman be, because everyone else reports to them. Are they fully in control, though, in practice? And what does the new alternative, behavioural view of risk have to say about that?

This is where anyone who has grown up with standard compliance and risk control systems may begin to recognize the shortcomings of conventional risk measures, and feel perhaps a little uncomfortable about it. The discovery that a measurement system you have relied upon is in fact presenting a false picture of reality *is* disconcerting. The changing picture of reality between behavioural and conventional risk vision is rather similar to how it feels to put on night-vision goggles for the first time or to take an infrared photograph. Everything in front of you is still in the same place, yet it all looks quite different. So it is when you apply a behavioural lens to risk, showing previously unseen layers of how things work. The behavioural lens reveals new shapes and patterns operating within your organization.

Formal and informal

For a start, every organization functions in two different modes: the formal and the informal. The formal organization produces artefacts that you can see with your standard lenses: published reports and structures, charts showing job titles and reporting lines, risk registers, annual reports, logos and mission statements. Most employees, and especially the board, tend to cling to these artefacts, these published versions of what's real, for reassurance.

Unfortunately for risk governance, however, it is the informal organization that dictates 'what actually happens' (WAH). My research concentrates on the WAH side of the divide, because it is a much better predictor of, well, what will actually happen when you impose any new form of risk control.

So it is WAH that informs the behavioural lens. It is rather like pointing a night-vision camera at your firm and saying: Where are the hotspots?

What actually happens (WAH) example realities

Look at your board meeting, and think: Who's really in charge in the room? Who has the most power here, in reality? Who commands the most attention?

Is it the CEO? (WAH view: Not necessarily.)

Is it the Head of Sales? (WAH view: Quite possibly.)

Does the chief risk officer have any authority here? (WAH view: Almost never.)

How about your sales operations or trading desks: Do the traders have any loyalty? (WAH view: Yes, but…). Who are they most loyal to? (WAH view: Normally, their own immediate team and careers.)

The learning point is simple enough. We can either cling to the comforting, but wholly misguided, view that published rules and codes work most effectively to curb human bad behaviour. Or we can work with real human behaviour to develop new forms of risk control that don't rely on systems and proxy measures of performance, such as monetary indicators. New controls based on a behavioural vision reject proxy measures in favour of directly observing how people behave. Direct observation of behaviour – using a behavioural lens – is the core of the WAH approach (behavioural science calls the technique 'relentlessly empirical'). Anyone seeking to impose a new risk control on people will get a far better response if they have already been watching closely how the same people responded whenever other controls were introduced.

Why don't people behave even worse?

The 'limit of agency' view

Unless they're psychopaths, or just seriously lacking in common sense and empathy, most organized groups of people (formal or informal) will restrain their own misbehaviour. They don't want to provoke strong intervention or a hostile reaction, losing all public support.

There's a practical element to this too: If Group A inflicted widespread harm on Group B, either there simply wouldn't be enough of Group B left standing, whose attention to grab, or the Group B survivors would turn all angry and vengeful. So there's seldom much long-term logic in Group A violently exercising its 'full agency' to wipe out Group B.

More normally, as an assertive group (such as your salespeople, maybe?) seeks to take control over what they see as their home territory, they limit their misbehaviour so as not to attract scrutiny which they'd see as likely to hurt revenues.

Now hold on a minute... didn't the mortgage mis-sellers actually fail to self-restrain in 2008? Didn't that wipe out a 'Group B' whose existence they rather needed: their customers? And this is exactly the point. When As fail to limit their provocation of Bs, they forfeit any external support.

Origins (2): Human tractability

One sad but pointedly useful finding of behavioural research among financial providers[8],[9] is that we really should be far less surprised when bad behaviour happens. There are several reasons why broad regulatory assumptions fail in financial markets in particular.

First, financial markets simply do attract more than their fair share of chancers. I think of this as the Willie Sutton Effect (after the gangster who robbed banks 'because that's where they keep the money').

Second, while it is true – thank goodness – that most people are honest in their ordinary lives, we know that a person's behaviour can and does change quite dramatically when their reference points for 'what's normal in life' are suddenly upset. One such trauma occurs when a large sum of money passes in front of anyone who has never seen such a thing before. Such a life-changing, behaviour-bending event happens frequently, of course, in financial markets.

Thirdly, and most important, is the action of informal groups; the financial service sector presents an exceptionally strong case of this. Whatever the formal rules and systems say, it is the informal behaviour of a person's immediate workgroup that most strongly determines what 'normal' means for them personally. It is perfectly normal behaviour (thanks to cognitive processes such as social proof and mirroring), that each of us quickly adapts to behave in ways that help us to fit in with our workgroup, even if privately we would prefer that they behaved themselves better. The workgroup includes people of equal status working in the same space and also – crucially – includes line managers. Perhaps most important of all, it *excludes* senior management – unless you are a senior manager yourself, in which case several more highly evolved forms of social proof come into play; most notably groupthink and the Dunning-Kruger effect (see box). Recent research offers a new explanation of groupthink processes[10], showing how these clearly apply to corporate boards, who risk 'group polarization', including denial of a present problem, since their 'salient shared identity' is 'a group whose members are already inclined in a certain direction'. Boards' 'affective ties… narrow the argument pool', creating a 'disproportionate number of arguments supporting that same direction'[11].

Dunning-Kruger

The word 'groupthink' may get all the news headlines, but its cousin, Dunning-Kruger is much more prevalent.

Dunning-Kruger is easiest to remember as the 'talent show effect'. It's the way that we all tend to think that we are good at doing something, just because we know how to do it at a basic level. As with wannabe singers who really can't sing, but nobody has told them; our inner Simon Cowell often goes missing.

For example, according to behavioural research, three-quarters of male car drivers rate their own driving skills as 'above average'; go figure.

One of the more recent behavioural insights has offered a specific explanation of how and why the informal workgroup operates in relation to financial markets traders: there's a 'tribal network culture' that drives their local loyalties[12]. This study showed how and why 'tribes' form, with their own loyalties that defy all forms of corporate control structures. The rate-fixers of LIBOR (2013) and foreign exchange markets (2015) operated as tribes, with their own language, social media, and even (criminal) codes of conduct. The study notes that where people used to feel loyalty (job security) from their employer organization, they no longer do so; so they 'stop caring about the organization' and care only for their 'tribe' – the contacts in other firms (or their close team) 'who will hire them or recommend them for jobs.'[13] The key point here is that the 'tribe' consists only of immediate workgroup and line managers, plus similar workers at other firms. Each tribe of financial salespeople develops an over-strong allegiance to their own immediate workgroup, plus a few close line managers, and industry peers – and a subversive attitude towards any more senior managers. That is, the tribe may choose to define itself partly by finding ways to 'beat' (put one over on, compromise, sabotage) senior management. And not a corporate mission statement in sight.

A final point of sabotage that frustrates aspiring regulators is biteback. Ironically, the harder a regulator pushes for change, the more some regulatees will regard attempts at control as a provocation, and respond with worse behaviour than before.

Biteback: SUVs and football hooligans

Researchers tracking human responses to control interventions have found a tendency for 'perverse' reactions.

When in the 1970s, British soccer regulators decided that spectators needed to be contained in fenced-off 'crowd cages' for their own good, many fans reacted badly and for a while levels of violence worsened: 'If you treat us like criminals, we'll behave like criminals.' The fallacy that people would behave better in cages was laid bare when those same cages set the horrific scene for mass fatalities in crowd-control disasters at Heysel (1985) and Hillsborough (1989).

For SUV (big, urban, off-road-type) car drivers, there's an analogous point: people who buy heavily crash-protected cars tend to drive less carefully.

Whether one is a hooligan or an SUV driver (or possibly both – see box), or just a regular person, it seems that we adapt our behaviour creatively – and sometimes perversely – to resist a new risk control. As a broad conclusion, therefore, it is necessary to strip out two unsound assumptions from our designs for conduct risk controls: first, the assumption that people's default setting is always good behaviour; second, that people will respond positively to the introduction of any well-meant new control. Human history repeatedly reminds us how such systems-thinking assumptions lead to things going badly wrong.

Origins (3): Macro structural factors enabling bad behaviour

All of which is very well, you may be saying, but all the factors mentioned so far operate at an individual human level; one might call these 'micro-cultural' risk factors. Turn the behavioural lens around, and at the higher level we may discern macro factors that are equally as important.

As one research study puts it[14]: while focusing on controlling the specifics of 'extreme risk-taking, mis-selling, and rate fixing', government and regulatory initiatives have taken attention away from larger, and darker, underlying factors that promote inappropriate tolerance for profitable but self-seeking behaviour. Focus on 'tone at the top', for example, for some years diverted attention away from duplicitous line managers and tribal loyalties among traders[15]. Attention on board governance and on specific enforcement actions in the early years of conduct enforcement left 'scant recognition' that there are 'common causes lurking beneath [many] types of misconduct' in financial markets, including 'a role in the facilitation of crime itself'[16]. These are serious charges indeed. It is important to understand the structural factors that underlie and support them, and to address these in any programme that genuinely seeks to embed good conduct.

Corporate longevity

Looking across the whole corporate landscape, one might assume at first that this is a far from certain point. Major brands disappear all the time, victims of market shocks, takeovers, technology change or customers simply walking away. While in the wider corporate sector it is very rare for a brand name to survive for more than a century, the financial sector retains more than its fair share of 'old' brands. Even after recent financial markets' collapse, takeover, and regulatory takedown, to a casual observer it still seems that many of the familiar established names still dominate the market.

Now, in cognitive terms, the world looks different if you are an employee looking out from inside the offices of one of these long-lived brands. One effect you would notice is that the political clock ticks at a much faster rate. In practice, here is what that means. Cognitive research has already taught us that small animals have faster body clocks than large ones: to a hummingbird, beating his wings 80 times a second, the world seems to move along terribly slowly. To a mayfly, 24 hours is literally a lifetime. To an investment banker whose firm has been around for a century, or maybe two, the four- or five-year term of a government is a transient irritation. Or, as one bank finance director once candidly muttered to me: 'If we don't like this government, it doesn't really matter – there'll be another one along soon enough.'

Decision science has not yet come up with a jargon name for this effect, although one might loosely describe it as Projection Bias. Working for a long-lived megabrand bank distorts employees' perceptions of what is significant in the wider world outside. In the worst cases, some staff come to believe that they are untouchable by outsiders – including law enforcers – simply because their brand feels as if it has outlasted everything else out there. This bias can quickly inflate into a grandiose self-belief that regulation does not matter. As with my cynical FD friend's analogy, governments can begin to look like buses; if the first to arrive isn't heading the way we want, we'll just wait for the next one. In practice, this means biding time by rear-ranging your budget, economizing on compliance efforts and beefing up your lobbying team to help you to keep on stalling any proposed reforms in the meantime.

Depth of resources

Closely related to longevity, as above, are firms' deep pockets. Any organization that has more capital and disposable cash than any sovereign government that is trying to regulate it, can play this tactic. And of course, they know who they are.

Those first two factors, longevity and deep pockets, are perhaps the strongest drivers of regulatory capture, as political scientists call it. Although that concept is a focus of numerous expert studies in regulatory theory, its underlying idea is quite simple: a well-established business sector has more resources than its regulator. Corruption will occur when any industry begins to take advantage of this skew (or 'structural asymmetry', in the jargon). The industry may start to find ways to outmanoeuvre the regulator, exploiting its own superior resources of cash, intellect, data and knowhow – some of the very same asymmetries that the regulator blames for driving product mis-selling. In the most egregious cases, an industry may capture its regulator so completely that the regulator stops serving the public interest and becomes an apologist for the industry's way of doing business, including its abuses.

Abstraction

The third factor is abstraction – the intangible, ephemeral nature of the product. Although the word itself may look awkward, again the idea behind it is simple enough: ordinary people like to interact with things that are tangible and solid – stuff we can see, touch, hear. Abstractions are the opposite. Business products or activities are abstractions if they are one or more of the following: complex, physically remote, virtual, subcontracted, or secondary-traded (derivative). Much financial product marketing clearly fits this profile.

For example, we now know that the more abstract a point-of-sale authorization feels, the less impression it makes on the consumer. So a chip-and-pin credit card transaction 'hurts' much less than handing over cash. A near-field card transaction 'hurts' even less than chip-and-pin. The result: as consumers switch to the most painless ways of buying stuff, they spend more, and faster, racking up ever larger debts which the provider is only too happy to charge interest on.

At a higher level, abstractions also give risk regulators a headache. It's not so much that financial markets are inherently complex (one might expect anyone trying to regulate them to have seen this problem coming). More, it is about kudos and public support: the regulator knows that a modest 'win' against a consumer brand will earn far more public approval than a higher-value enforcement against an obscure wholesale derivative contract.

In a related, and rather depressing, form of cognitive bias, many people (including many bankers) have no mental conception of what a large number means – for example, they can't imagine a billion of anything, or that 3 billion is 3,000 times bigger than a million. And *that* form of cognitive blindness also gives rise to the next structural risk factor…

Absence of concerted challenge

In spite of the many scandals of recent years, compared with other sectors financial services enjoys a distinct lack of concerted challenge from outside the industry. Unlike other industries – and whatever its advocacy groups maintain – it faces weak commercial competition, and no single-issue coordinated criticism from consumers, politicians or businesses. One aspect of Agency Theory of consumer protest (see box: Why don't people behave even worse? above) is that if the protestors want to really change anything, they need to pick on a social harm that's plainly defined and easy to see. In the United States in the 1960s, a major auto manufacturer was content to produce cars that spontaneously exploded in some traffic situations; campaigners responded with *Unsafe At Any Speed*[17], and after some adjustment pains, the carmaking industry was forced to change.

Evidently, financial products do not present the same kind of easy targets for protest; if anything, they are the exact opposite. Anyone marketing products that the general public cannot understand – or, dare one suggest, that it is a marketing strategy that the product is hard to understand – is already operating in an ethically unsound zone. The credit crunch, apart from being called a crunch, is wholly unlike Mr Nader's unsafe cars. In the fully virtual landscape of credit derivatives, there is no easy-to-find target for personal protest; no exploding car, no charred bodies on the highway. Lacking any such focus, what's a consumer protest group to do? This insight may help to explain why the Consumers Association continues to thrive, 50 years on, while the Occupy anti-banking movement has struggled to gain traction.

Not territory-dependent

Financial service businesses are often not territory-dependent; that is, their offices have no need to be located anywhere in particular. This is clearly the opposite of (conventional) shop-based retailing of consumer goods.

Together with the longevity and abstraction factors above, this can encourage providers to reason that 'because we don't need to be in this country, we don't need to worry about its laws'. Not being dependent on any one country for infrastructure, they shop around – typically for the cheapest labour and the lightest supervision; so-called 'regulatory arbitrage' or 'jurisdiction-hopping'.

An entire international service economy, known simply as 'offshore', has sprung up to cater for this. For example, one offshore territory, the Cayman Islands, happily markets itself as a place to bring 'complex financial deals which might not otherwise happen onshore'[18].

As a provider looking to exploit any ambiguities in defined good conduct, once one can convince oneself that such rationales are good for business, behavioural norms are readjusted in a range of ways. The organization becomes ethically flexible, less concerned to comply with rules in any one jurisdiction; indeed, other jurisdictions may offer greater flexibility. Games of regulatory arbitrage and jurisdiction-shopping may occasionally be played hard by ethically neutral boards.

Regulatory arbitrage takes many forms, but for our purposes here it is sufficient to look at two broad types: passive and active. In the passive game, the company sets up shop only in territories that offer the most favourable version of the law: for example, licensing intellectual property out of a holding company in Luxembourg or Eire, repatriating profits there for tax efficiency. In the active game, the company uses its presence as a national mass employer and/or tax contributor to insist that the government make favourable changes in the law, against a blackmail threat of job cuts and relocation to elsewhere.

Granular regulation

It is a truism that the more the detail, the more the loopholes; so-called 'granular regulation' offers more opportunities for gaming the 'spaces in between the rules'. There is also a deeper structural factor here. As seen in Chapter 4, a universal systemic weakness of regulation is that regulators can never have access to the same resources of information or intellect that the industry does. Such 'resource asymmetry' is inevitable. Governments and regulators argue from time to time that forcing an industry to provide more detailed information will create more opportunities to reveal and prosecute misconduct. There is no good evidence that this succeeds, and plenty of evidence that it achieves the exact opposite: the regulator succeeds only in building up such a vast pile of management information that they will never find enough staff time to analyse it.

There is also an obvious paradox designed into this model of so-called 'enforcement self-regulation', in which the regulator relies on the industry to produce the management information they need to determine whether to mount an enforcement action. Unsurprisingly, regulatees are in absolutely no hurry to incriminate themselves by self-reporting any problems.

Origins (4): Team-level risk culture

As recent behavioural research has been finding, it is less 'tone at the top' than 'tone in the middle' that legitimizes bad behaviour, confirming why the regulator needs to take a behaviour-based approach[19]. A key determinant of good behaviour and compliance, and hence potential costs of misconduct, is how far staff regard governance and risk structures as personally relevant to themselves, and socially supported by everyone around them. It is not enough that staff make their own sense of any standards shown to them, or even that they are trained in; they must also look for supportive (non-verbal) signals from people close to them, confirming that 'this rule really does apply to me'. Although conduct risk *is* a matter of culture, it has almost nothing to do with any carefully formulated artefacts that senior managers hand down. As a matter of intuition and common sense, if the central rules say one thing, but the line manager or colleagues at the desk say another, the local version will usually win – especially as long as financial rewards for 'making the numbers' remain the key measure of success.

The behavioural research[20] has also shown that senior managers invariably have a more optimistic view of their organization's risk culture and compliance than the reality can support; and that middle managers invariably 'filter' upwards reporting when they are non-compliant. To put that another way: the most powerful predictor for bad behaviour turns out to be that people won't talk about bad behaviour.

Finally, to support this understanding, it helps to be aware that research continuing[21] in the related field of corporate corruption (FCPA [US] and Bribery Act [UK]) shows parallel findings. This research confirms earlier reports about rational non-compliers (aka 'rational calculators'). In many a regulated community there will be a subset of individuals who do a quick mental sum, weighing up probabilities and costs of detection, against the normal return on profit from bending the rules. As so often with behavioural research, one research respondent has already summed up this point perfectly: 'If I violate the Code of Conduct (or FCPA etc), I may or may not get caught; if I miss my numbers for two quarters, I will be fired.' This is the logic of control failure under the 'what actually happens' effect.

As the behavioural research net casts ever wider, we are finding more and more instances and places where this effect occurs. New understandings of the supply and demand forces in the 'market' for corruption are a significant parallel step in the creation of universal conduct risk understanding.

Conclusion

This chapter has considered some internal origins of misbehaviour in organizations. Many of these effects spring from traditional structures and habits that persist in the financial sector. These include powerful informal and 'tribal' groups; regulators who lack resources and are susceptible to deal-making; firms' relative longevity, deep resources and mobility; and a lack of concerted challenge by disadvantaged customers.

The next chapter will move on to examine how regulators' political sponsors – and the voters who empower *them* – are pushing for behavioural regulation as a way to remedy these failings.

Notes

1 Cambridge Judge Business School/CCP Research: *Conduct Risk 'Grey Areas' Project,* in press (2017), with this author's participation

2 Sheedy, E and Griffin, B (2015) *Risk Governance, Cultures, Structure and Behaviour,* MacQuarie University, at papers.ssrn.com/sol3/papers.cfm?abstract_id=2529803

3 Sheedy and Griffin, ibid

4 Adair Turner, interview in *Prospect* magazine, 27 August 2009

5 Mark Carney, national press interviews, 28 May 2014

6 Montague Norman, speech to the US Bankers' Association, New York, 1924

7 A term explored by Laureen Snider (in *Corporate Crime,* 2009, etc)

8 Platt, S (2015) *Criminal Capital,* Palgrave Macmillan

9 Miles, R (2013) *From Compliance to Coping,* University of London

10 Sunstein, C, *RSA Journal* 2014/4

11 Sunstein, ibid

12 See *Tribal cultures in large banks,* Compliance Complete, 5 January 2015: Stephen Mandis, a former investment banker and now professor at Columbia University, discusses his study of how 'tribes' form within banks

13 From *Tribal Cultures* study noted above

14 Platt, as above

15 From *Tribal Cultures* as above

16 Platt, as above

17 Nader, Ralph (1965) *Unsafe at Any Speed: The Designed-In Dangers of the American Automobile,* Grossman Publishers

18 Platt, as above

19 Sheedy and Griffin, as above

20 Sheedy and Griffin, as above

21 Richard Bistrong and Alison Taylor, *Behind the Bribe* project, at The Network/Columbia University: see tnwinc.com/13686/whitepaper-behind-the-bribe-2/

The politics of prosecution

06

Conduct rules go global

Introduction

Each board director of a financial firm in the UK is now a target for direct, personal prosecution, under the conduct regulator's Senior Managers (and Certification) Regime.

We should recall that it was only a few short years ago, in 2013, that the Financial Conduct Authority (FCA) led the way to this as the world's first financial conduct regulator. Yet, within that short time, the FCA's initiative has itself been overtaken by faster moving new 'behavioural enforcers' in other countries around the world. Conduct controls have been a surprise hit, with revenues from enforcements creating a gold rush among national governments. There is much that this implies for firms' future management of risk. To see properly what all this means from now on, we need first to understand how and why an underlying change in political attitude has come about.

This chapter will also consider the globalization of conduct rules, as other jurisdictions bring in their own controls, similar to the UK model but with new entrants also bringing their own local agenda points. Other countries implement conduct regulation with local interpretations of core value-systems, with a global taxonomy of conduct risk emerging.

Themes and concepts in this chapter

authority – careless record-keeping – cognitive failure – conduct regulation – customer care failure – 'Econs v Humans' debate – empathy-deficient – fundamental attribution error – the global taxonomy of conduct risks/enforcements – irrational behaviour – legitimacy – market abuse – mirroring behaviour – nudging – oversight failure – political theatre – predictably irrational – 'real people'/'normal people' – relentlessly empirical – self-reporting – shaming – symbolic enforcement

Points of origin

Surveying the debris of wholesale and consumer financial markets post-2008, politicians needed urgently to reassert their authority and legitimacy. Voters everywhere, even as they often struggled to understand what had just happened, nevertheless were feeling the pain of evictions, foreclosures and tax-funded bailouts, and were beginning to turn their rage towards their elected representatives who seemed to have caused it all, somehow, by losing control.

Casting around for a new template for regulation, public officials seized on an unconventional branch of science that seemed to offer hope: behavioural economics. This suggested that by regulating the *behaviour* of people in financial markets, rather than the products they sold, all would be well again. There was another political payoff: the new behavioural alchemy of 'nudging' would give politicians a kind of super-heroic power to make big social changes without having to spend public money. It didn't seem to matter that, back in the early 2000s, behavioural science's most talked-about successes were the (much debated) Black-Scholes options pricing system, and a design scheme to discourage male travellers from urinating on the washroom floor at Schipol Airport. Then again, all innovators have to start somewhere[1]. A big draw for the politicians was that possibility of using 'nudges' to 'do more with less – the permanent task of a leaner, more efficient state'[2], true to the manifesto of a newly elected austerity government.

That same behavioural science, repurposed into financial regulation, has since globally yielded more than US $300bn in penalty and restitution payments[3]; an economically significant sum on a global scale. As a new revenue stream – a flood, even – for the governments backing this policy, it has far exceeded its political sponsors' expectations. (Admittedly, the sum received a boost from recurrent bouts of bad behaviour as certain firms mis-sold personal insurance products and tampered with market benchmarks.)

The new regulators' blockbusting fines present a form of political theatre. So too are their prosecutions of individuals: these are a modern form of public shaming, cheered along by a questionable ethic of revenge for the suffering caused to consumers. Never mind that, to cognitive science, personal prosecutions are a form of fundamental attribution error (the bias-compulsion to 'give every story a human face')[4] – or, if you're legally minded, a *circumstantial ad hominem fallacy*[5].

Then there's the straightforward conclusion from doing a cost-benefit analysis. Besides generating a heap of cash for governments, conduct prosecutions save on regulatory agency running costs. By going after individual managers, the new generation of enforcers needn't waste public money building a case against entire organizations or product ranges.

All of these political trade-offs would seem to encourage any conduct regulator's government sponsors. Which, in turn, comforts those sponsors about their own political party's prospects of re-election – assuming, of course, that voters have time to notice any of this happening, as (for example) the tectonic plates of the European Union shift uneasily beneath us all. To help explain the rush to regulate conduct, we will need to look at a little economic theory, but mainly take a straightforward overview of behavioural research into the human viewpoint that we mostly know as 'what actually happens'.

Is this science at work, or something simpler?

Back in 2008, taking stock of what just happened, legislators and market-watchers saw a systemic failure of risk controls that had rested heavily on certain assumptions of traditional economics: notably that markets are self-correcting and populated by rational 'resource maximizers'. These 'maximizers', such as traders in a financial market, were seen as wanting to take as much as they could from an opportunity, and contrasted with 'satisficers', who by being altruistic, lazy, or simply unmotivated, would only take what they needed or could survive with[6]. This viewpoint had failed to explain, let alone foresee, irrational behaviour in markets, such as bubbles, liquidity failures, runs, and crashes. Indeed, the traditional viewpoint – 'Econ', to its critics – hardly distinguished between *irrational* and *unpredictable* behaviour[7].

Although events such as liquidity droughts and customer runs on banks were unusual pre-2008, they certainly weren't unknown; clearly some new form of early warning system was needed. To be able to understand and predict these effects, we all needed to see them in a different light. It was time for the old economic order to stop pretending that markets are rational and self-correcting, and that panic effects are outliers; time, in short, to get on with 'understanding normal people', as one of the new sceptics[8] pithily put it.

With the power of hindsight, we have since been able to uncover many of the flaws in traditional regulatory control designs, with their fatal reliance on econometrics. Looking back, it now seems strangely optimistic, not to say wrong-headed, that anyone would design a system of market restraint around the idea of asking sellers to self-report on their contract volumes and prices, calibrating the probity of their trading in terms of historic movements of money. As an approach to control design this seemed almost to invite abuse, failing completely to register, for instance, the real-time human truth of how traders mirror one another's behaviour.

And abuse is exactly what happened, in numerous cases that have since come to light. The reporting of risk was widely 'gamed'; traders manipulated market benchmarks; salespeople oversold; trading line losses were buried deep inside aggregated reports; proscribed trading partners were given anonymous accounts. There was no transparent account of how salespeople were behaving day to day; if there had been, perhaps alarm bells might have rung sooner.

During the political maelstrom that followed the global crash, public officials pulled behavioural economics from the fringes of science into the mainstream, largely because the new science seemed intuitively to have some helpful things to say about what human beings actually get up to. The new science was certainly different from the old stuff. For a start it described us all as *predictably irrational*[9]. It also held out the hope of overcoming the cognitive failures of classical economics, the 'Econ' legacy. What mostly mattered, though, was that governments in every major economy were in a state of some alarm about rising public anger, and so were super-receptive to – indeed, urgently needed – a change of strategic focus. Less than a year after the market implosion, future Prime Minister David Cameron urged his leadership team colleagues to read a pop-science book called *Nudge*, which promised to deliver big social changes against a small public-sector budget.

Since then, the political dividend of applying behavioural economics to financial regulation has outpaced its sponsors' highest expectations. For the politicians, US \$300bn+ of windfall revenue is a lot of cash for indebted governments to suddenly find they are free to redeploy. That new regulatory jackpot positively shouted for attention, and other jurisdictions have joined in with enthusiasm. To the objective behavioural analyst, the rocketing global rise of conduct regulation is simply explained: it is less about the science (whether of human behaviour or regulatory design) than about *realpolitik*. True, the old econometric system of regulation failed us badly. True also, that any system of regulation that reveals bad behaviour at point of origin and as it happens, ought to represent an improvement. However, there is both more, and less, to the new regime than that: to explain, let's take a step back for a broader view of what is happening.

The place where all regulation comes from

The long view, always worth bearing in mind, is simply this: all regulation is the product of failure. No national leader has ever woken up one sunny morning with the thought that 'I fancy a spot of regulatory drafting'.

In the aftermath of the financial crash, every government that had been affected by it – which included most of the developed world – faced not just a financial crisis, but an existential one, as voters asked: How effective is my government, these people who let *this* happen on their watch?

As with any crisis in national life, after a financial crash a government looks to reassert its authority and legitimacy. To succeed, it needs to make its assertion in plain terms, free from the jargon that public administrators normally use. Just as citizens caught up in a tsunami don't much care about hydrodynamics – they are too busy trying to stay alive – so voters hurt by the financial crash had little interest in the mechanics of collateralized debt instruments; they just wanted to find cash to pay the household bills. To a voter who has just lost their job, a taxpayer-funded bank bailout looks suspiciously like an imposed social injustice. Voters were (and many remain) deeply troubled by the thought that their elected representatives seemed to have lost traction over financial firms, or worse, to have ceded power to 'big finance' interests.

Standing on a cliff-edge of public trust, politicians needed to find, quickly, a new regulatory concept that offered a way to displace public anger elsewhere and to overlay this concept on existing control agencies – to create a new regulatory 'narrative'. Against that somewhat desperate brief, behavioural regulation must have seemed very like a perfect answer to the politicians' prayers.

Meanwhile, on campus...

Faced with the new exotica of behavioural science, the Compliance and Risk traditionalists might be forgiven for wishing it would all go away, in favour of a return to the (relatively) cosy certainties of credit default probabilities and Value-at-Risk. But the 'Econ' view is in a diminishing minority now that even the business schools are teaching BE in Economics 101[10]. The behavioural toybox is open, and nobody is going to shut it again any time soon.

For any who had eyes to see, that behavioural science toybox, or more properly toolbox, had in fact been around since the 1700s. Yet for most practitioners, BE operated just below the surface: for example, since the 1980s, any traders using the Black-Scholes options pricing model have been relying on behavioural science, possibly without realizing it. By the early 2000s, while financial markets were busy inflating a global bubble, over in academia an evangelizing group of scientists began to believe that the power of their behavioural findings could reach far beyond the laboratory; Nobel Prizes for pioneers including Nash (1994) and Kahneman (2002) strengthened that belief. Around the same time it dawned on mainstream media owners and news editors that, if science was now ready to explain to us all why so many people seem to act so stupidly, here was a rich new source of human-interest content.

On cue, therefore, when the financial bubble burst in 2008, behavioural scientists stood ready with a breezy new narrative to explain what had just happened. They also offered some fun new phrases we could all start to use to describe human weaknesses: sticky bias, halo effect, social proof, hedonic treadmill, and many more. Significantly, even though these explanations were new, they looked simple and felt familiar – common sense, even, in a welcome contrast to the obscurantism of classical economics. The new science made us all feel wiser, by seeming to support our intuitive, folkloric view of human nature. (So, most *X-Factor* contestants can't actually sing? That'll be the Dunning-Kruger Effect, mate.) All of which appeals hugely to the general public – and of course to the political classes who know a headline-grabbing story when they see one.

Boom times for publishers, too

Putting these pieces together, we should not be surprised that behavioural science – or at least its pop-science variant – took off in such a big way directly after the market crash. In next to no time, titles such as *Nudge*[11], *Thinking Fast and Slow*[12], and *The Art of Thinking Clearly*[13] shipped more than a million copies each. Web resources such as *Predictably Irrational*[14], *Understanding Uncertainty*[15] and *The Behavioral Economics Guides*[16] have become viral hits.

Besides giving booksellers and bloggers a welcome boost, this new tide of science has made us all feel more comfortable indulging in the armchair sport of criticizing the behavioural traits of public figures. It's gossip, but with added science, so that's OK then: that politician lost the election because of his False-Consensus problem; that other one, she's a bit on the empathy-deficient spectrum; here's why this CEO is quite like a school bully; look, derivatives traders behave just like primeval tribesmen!; and hey, here's why my board meeting is just like a children's party. What's not to like?

Of course, this may all simply be the latest resurgence of a prurient herd instinct that made earlier titles such as *The Naked Ape*[17], *Influence: The Psychology of Persuasion*[18], and *Watching the English*[19] into huge pop-science hits. Anything that helps us to understand our collective selves is probably good for society as a whole.

Where next: Trends in enforcement

After behavioural financial regulation was first introduced, several things happened quickly. First, conduct control was an easy sell to the electorate, with its individual attacks on senior managers. Next, it emerged that the potential for revenues was enormous. In the United Kingdom, since its inception, conduct enforcement alone (net of clear-up costs) has yielded more than £30 billion[20] – that is, all the capital raised by banks in the previous three years. Finally, this succeeded in getting bankers' attention where previous regulators had failed: some of the mega-fines even dented firms' Tier 1 capital adequacy.

Wider consequences then rippled out. Around the world, new conduct regulators started to roll out their own conduct control toolkits – with varying degrees of respect for the underlying behavioural science.

Amid this storm of activity, some researchers have been quietly analysing the event of every single conduct enforcement across the world's major financial centres. Their findings enable us to better predict future costs of conduct compliance and to uncover the hidden policy levers that determine it. The researchers' taxonomy of conduct risk enforcements worldwide[21] shows how each enforcer's own behaviour is changing, and whom the enforcers are most likely to be calling on in the near future. Some of the more eye-catching trends are summarized here.

The future of conduct enforcement: six trends[22]

1   Regulators will '**hunt in packs**': Regulatory agencies will now seek 'multilateral enforcement', using 'co-operative memorandums of understanding'[23]. The FCA is already the most sought-after partner by other enforcers globally. Multi-agency coordinated international prosecutions have begun to happen: during the prosecutions of LIBOR and foreign exchange abuses, the various enforcers involved compared notes; as one result, the UK's FCA, US Federal Reserve and CFTC all levied very similar recent fines against foreign exchange market manipulators.

2   A '**revolving door**' of regulatory talent. Successful senior enforcers are becoming global citizens, headhunted between the jurisdictions that lead the practice of conduct risk enforcement: Singapore, Hong Kong, Australia, South Africa, the United Kingdom and the United States. Big-hitting enforcers will go wherever on the planet their behavioural wisdom may be of value to reform-minded governments.

3   Enforcers will focus on **hit-lists**, trebling the number of highlighted 'instruments of interest' – products and sales operations that appear to present high risk of misconduct. These currently include client asset handling, record-keeping and segregation of duties.

4   They will also look upstream of providers' current activities, to consider future product pipelines. For example, they will target **product designers**, who will now be committing a conduct offence if they fail to involve 'product governance' risk specialists from the outset.

5   '**Heads on spikes**': Product-based fines against corporations will decline, to be replaced by tougher personal prosecutions; during the first half of 2016, *all* the FCA's fines were against individuals rather than product classes or corporate brands. Under the new Senior Managers Regime of regulation, mis-selling by salespeople is becoming a lesser offence than board members losing control of risk governance.

6   Automatically **criminalizing** misconduct. This is being tested, notably in Australia where the securities regulator ASIC imposes prison sentences for mis-selling, and has doubled its conviction rate. Other enforcers globally are set to follow suit, with lifetime senior manager bans routinely followed by criminal convictions.

Science or populism?

To a pure behavioural analyst, it appears that the boom in behaviour-based regulation owes less to scientific principles than to *realpolitik*. Conduct regulation has handed governments a low-cost, tax-neutral way to 'nail' the business leaders who had previously 'got away with it', while also reducing public deficits, and recasting themselves as fearless champions of consumer rights.

Behavioural scientists meanwhile lament that their 'beautiful' research field has been hijacked by governments whose only motives are 'lack of funds and political helplessness'[24]. Even public auditors are sceptical of government motives; the UK public auditor's review[25] has questioned enforcers' 'lack of evidence' that conduct prosecutions actually reduce mis-selling.

Conduct-based enforcements have pressed ahead anyway, with agents making the most of lower thresholds of proof, and personal focus, to prosecute token senior individuals (see *Enforcement as theatre*, box below).

Enforcement as theatre

Predating the mega-fines and personal pursuits of conduct risk, most regulators of course knew all about the power of symbolic enforcement. In the United States, for example, enforcers had pioneered two performance skills that became Wall Street legends: the 'perp walk' and 'yacht day'.

Perp walk: enforcers arrive at a suspect's office, handcuff them and walk them for a lap around the trading floor before taking them away for questioning.

Yacht day: the prosecutor locates the suspect's biggest dishonestly gained asset – ideally a yacht – then arrests the suspect and has them photographed, in handcuffs, standing in front of it. Finally, the resulting picture is displayed on the agency's office wall, in the manner of Employee of the Month, and sometimes also shared with friendly news media for extra impact.

To expedite this, British regulators had wanted to 'reverse the burden of proof' – that is, presuming every suspect to be guilty unless they could show otherwise – until someone pointed out that this also reversed exactly 800 years' worth of defendants' rights, as originally enshrined in Magna Carta (see box). 'Nailing' a single senior manager for a loosely defined conduct infraction clearly remains a tempting enforcement option for any trust-deficient government seeking popular support; along with the use of fines as a form of vicarious vengeance for the suffering that firms have caused to customers.

Freedom from assumed suspicion – an ancient English right

The Great Charter of Liberties (*Magna Carta Libertatum*), signed in the year 1215 CE by a reluctant King John of England, protected prominent citizens against illegal imprisonment and trumped-up charges.

Designated an 'Icon of Liberty' by the American Bar Association, as the model for the American Declaration of Independence, and later the US Constitution and Bill of Rights, the text of Magna Carta is displayed in the US Capitol building, Washington, DC. The original document is an official 'Treasure' of the British Library in London[26].

Conduct enforcement, an exportable asset

As the United Kingdom's conduct 'project' appeared to be solving its sponsor government's problems, both of reasserting control and of public perception, the stance of other financial regulators around the world changed from curiosity to replication. Of course, regulators around the world had known for years about the power of symbolic enforcement (see above) but this new regime offered every government something better. Whatever country you called home, if you were a finance minister still stuck on the back foot after the crisis, or a discredited regulator looking to retrieve a few quick wins, the behavioural approach could take care of it. By allowing you to prosecute any individual who simply looks as if they are behaving badly, it plays to an enduring public preconception that bankers are bad people. (And propagandists well know, a sure way to bond with the mass electorate is to 'respect' their existing prejudices.) Morally, it also appears unchallengeable: the regulator can always present itself as valuing the interests of the customer above all other concerns. How the customer experiences a transaction becomes the paramount measure of acceptable and expected conduct; regulation then makes it enforceably so.

We should see this change of perspective for what it is: a system of customer-centric regulation that begins (literally) to account for human misery suffered, and equally to 'price in' social benefit. It is these points that the behavioural lens addresses, and that have not been considered in any previous guidance on risk management.

The new inversion of regulatory focus, from producers to customers, one could see positively as a reasonable and overdue change, recognizing customers' real needs. The new approach explicitly requires producers to turn their own compliance lenses inside-out, or more accurately, outside-in, after decades of introspection and self-certified assurances.

In the end though, it has been the money raised and the populist manager-bashing, far more than the philosophical merits of behavioural science, which has endeared conduct regulation to governments wherever financial services operate – and increasingly in other regulated sectors too. We should expect the surge of behaviourally informed activity among regulators in jurisdictions globally to continue, regardless of elections and referenda; in a time of increasing public scepticism about politics, this activity retains an all-party appeal.

At a national level, research into 'global taxonomy' of conduct risk reveals each regulator beginning to codify conduct offences and to group them under conceptual headings, such as market abuse, oversight failure, customer care failure, careless reporting or poor record-keeping. Intuitively, these conceptual group labels are often consistent across many territories. The taxonomy study is now developing *predictive* power, taking real data from conduct prosecutions and synthesizing this to begin to foresee hotspots of liability in other jurisdictions (see the 'six future trends' box above). Most useful of all, the global taxonomy approach is one way to start to answer that stupid-sounding yet vital question that everyone asks at conduct risk conferences: 'What does good behaviour look like?' With, as ever, vast sums of compliance budget riding on the right answer, we are now in the age of the conduct risk analyst.

Key terms recapped

- **Behavioural science** – essentially the study of 'what actually happens' when humans interact and respond to real events. It focuses on observing real human behaviour and interrogating why this does not conform to rational expectations. Humans behave irrationally much of the time – but fitting a variety of patterns, based on our biases and social influences, that make us 'predictably irrational'.

- **Behavioural economics** – how this understanding helps us to predict people's decision-making, especially when they're trading (buying, pricing, selling).

- **Behavioural risk** – the potential cost that may result from any things that your staff do, that undermine trust or value in your business.

- **Conduct risk** – the potential cost resulting from any of your employees or suppliers committing any of the newly regulated conduct offences.

- **Behavioural regulation / Conduct regulation** – disciplinary offences as framed by regulators using ideas from cognitive and behavioural science (such as *biases* and *information asymmetry*).

Conclusion: Getting worse before it gets better

Should we believe that multi-billion amounts raised by conduct regulators in their debut years represent a high-tide mark of enforcement, and that firms may now expect 'an end of banker-bashing'[27]? One could believe so, following abrupt changes of leadership[28]; the softening of prosecutors' powers under SMR[29]; and the dropping of plans for public investigations into bank culture[30] and tax evasion[31].

Four reasons why 'conduct enforcement' makes politicians happy

- Earning power – enforcements raise big revenues from fines
- Populist appeal – 'banker-bashing' placates angry voters
- Low barriers to entry – it's cheaper and quicker to prosecute individual managers than whole product classes or firms
- Exportability – concentrating on just chasing individuals' 'bad behaviour' is an easy sell to other jurisdictions, helping the world's regulators to work together

Yet there remains a rare degree of agreement among politicians, publishers, enforcers and customers: everyone wants to use more behavioural science – whether as raw material for pub-psychology conversations or as a tool for populist reprisals against 'bad bankers'. Amid all the ructions of the European Union and elsewhere, politicians remain anxious about becoming targets for still-boiling public resentment over tax-funded bank bailouts. That there is a reservoir of public anger over this is beyond doubt: in several countries more than three in every four voters still want to see tighter regulation of financial firms (very few, anywhere, want to see the rules relaxed)[32]. From time to time, overflows of public anger have disrupted the political sphere: the issue clearly continues to raise temperatures in public debates, as seen in the unprecedented fracturing of the United Kingdom's two main political parties in mid-2016.

Among regulators, the response has been to spread discussions about conduct control across a wider (and increasingly supranational) group of enforcement agencies. 'Deterring misconduct'[33] has begun to lead the agenda at, for example, FINRA[34] and super-regulators FSB[35] and IOSCO[36].

So while conduct-based regulation may indeed work, far more significant, if you're a politician facing electoral meltdown, is how well it signals your sincerity to a deeply sceptical public (see *Four reasons* box above). The conduct enforcement option is a quick way to 'nail' a token senior manager; its massive fines may be portrayed as avenging customers' suffering, and they also deliver big windfall revenues.

On that last point: strikingly, after UK banks raised a total of £30bn in private equity (2009–15), they expended *all* of this hard-won investment in settling fines and redress payments. That startling fact led the central bank to comment that high levels of misconduct have not only drained capital resources; they have 'undercut public trust and hindered progress'[37]. Across continental European banks in the same period, misconduct fines alone totalled 50 billion euros, a lost resource that has 'direct implications for the real economy... [that wasted] capital could have supported 1 trillion euros of lending'[38]. Going forward, central banks will include potential misconduct costs in stress tests; the Bank of England has predicted that UK banks alone will have to find at least a further £40bn to provide for this in the years ahead.

For principled advocates of behavioural regulation, there is now an ironic tension between its idealistic aims – to, well, encourage good behaviour by regulated people – and the cold political calculus of how it is now applied in practice. For governments of countries with active financial markets, the apparent 'quick win' attractions of personal enforcement against senior figures in an unpopular industry have been hard to resist.

Despite all the politics, and the background science, the behavioural approach has become a topic of mainstream public interest of its own. That is most likely because people intuitively want to trust any research that seems to help us see our own human nature. That research may yet produce the wider, real benefits to society that its mid-20th-century pioneers would have wanted: we might aim higher and try to use the new science to pursue its original, more pro-social aim. Behavioural understanding is essential to answering the naïve yet vital question on every provider's mind: 'What does good behaviour look like?' Vast corporate budget decisions continue to depend upon conduct risk analysts' answer to this question.

The behavioural lens approach presented in the following chapters answers this urgent need and, over the longer term, may even help financial providers to revitalize their misplaced social purpose. Whatever is by then happening among politicians, if firms discover a fresh sense of social purpose *that* is a change that could revolutionize their engagement with risk management, and with the wider world.

At which point, it seems right to move on in the next chapter to consider that naïve-but-vital question: What does good behaviour look like?

Notes

1 Richard Thaler, When Humans Need a Nudge Toward Rationality, *The New York Times*, 8 February 2009, at nytimes.com/2009/02/08/business/08nudge.html?_r=0

2 Prime Minister David Cameron, *Mansion House speech*, 11 November 2013, at gov.uk/government/speeches/lord-mayors-banquet-2013-prime-ministers-speech

3 Source: *Conduct Costs Project* briefing, January 2016 (LSE–Cambridge University–CCPResearch) at conductcosts.ccpresearchfoundation.com/

4 Dobelli, R (2013) *The Art of Thinking Clearly*, Sceptre/Hachette

5 For context see *Encyclopedia of Philosophy* (Stanford Law) at http://plato.stanford.edu/entries/fallacies/

6 Simon, H A (1956) Rational choice and the structure of the environment, *Psychological Review*, 63 (2)

7 Richard Thaler expands on the 'Econs v Humans' debate in *Misbehaving* (2015) Allen Lane

8 Camerer, C (2003) *The Behavioral Challenge to Economics: Understanding normal people*, Caltech, Pasadena, CA; proceedings of the Federal Reserve

9 Ariely, D (2009) *Predictably Irrational: The hidden forces that shape our decisions*, Harper

10 Source: author's own interviews with Financial Services Club members, London (March 2016)

11 C Sunstein and R Thaler, 2009

12 D Kahneman, 2011

13 R Dobelli, 2013

14 Dan Ariely's (2009) book, *Predictably Irrational*, and blog at danariely.com/tag/predictably-irrational/

15 Prof Sir David Spiegelhalter's blog at the University of Cambridge at understandinguncertainty.org/

16 A Samson, series editor, R Miles co-editor: behavioraleconomics.com/the-behavioral-economics-guide-2016/

17 D Morris, 1967

18 R Cialdini, 1984

19 K Fox, 2004

20 Mark Carney, Governor of the Bank of England, 2015: *Opening statement at the European Parliament's ECON Committee* (European Parliament, ECON Committee, Brussels 7 December 2015, at bankofengland.co.uk/publications/Documents/speeches/2015/speech869.pdf

21 Corlytics, University College Dublin at www.corlytics.net

22 All findings: Corlytics, University College Dublin, as above

23 See, for example, the US SEC's current roster at sec.gov/about/offices/oia/oia_cooparrangements.shtml; the UK Conduct regulator (FCA) has standing agreements with, among others, its fellow UK regulators for Prudential (PRA) and Competition (CMA) matters

24 Prof Eldar Shafir, Princeton University, quoted in *The New York Times*, 26 February 2016, at http://www.nytimes.com/2016/02/24/business/economy/

25 UK National Audit Office, 2016: *Regulation and Redress*, review of the UK Financial Conduct Authority (National Audit Office, February 2016), at https://www.nao.org.uk/report/financial-services-mis-selling-regulation-and-redress/

26 http://www.bl.uk/magna-carta

27 Widely reported, for example in *Financial Times*, London, at ft.com/cms/s/0/e926e9e2-aef1-11e5-993b-c425a3d2b65a.html#axzz43faysxJk

28 *Top FCA watchdog: I regret…* , 28 January 2015, at cityam.com/208129/

29 *Business welcomes changes to SMR*, October 2015, at economia.icaew.com/news/october-2015/

30 *Banking culture inquiry shelved*, 31 December 2015, at bbc.co.uk/news/uk-35204010

31 *FCA ends HSBC tax evasion probe without further action*, 5 January 2016, at citywire.co.uk/new-model-adviser/news/fca-ends-hsbc-tax-evasion-probe-without-further-action/a871524

32 Edelman *Financial Services Trust Barometer*, 2015. Public responses to the question: 'Is Government regulation of the financial services

industry not enough, or too much?' UK response: not enough:
77%; too much: 2%. (Global benchmark: 54% / 15%. US: 45% / 27%.
Hong Kong: 58% / 7%. Gaps accounted for by 'don't knows').
Financial services meanwhile continued its eight-year streak as the
'least trusted sector'. (Edelman, *Global Trust Barometer*, 2016)

33 FINRA's first declared objective

34 The US Financial Institutions Regulatory Authority, which polices
investment brokers

35 The Financial Stability Board, comprising central bankers from the
G20 nations, in 2016 prioritizes 'addressing new and emerging
vulnerabilities in the financial system, including potential risks
associated with... conduct' (fsb.org/wp-content/uploads/
Chairs-letter-to-FMCBG.pdf). The FSB is chaired by Governor
of the Bank of England, Mark Carney.

36 The International Organization of Securities Commissions, the global
standard-setter for the securities sector. As a super-regulator, IOSCO
prefers to devise its own language for conduct risk, designating it
'harmful contact' (IOSCO Risk Priorities 2016: iosco.org/news/pdf/
IOSCONEWS421.pdf)

37 Mark Carney, Governor of the Bank of England, 2015: *Opening
statement at the European Parliament's ECON Committee* (European
Parliament, ECON Committee, Brussels 7 December 2015 at
bankofengland.co.uk/publications/Documents/speeches/2015/
speech869.pdf

38 Carney/ECON, as above

Establishing what your 'good behaviour looks like'

07

Introduction

As we approach using the behavioural lens, this chapter looks first at how various parties 'see' the business of taking risks. There are clear differences between expert and layperson views of risk – but this does not mean that the lay view has less value than the expert, or more. It's just different, and we need to understand these differing values.

There is also a clear difference in how the notion of risk is understood by people working in different sectors. Most notably, there's a big cognitive gap that we will now look at, between the whole of the public sector (including regulators) and the whole of the private sector. This has serious implications for what matters to each side, and for what actually happens when one side interacts with the other.

Next, this chapter examines why, if regulators want us all to exhibit good behaviour, they don't simply tell us what to do. To the average compliance-minded provider, life would be so much easier if they could just work through a prescriptive list of good behaviour stuff... but this is never going to happen, for some good reasons I will discuss shortly.

Yet just because the regulators won't (or shouldn't) publish such things, does not mean that we can't look at them here; so we will. By a slightly roundabout, but highly instructive, tour of 'bad behaviour' types found through the author's personal research conversations with practitioners on the dark side, we can begin to characterize what regulators see as 'good', by contrasting it with the 'bad'.

You may or may not have ever wondered where regulators get their own ideas about conduct from. Surprisingly for some in the industry, as will shortly be seen, regulators are often deeply interested in how society itself builds a sense of what is acceptable behaviour – and, of course, 'detrimental' behaviour too. Through probing conversations with regulators over the years, as with practitioners, I have built up a picture of how regulators' own curiosity works, and will now share this with you. All of this informs the creation of conduct offences, which should in turn inform your understanding of how better to manage conduct risk. With that understanding in place, we're ready to put the behavioural lens to valuable use.

Themes and concepts in this chapter

acceptable and expected behaviour – affective/affect – amoral calculators – blame-shifting – box-ticking – chancer – cherry-picking – conditioned – confirmation bias – constructed ignorance – creative compliance – customer detriment – customer-centric – dark side research – delusion of adequacy/Dunning-Kruger effect – econometric measures – expert bias – fit and proper persons – gaming of rules/compliance – groupthink – hot-button issue/hot topic – juniorizing – legitimizing / legitimated misconduct – manipulation/'rigging' – motivated reasoning/cultural cognition – mystery shopping – neurochemical reward – no-answer excuse – 'normal people' – normalizing – ombudsman – overselling – performative behaviour – perverse effects – playing to the test – pre-notified inspections – proprietary trading – rational compliance – reciprocity – reframing – regulatory capture – responsible person – risk appetite – risk culture – risk engagement – risk-aware working – rogue trader – signal value – skilled and competent – social proof – sociopath – spotlight effect (bias) – 'tell' signs – three lines of defence – tone at the top

Differing conceptions of risk-taking

As already seen, regulators proposing new controls may wrongly assume that regulatees will respond positively to a call to support newly published rules, reasoning that rules are for the common good. A rule-maker's optimistic forecast of rational compliance imagines that regulatees will conduct themselves well because they agree with the rules' broad intent and so will look for practical ways to implement them. Drafters of controls tend to be hopeful, but frankly deluded, in assuming that everyone else shares their outlook and rationale[1] as to the best way to change a situation for the better. This fond belief by rule-makers, that 'other people think like us' and will 'see things our way', is their particular version of expert bias.

Consider the profound implications of that; that the people who design the controls think that everyone thinks as they do, processing information, arranging and making sense of the various problem factors in the same way. Although this attitude is prevalent among public officials everywhere, this type of expert bias – associated with confirmation bias, people's common tendency to seek and absorb evidence that reaffirms their existing view of the world – is just one scion of a pernicious family of bias effects that have been described as 'motivated reasoning'[2]. (Other close relatives include cultural cognition, groupthink, delusion of adequacy and Dunning-Kruger effect – see Glossary for all definitions).

It is time to challenge this, with a better and more practical alternative. Our aim should be to devise controls that are both more robust, and that more people will spontaneously support. A fruitful way to approach this is to look first at the things that regulatees prefer to do when left to their own devices – one of the new 'relentlessly empirical' methods that behavioural scientists recommend. As the behavioural lens technique will explain in Chapter 8, people prefer not to be forced to modify their established patterns of behaviour, and will go to some lengths to avoid having to alter their preferred routines. We need to acknowledge this, and work with it.

So, rather than start the regulatory design process from the cheerful (and shaky) assumption that regulatees will want to engage positively with the outcome, a more pragmatic approach is to start by looking at how regulatees prefer to behave. Why do people do what they do? And in particular, what is their past form on adapting their behaviour to comply with new rules?

Before beginning to draft any new form of control or rule, it is always instructive first to research the 'dark side' of compliance – that is, what the mainstream population of regulatees gets up to, when they think no one is watching. Having observed what regulatees actually do, and reflected on what one has seen, the drafter is starting from a more reliable reference point than any blindly optimistic expert colleague's. By getting into the habit of observing what actually happens, we also equip ourselves with a sounder view of how humans in general are likely to respond to anything we might ask them to do, especially when we are asking them to change the way they behave.

Expert v intuitive: a family example

The US guru of behavioural threat assessment, Gavin de Becker, gives families with young children a piece of advice that at first seems contrary: *Do* talk to strangers[3]. This appears to cut across conventional wisdom that children are safer if they are taught *not* to talk to strangers. Why should de Becker's advice work better than the old wisdom?

Actually, if you apply a little behavioural analysis, the benefit of this approach is plain to see. A child who grows up conditioned to believe that all strangers are dangerous is more likely to grow up to become a suspicious, even anxiety-prone adult. By contrast, a child who grows up with the daily habit of striking up friendly conversations with adults – as many children spontaneously do anyway, until 'rational' adults tell them not to – is internalizing two vital life-lessons. First, to know what a normal conversation with an adult feels like. Second, to know intuitively when a conversation has turned *abnormal* (creepy, or coercive), and so to avoid the speaker. By growing up with a respect for their own intuition, the child has gained a useful life skill in managing risk, making a sharper intuitive appraisal of the hazards present in the world around them.

Moving on, we may apply this simple behavioural insight to consider how regulators go about their business. Starting with a point so obvious we may have overlooked it: people who work in the public sector, including regulators, tend to be motivated by rather different aspirations and rewards from people who work in profit-making, regulated commercial businesses. While there is a huge research literature on this theme[4], its core point is easy to grasp and may be readily confirmed with a quick real-time probe that I have used often over many years. Simply assemble two groups of people: one group public sector employees, the other private sector. Ask them, 'What is the purpose of risk management?', and also ask each group to produce some images and ideas of what the word 'risk' signifies to them.

The public sector people (including regulatory staff) tend to see risk primarily in terms of threat; they see risk analysis as a vital tool to help with civil resilience and disaster preparedness, to contain and prevent hazards to public health and safety[5]. Commercial people, by contrast, conceive risk as a structured way to pursue opportunities for profit – while still, of course, trying to reduce the impact and likelihood of hazards. Although these two different cultures of risk are not polar opposites, they do reveal a difference in emphasis that helps to explain why there are persistent gaps between optimistic regulatory design and the reality of compliance. This in turn helps us some way along the road to understanding why, in the real world, commercial people break the rules that public-sector people have designed.

When asked for visual images that sum up what risk means to them, the difference between private- and public-sector groups is especially striking. From among dozens of images offered, I return again and again to one contrasting pair of pictures that offers the strongest visual metaphor for why the two groups engage differently with risk-taking. Each image speaks to its own side of the cultural divide about what 'risk' really means. For the public-sector people, their icon of risk engagement is a recent news photograph of a firefighter rescuing a child from a burning building (Figure 7.1).

For the private sector, 'risk' is an antique engraved picture of a gold prospector in 1848, tooling up and saddling his mule to head for California (Figure 7.2).

Figure 7.1 Professionals' conceptions of risk (1): Public sector: 'Stopping bad things from happening to vulnerable citizens'

Figure 7.2 Professionals' conceptions of risk (2): Private sector: Private enterprise – setting off across the desert in pursuit of profit

Here is why these mental images of risk matter. Behavioural research shows that our choice of career is heavily influenced by the brain structures and in particular by the workings of our personal neuro-chemical reward system[6]. We self-select and pursue a career in either the public service or commerce according to whether our brains are more inclined to reward risk-taking or risk-aversion. One unfortunate outcome of this effect is that people whose brain chemistry rewards risk-taking are often drawn to work in financial services. At the extreme end of the scale, people with an unnaturally high appetite for risk-taking find the financial sector powerfully attractive. Should we really be surprised that a sector where money is a constant presence is skewed towards attracting thrill-seekers?

Why it's useful to study 'gamers'

Financial services, then, suffers as a realm of organized activity that excites the attention of chancers (sociopathic risk-takers), despite the best efforts of HR and security departments to bar the door to them. The chancer has a simple rationale, immortalized in an (apocryphal) account of a courtroom exchange involving bank robber Willie Sutton, back in 1951 (see box).

Rational misconduct: robbing banks

Before sentencing career bank robber Willie Sutton to yet another term in prison, the judge asked him, 'Why do you rob banks, Mr Sutton?' Sutton replied: 'Because that's where the money is.'

Places and commercial activities where there are large concentrations of money naturally attract criminal enterprise – which may find its outlet through all kinds of activities that go on there, ranging from simply handling cash, through to marketing complex contracts. This 'Willie Sutton effect' is not, of course, unique to financial product providers: in the public sector, Sutton fans may be attracted to the cash-rich business of government procurement, especially in countries where democracy is in short supply. Anti-corruption analysts confirm[7] that a kleptocrat (thieving dictator) likes nothing better than to start up a big infrastructure project, such as building a dam or a highway, ideally hidden away somewhere remote, to provide a conduit for quietly siphoning public funds into a private offshore account[8].

As a primer to help set good conduct in context, this chapter sets out next some significant patterns of bad behaviour. These patterns are as identified by primary research among regulatees, by this author[9] and others[10].

By contrast, the second half of the chapter then highlights a range of desirable types of behaviour that the regulator has indicated will meet with approval. A note of caution is necessary about regulators' own engagement with the latter point: we should expect that conduct regulators will continue to resist calls to publish or endorse any checklists that prescribe good behaviour. Regulators have at least one sound reason for this stance. In the past, publishing prescriptive approaches has tended to discourage intelligent evaluation of risk culture, perversely encouraged 'playing to the test'[11], and led to mindless box-ticking. That said, personal research into conduct regulators' private views suggests strongly that they are receptive to firms' own independent initiatives to promote some specific patterns of good behaviour, as outlined at the end of this chapter. More than simply fitting into some notional template of 'what good behaviour looks like', these patterns are about engaging in qualitative discussions throughout the firm, and between the firm and the regulator, to develop a wiser and more intuitive appreciation of good conduct in various forms, and of the links between misconduct and customer detriment.

First, then, a tour of some prevalent patterns of misbehaviour. As brief summaries of this author's first-hand research among financial practitioners over more than a decade[12], these examples are gathered together under a general label of 'rule-gaming', since this broadly describes many of the recurrent patterns of behaviour found. Although the gamers' intent varies between mild subversion and full-on deception (that is, fraud), they may not always themselves be aware of which end of that scale their own efforts place them at. For all that the degree of subversive intent varies, all the games flow from the same precondition: an assumption by commercial people that it is acceptable to bend out of shape the controls that compliance and risk people try to impose, because commercial interests trump all other considerations.

As will be seen, sometimes the focus of a game is the specific routines and activities of compliance itself, such as generating reports; at other times the game is more broadly subversive, resisting any outside attempt to modify preferred ways of working. The behaviour may result from a preference for passivity ('anything for a quiet life'/'leave me alone'); or from a desire to assert special group status or untouchability. There is an inglorious history[13] of sales-side staff acting up, disrupting and undermining the authority of compliance officers, to signal that profit remains the prime cultural value in the organization. While none of these attitudes is acceptable as a response to the new conduct imperative, they remain present in some systems, and all too familiar. The reader may have witnessed some of these situations, as in the past personal tension has been common between sales and compliance people[14]. Whether or not the following examples remind you of anyone in particular, they are intended to provide a useful summary of behavioural challenges that conduct programme leaders commonly face.

Framing the gaming

A number of major providers have learned already – through hefty fines[15] – how costly it can be to underestimate the importance of good conduct. Regulators are deeply concerned to overcome the culture of carelessness that characterized some firms in the past, and that has contributed to a long-term decline in public trust in the financial sector[16].

It is worth recalling, as seen in previous chapters, that non-compliance and other failures of risk control are also a consequence of poorly conceived control structures. Badly designed controls, including unwieldy risk and compliance report formats, are in turn created when organizations fail to realize or to pre-test how a new control measure will work in practice, when it is rolled out for use. For the purposes of regulatory compliance, any of the workforce who are not dedicated compliance officers may be pragmatically treated as 'normal people' – that is, they will exhibit non-expert, 'outsider' reactions to expert-led demands to modify behaviour and conform to rules. The list reminds us what to expect and to have to manage. Many of these are (sadly) predictable 'what actually happens' effects among staff, especially on the sales side.

We have just seen how there is a clash of conceptual purpose, as even the core phrase 'risk management' holds different shades of meaning for regulators and practitioners. Regulators conceive risk management mainly as activities to minimize market turbulence and to protect buyers from harm. Firms see risk management as the art of ensuring that their risk-taking continues to turn a profit – or, to reduce it to cashflow basics: because compliance activity takes up a lot of expensive resources, some people will see it as diverting resources away from the higher priority activity of making sales.

Where practitioners resent spending on compliance, for some the unethical alternative is to do 'creative compliance' – that is, presenting a compliant public face while not actually changing one's behaviour. If one's view is that compliance is a cost to be avoided, since turning a profit trumps all other considerations, then the behaviours listed in the following section of this chapter may be seen as legitimated; that is, rationalized as acceptable or even normal. For regulators – and indeed all of us who have any kind of moral compass – the following behaviours clearly fall outside a definition of acceptable behaviour. For a shrinking minority of practitioners, however, risk management remains unconnected to ethical values. The following list therefore offers the rest of us a few hints at 'tell signs' that this type of practitioner is at work, and needs to be challenged. Among the myriad forms that creative compliance (also known as performativity) may take, these are some consistent patterns encountered[17].

Types of gaming behaviour

Types of games of compliance may be loosely divided into three categories: people-games; reframing; and gaming the system. Because real life is messy, there are of course some overlaps between those three sets.

As will become clear, people-games involve personality types and shuffling human resources. Reframing entails adjusting one's own systems of measurement and/or reporting to disguise inconvenient data. Gaming the system involves manipulating the processes that external control agencies are using, or exploiting their poor design. In any event, these groupings are only this author's suggestion to help to identify common patterns among similar events of misbehaviour.

Besides being very much in the public interest, it is also quite entertaining to watch for and report new examples of each of these games[18]. The game examples in the following list are all – unfortunately – confirmed as extant by research, as well as arising daily in news reports across many sectors, not just finance.

Games with people

- **Little birds:** Seconding a firm's staff to and from the regulator's office, to sound out what's going on there, and in particular who is most/least respected. Of course, argue many firms, experience on both sides of the regulatory divide is helpful for all concerned and can only improve dialogue, and ultimately the framing of regulation itself. Up to a point, maybe so.

- **New best friend:** Making all regulatory inspectors, including external auditors, feel extremely welcome when they visit the firm's office, as a way of building up an expectation of **reciprocity**. In extreme cases (as with Enron's 'independent' auditors, Andersen[19]), the visitors end up 'going native' while working in-house; and end up co-indicted as a result.

- **Bad apple:** A classic blame-shifting tactic used by senior managers. The firm cynically rewards risk-taking as long as this is profitable, but if a large loss event occurs it is disowned as the work of an unlicensed junior 'not adhering to our values', 'acting alone' or 'going rogue'. It is worth noting that several notorious rogue traders – famously including Nick Leeson, who brought down Barings Bank (see Chapter 8) – had previously earned their employers' high praise for making them high profits[20].

- **Rationally bad:** Displacing blame and disowning personal responsibility for their bad behaviour, rule-breakers use a predictable suite of justifications[21], including: the mis-sale is the victim's fault ('they were asking for it'); it is the firm's or market's fault ('for putting temptation in my way'); it doesn't really count ('no one was really hurt'; 'losses are insured anyway'); or, dishonest income is a normal entitlement ('just doing what everyone else does').

- **Rock star:** No need to obey the rules, apparently, if you're an 'exceptional' trading talent or supersalesperson. The rock star argument is essentially: 'as long as you enjoy what I produce, you can't question how I behave'. Rock stars on the trading floor may even bend reality by invoking an imaginary future in which short-term failure is irrelevant ('oh, of course that contract's losing money *now* – the market just hasn't found us yet').

- **Amoral calculator:** The team selling a dodgy-but-profitable product do a quick sum: A times B, on the back of an envelope. 'A' is: how likely are we to get caught?, multiplied by 'B': what's the cost of the fine if we get caught? If the resulting figure is a lot less than this year's profits on the dodgy product, they keep on selling it.

- **Forced teaming:** Coercing reluctant colleagues to support a dishonest sales scheme, by appealing to a (spurious) local loyalty: 'we need to stick together on this'; or threat: 'if you're not with us you're against us'.

- **Violent innocence:** Where a wrongdoer perceives that an enforcer's suspicions are based on weak evidence, he/she aggressively counter-accuses the accusers (for example, of improper process), to try to make the enforcers question their own judgement. See also '**Blink**' below.

Games of reframing and measurement

- **'Reset'** (aka normalizing bad behaviour): This exploits the wide-ranging bias effect of social proof (we might also call it 'social justification' – as in, 'everybody does it'). For example, a dishonest sales team encourages others around them to tolerate, and then to condone, their unqualified risk-taking or high-pressure selling. Eventually the team's results come to be reported as routine successes.

- **Nelson's eye**: Named after the famous one-eyed English admiral who opted out of obeying orders by placing his telescope to his blind eye and telling his staff 'I see no signal'. Among our regulated providers, there are several variants (look the other way; misdirect auditors' attention; deny any irregularity). The game's the same in all cases: to ignore any outside instruction that contradicts one's planned course of action.

- **Moving the goalposts**: If the reported results don't fit expectations, re-base your system of measurement; or redefine your key risk indicators.

- **Cherry-picking**: When required to publish any form of compliance test result – especially risk simulations – run lots of extra tests until there's a wider range of results to choose from. Then select and report the most favourable result.

- **On-target:** Justifying any behaviour, however bad, by referring to the narrowest possible (numerical) indicator, ideally a headline sales figure; avoid reporting any human factor indicators (such as levels of customer satisfaction – or complaints).

Games with systems (including regulatory–political regimes)

- Colluding to arrange **pre-notified inspections**: Some regulators in the past have provided advance warnings of a visit, so that the inspection goes unnaturally smoothly. A genuine inspection needs an unannounced audit visit. Pre-notified inspections give regulatees time to hide any awkward issues; but they also give overworked regulatory case officers an easier time and make for quicker approvals. One can see how gamers on both sides might be tempted to collude. No surprises that pre-notified inspections find far fewer problems than random audit visits.

- **Revolving door – home:** An executive 'responsible person' arranges not to hold his or her job long enough to be held accountable for any errors or wrongdoing. (A game partly eradicated by the UK Senior Managers Regime, although see variants below: juniorizing and temporizing).

- **Revolving door – away**: Where a firm is troubled by the persistent attention of a keen regulatory case officer, the firm delays contact and waits for the regulatory agency's routine rotation of staff, which will see the case officer replaced by someone (hopefully) more amenable.

- **Juniorizing**: Where senior managers demote themselves, at least fictitiously for compliance reporting purposes, so that they do not hold a job title or function that the regulator designates as a **responsible person**.

- **Temporizing**: Similar to juniorizing, above; converting one's contract of employment from permanent to temporary, as a method of avoiding the responsibility (and/or blame) attaching to a **responsible person**'s regulated function.

- **'Blink'** (aka 'chicken', 'who blinks first', 'block-bluff'): This is a corporate version of the children's playground game, where the winner is whoever doesn't flinch in the face of a challenge or threat. Among regulatees, this means facing down a regulator's request for disclosure. A badly behaving regulatee knows at the outset that his firm has certain strategic advantages over the regulator, such as longevity and deep pockets (see Chapter 5). Knowing this, they can call the regulator's bluff. At its most brutal, this may entail the regulatee challenging the enforcer's jurisdiction or credentials ('You have no business asking that'), simply presenting a straight block: 'Or else what?'

- **Constructing ignorance**: Designing a new risk control measure in such a way that it provides 'deniable spaces' or 'firebreaks' that exempt its sponsor from blame in the event that the control fails[22].

- **Fake Academy** (a form of **regulatory capture**): Where a regulated firm or firms own, or effectively control, the means of certifying their own good behaviour. Funnily enough, everyone gets a certificate of compliance.

Positive resetting towards 'good'

While we were chatting about the importance of behavioural research, a conduct regulator said to me recently that she wished that her agency had a more positive reputation for being supportive of practitioner initiatives for good behaviour. She was weary of always being seen as the 'tough guys', enforcing prosecutions against misbehavers. I found this revealing, and an encouraging sign that the new type of conduct regulator is genuine in their desire to engage positively with practitioners. Of course, regulators are understandably reluctant to publish best practice guides – that is, advice on what they would accept as good behaviour – for fear that these will be converted into simplistic checklists which get reused as 'gaming' playlists by the people we met at earlier in this chapter. Despite that problem, it is clear to me, wherever in the world I've talked to the newly emerging conduct regulators, that they have this desire in common: to see the industry itself come forward with leadership ideas that identify and promote best practice, so that others start to follow a better-behaved 'new normal'.

Meanwhile we remain in a transitional period, with some of the bad old patterns of behaviour persisting and few exemplars of best practice leadership yet emerged. The games of compliance above are all taken from practitioners' first-hand accounts of actual experiences during the past decade. These examples are just a brief selection from a much longer analysis, summarized from both my proprietary research among bank Chief Risk Officers and others, and research colleagues' findings in other regulated industries[23]. As the collective stance shifts – we must hope – from defensive to exemplary, it is more than ever useful to take stock of forms of bad and good conduct practice. Before attempting to design any new conduct rule or behavioural control, it is always good preparation to review behavioural dark side research generally, and to study gaming responses in particular.

With the coming of the conduct regime, regulators around the world are now looking to reset industry and public expectations of acceptable behaviour. Regulators have already started the push-back against a range of commercial activities that in earlier years were accepted as normal, such as proprietary trading. More assertive regulation tends to make regulatees more defensive (or sometimes, defiant), leading the more cautious firms to de-risk a swathe of activities that they fear may later be caught in the conduct regulator's spotlight. For any old-school providers who still expect to outmanoeuvre the enforcers, gaming moves are beginning to look 'so last century': times have moved on.

The conduct regime asks providers to develop a new understanding, including being ready to look beyond their own organizations for proof whether their own behaviour is, or is not yet, acceptable. What techniques they will need to use to achieve this outside-in view, in order to keep a conduct regulator satisfied, the rest of this chapter, and indeed the rest of this book, will reveal.

At this halfway point, take heart. Reading the section on gaming, above, you might perhaps have been reminded of one or two scenes you have witnessed: perhaps, of a regulator's case officer being outmanoeuvred, or a sales manager getting away with reporting a technical half-truth. If any of that felt familiar, and made you feel uncomfortable, good for you – this shows that you are sensitive to conduct risk issues. Just by realizing this intuitively, you have taken a significant first step on the road to understanding good conduct. Soon you will be ready to champion it. The simple fact that you paused to think about 'how it feels to do the right thing' is a good indicator that you already have a healthy intuitive capacity to look ahead and develop an organization that collectively behaves well.

What the regulator really wants

As a starting point for this, let's think about why the regulator said what she said to me about wanting to spend more time applauding good behaviour. Have you ever wondered where the regulators themselves look for new ideas? Like all of us, they want to understand and get a clearer sense of those important but broad notions, 'acceptable behaviour' and 'detriment'. As a source called in for these briefings, and having had a hand in designing several research programmes that regulators have referred to in recent years, this author can offer some guidance here.

You might think that, as many of them are qualified lawyers, the regulator's staff must be fixated on reading the law reports, Hansard, and such like. Really, they're not. The modern conduct regulator is much more likely to be reading the latest behavioural pop-science book, or real science research journal; or to be sharing intelligence with watchdogs of all kinds – consumer campaign groups, independent mystery shopper research firms, complaints bloggers, and ombudsmen's offices.

With good reason, conduct regulators also see themselves as pioneers and enjoy sharing insights and experiences with their peers in other jurisdictions and sectors; they even have their own forum just for financial regulators, IOSCO[24]. They are also, as you might expect, keenly attuned to the political climate and may jump on a popular hot button issue if there is a good positive story in it for them.

A financial regulator is lucky – in this respect only, perhaps – that they are regularly gifted high-profile opportunities to champion consumers' rights, thanks to an endless reservoir of consumer-friendly news stories. Practitioner individuals and firms will, it seems, always continue to do careless, devious, or just plain stupid things with customers, so laying themselves open to a hostile scrutiny by news and social media who like to ask for the regulator's view of the miscreant. As we will see in Chapter 8, a single customer's detriment story can very quickly morph into a mainstream hot topic, as evidence of wider problems. In next to no time, as the behavioural lens shows, signal value turns minor local incidents into popular causes, simply by tapping into one or more of the public's ever-present intuitions about 'imposed' changes, unfairness, danger, 'not getting it', and so on.

Having topped up their think-tank with new ideas from these various sources, a regulator will typically then go back to first principles and build outwards from them. In the case of a conduct regulator, the first two principles of general regulation were mostly well established by an earlier regime, but the third now adds a behavioural slant. Those first two commercial principles that remain the same are to support fair markets and to preserve corporate stability. The third, with its new spin, is not simply to ensure that providers (and the regulator) give *fair* treatment, but to *prevent detriment* to customers. It is this last principle that most exercises the many providers who attend conferences where conduct risk is earnestly discussed with analysts, this author often included. They ask: What things do I do, that could be called 'detriment'? If good behaviour is the opposite of that, what does good behaviour look like, too? The principles are well and good, but what do they mean in practice?

The book you're reading now is unusual, in that it is not reductive or technocratic. The aim here is not to attempt to reduce conduct risk to a prescription or checklist of operational assurance points. If that's all you need today, fair enough – and sorry; there are plenty of other technical manuals out there that aim to do just that – some of which I contribute to, along with several projects that inform the regulation itself – but this book is not one of those. Instead, using a combination of analysis and direct experience that is very rare outside the regulator's office (and indeed, fairly rare within it), this book's approach offers a more intelligent way to see the risk from the other side: to appreciate the regulator's motives and sources, and how the customer's personal cognition gets to work to critique your conduct and decide whether what you do is expected, acceptable, or otherwise. We will take this approach because that's where conduct regulators themselves are coming from, now and in the future. The future will be less about modifying or re-labelling old oprisk rules, and more about rule-making that is premised on a truer understanding of human behaviour.

Which feels like the right point to move on and look at what the regulator's own understanding of good behaviour is. Remember, the regulator is never going to write you a prescription for this; you are reading it here.

Patterns to avoid...

First, here are some forms of past bad behaviour that the regulator does *not* want to see recurring, in any form at all. For practitioners, the point is not just 'don't do it', but 'don't even give the appearance of doing it' – or, as they say over there, 'don't even think about it'. Here are some items on the regulator's personal Naughty List.

Any attempt to manipulate a market, or even to be seen to share information inappropriately, would be very unwise in the wake of the LIBOR, foreign exchange and other market-rigging cases.

Remembering the regulator's second principle of preserving stability, providers can no longer offer a no-answer excuse ('we haven't had to think about it') when the regulator asks about quality of a firm's systems for supporting stability. As just one example: most banks suffer occasional problems with their ATM networks, but repeat offenders should now expect to be fined for detriment[25]. Where any financial delivery system is fragile, or recovery plans non-existent, the firm is now liable. A striking feature of the new enforcers' agenda is their willingness to prosecute the *non-event* of risk controls, rather than just the failures of extant controls. Above all, any of a firm's systems that help preserve acceptable levels of risk, capital and solvency must be sound, as must the operational controls that surround them.

Again in the wake of past scandals, any hint of overselling will not be tolerated. Granted, the industry has already paid heavy restitution for past excesses (including endowment mortgages, pensions and purchase protection insurance [PPI]), yet new abuses may be lurking just over the horizon: watch out for prosecutions against providers' roles in unwise pension transfers, splits, client money accounts and mortgage affordability.

A final category name here I have had to invent, again following a conversation with a regulator who has not yet come up with their own term for it: let's call it self-serving products. (A self-serving product is one whose sale makes a profit for the provider but does little, if anything, to benefit the customer; such as the many worthless 'purchase protection' insurance contracts.) Although the term 'self-serving' is not used officially, it is clear that at least one regulator uses it privately; there are plenty of phrases that support the idea behind it; and as a cluster of abusive patterns it is already documented. The tell signals for this form of misconduct are, in the regulator's informal words, 'short-termist selling' (or as I tend to think of it, 'hit-and-run' selling); a 'disconnect' between seller and customer; and any sale which produces 'early revenue' to the seller – including many of the front-end-loaded contracts of yesteryear.

Patterns to aspire to...

Having approached the task of defining good behaviour (in the regulator's mind, as it were) by seeing what it is *not*, let's turn now to the positive side.

Conduct risk is conceived by the regulator as, in one of their informal briefings, 'TCF-plus'. In other words, the old points of the Treating Customers Fairly initiative still apply but now with added 'teeth' for the enforcer. It is a good idea to review the key components of TCF with this change of emphasis in mind.

When hiring and training, firms should carefully observe and test for employee integrity. At the higher levels, managers must be both 'fit and proper persons', meaning in simple terms that they don't personally have (for example) criminal records or other antisocial or sociopathic traits; they must also have, as professionals, the skill and competence needed for the role they are hired to perform. While that last point might seem obvious, a recent parliamentary review of directors' competencies following the collapse of three major institutions highlighted the fact that the senior people responsible had, variously 'no technical expertise... no qualifications in banking... no financial services experience' and 'no relevant [derivatives] product knowledge'[26].

The regulator is very serious about realigning financial services providers' outlook to be, as they call it, customer-centric. One way to imagine this, if it helps, is to remember how the shape of the known universe changed in the age of Galileo: previously, humankind thought that the sun, stars and the other planets revolved around the earth; afterwards, we all knew that the earth is just one of the planets orbiting the sun, within a great big universe. In the same way, financial firms have tended to think of themselves as the centre of attention, with customers revolving around them; the regulator now proposes that providers should make customers the centre of attention. In the language of behavioural science, we are striving to overcome spotlight bias.

If that seems fanciful, just recall that under the historic model of financial product marketing, firms would raise funds, then push products out towards customers; in the new financial sector cosmos, and especially the spaces where challenger-banks and online disruptors play, funds may be raised through crowdsourcing, and customer defections are only a click away. The regulator is especially concerned that providers think harder about *designing in* customer-centricity; that is, making sure that rewards and incentives are geared to support customer satisfaction, not simply notching up quantities of product sales. How many firms have awarded staff bonuses based on customers' reported satisfaction? – Outside the financial sector, plenty; within, few if any. How many financial providers have *ever* modified a product in response to a customer complaint? – Having put that question to many conference audiences, totalling thousands of providers, I have yet to hear a single positive response to that. Which brings us to…

The culture of the firm is a huge topic in its own right, but one we may capture straightforwardly for behavioural purposes, and as envisaged by the regulator, as 'not taking advantage of biases', whether with customers, suppliers or staff. Until recently there was much talk of how setting an appropriate 'tone at the top' would foster a culture of pro-social behaviour throughout an organization. Unfortunately for regulators (though as no surprise to this author, who was involved) a major behavioural study[27] showed in 2015 that tone at the top has *no positive correlation whatever* with the ethical behaviour of salespeople, and may even be negatively correlated – that is, sales staff may even view pious claims by their company chairmen as a perverse invitation to game compliance more vigorously. Since that finding, regulators have been careful to rephrase the culture challenge as concerning 'tone from top to till' and, somewhat clumsily, 'tone in the middle'[28].

The three lines of defence for oversight and control have already been discussed in detail in Chapter 3. The conduct regulator expects these activities to be deployed not just to reflect the letter of compliance requirements, but the spirit of customer-centric good behaviour.

As with the recent rethink over 'tone at the top', conduct regulators are also interested to hear intelligent debate over control concepts that may have been proved unsound. There is much discussion over whether the oprisk concept of risk appetite should or should not be applied to conduct, as in 'conduct risk appetite'. While some practitioners and professional advisors argue that the concept is useful as it helps to focus attention on 'zero tolerance of misbehaviour', this author is firmly set against adapting an operational control indicator to a behavioural setting. To put it plainly, one possible translation of the phrase 'conduct risk appetite' is: 'pricing misbehaviour into your product'. While customers might reasonably expect the provider to recover the cost of maintaining good operational controls (such as systems to protect against fraud), it is hard to imagine that any customer would welcome paying a service charge for good behaviour. If conduct risk appetite is in any case always determined to be zero, it would seem to be a worthless indicator anyway.

This raises the wider question of how (and whether) to try to adapt past econometric measures for use in the new behaviour-control context. The regulator is mindful of how over-reliance on money-based indicators[29] has in the past blinded market participants to the human affective factors[30] that, for example, hastened the onset of the liquidity squeeze in 2008, and which still have a big impact. Indeed, the theme runs through this book: numerical measures of sales volume fail to capture important behavioural aspects of what's actually happening as salespeople interact with customers and with each other – including effects such as bias, tribalism, and gaming.

Another aspect of this behavioural awareness that the regulator expects firms to consider is the effect of incentive structures. How a firm approaches designing its rewards for selling, and its choices of performance indicators, say much about whether its culture is truly customer-centric: are bonuses awarded for good customer outcomes (high rates of satisfaction), or simply outputs (shifting quantities of 'product')? This is a significant warning sign for a culture gap between published rules and real behaviour – the 'what actually happens' gap, if you like.

The gaming of targets also falls within this area of regulatory concern. You may know this common perverse effect from other regulated fields, such as teaching or healthcare, as well as finance; popular phrases to describe it include 'teaching to the test', and 'what's measured is what matters'. Economists know it as Goodhart's Law. In this context it means doing only the bare minimum of what the control measure requires, in order to satisfy an audit, and crucially not modifying or stopping one's underlying (poor) behaviour. Conduct regulation seeks to improve practitioner behaviour, not just induce gaming of test results.

By contrast, the good behaviour that the regulator expects is about looking forward and taking an outside-in view of one's firm to get others' opinions of what is now acceptable and expected behaviour (these are expanded on in Chapter 8). There are several broad patterns of good behaviour within this, as follows.

Learning to see and respond

All human behaviour is dynamic – that is, the way that we react to the world around us varies, with the changing context of where we are and who we are with. As a part of this, what we regard as acceptable or expected behaviour changes over the course of our lives. We age; we move home; we learn, acquiring knowledge and skills, formally and informally; we move jobs; our circles of family and friends change; our spare-time interests change. All of these changes inform and modify our personal view of what constitutes good behaviour. The conduct regulator is keen for practitioners to understand the views of those people whose tolerance (and sometimes active support) is essential to a firm's survival. The views that the regulator wants you to understand better are threefold.

First, the regulator's own view. A recurrent theme of this book has been how the regulator's own outlook has changed in response to financial crisis. To this, now look for and add your own understanding of how a modern conduct regulator informs themselves, for example by talking to and sharing data with ombudsmen, consumers and campaigning groups.

Next, and taking your cue from the regulator's own newly customer-centric outlook, see the customer's view. Ask customers (yours, and other providers') directly what kinds of provider behaviour upsets them; what do they accept and expect, as at today? – Keep on asking, and expect to find many changes over time. The behavioural lens in the next chapter is a vital tool for this.

Finally, open yourself to your employees' view. A healthy risk culture encourages constructive criticism and frank discussion, for example about near-miss events. As conduct risk research shows, there are various signs that you have an unhealthy risk culture, such as that nobody wants to discuss conduct risk; or that the risk team never get asked to collaborate with the product developers; or that everyone has (informally) a story to tell about how pious 'tone at the top' announcements make the salespeople smirk in disbelief. Look at controls and rewards, perhaps as through the eyes of junior counter staff, or of ambitious sales people, or of long-serving back office staff. Are they encouraged to raise concerns? If they want to discuss a 'difficult' issue, does that get them thanked or punished? If your firm is typical of many, some of your staff probably believe that it is better to stick to using a checklist, even if this makes no sense in context, rather than use intuition and common sense when facing a problem. Risk-aware working, using the behavioural lens, is the answer, as will be seen.

Conclusion

The key to pleasing the regulator is thus not to codify 'good behaviour' into a template, but to loosen your thinking, allowing and rewarding staff for using their intuition to spot and overcome problems. Along the way to problem-solving, as the regulator now knows and will expect to see, there is a process of thinking intelligently and with risk-awareness at every level throughout the firm. To do this requires everyone to maintain an appetite for risk information – which may include new behavioural ways of seeing problems, as in the next chapter; or better ways of modelling risk; or sharing information and experiences of problems solved in other parts of the business or the sector.

At the root of this new understanding is a new willingness to ask what informs the regulator's view of what constitutes customer detriment. Ask, and keep asking, simple questions about the behaviour that customers look for: What pleases or upsets each customer (and therefore the regulator)? What's accepted and expected good behaviour – today? Who is saying so – not just us, of course – and how do we know? If your firm has no track record of directly researching the customer experience, and this does not just mean handing out customer satisfaction questionnaires at point of sale, try for example appointing a mystery shopping research team; or joining your customers' online complaints forums; or talking to customers' advocacy groups (whether consumer, or wholesale trade bodies). Even if you do have some or all of these in place, do your product designers ever take account of customers' views, including complaints? Are your products and services customer-centric, based on demand pull rather than marketing push? How early in your product design and marketing does your risk team get involved?

Finally, if you haven't already, you will need to invest some time, effort and resources in understanding biases and 'design asymmetries' – for which the next chapter is as good a starting-point as any.

Notes

1   Margolis, H (1996) *Dealing With Risk: Why the public and experts disagree*, University of Chicago Press

2   Kahan, Dan M (2015) Ideology, motivated reasoning, and cognitive reflection, *Judgment and Decision Making*, 8 (4)

3   De Becker, Gavin (2000) *The Gift of Fear: Survival signals that protect us from violence* (new edition) Bloomsbury

4   Katz, D and Kahn, R L (1978) *The Social Psychology of Organisations*, Wiley; also Horwitz, F M (1991) Human resource management: an ideological perspective, *International Journal of Management*, 112 (6)

5   See 'Resilience UK' and related initiatives at gov.uk/government/policies/emergency-planning

6   For example, Van Ryzin, G (2014) The curious case of the post-9-11 boost in government job satisfaction, *American Review of Public Administration*, January 2014

7   Richard Bistrong and Alison Taylor, 2016, in *Organisational cultures of corruption*, at richardbistrong.com

8   Platt, S (2015) *Criminal Capital*, Palgrave Macmillan

9   Miles, R (2012) *From Compliance to Coping*, King's College London, at kclpure.kcl.ac.uk/portal/en/theses/

10 Bloor, M, Datta, R, Galinsky, Y and Horlick-Jones, T (2006) Unicorn among the cedars: On the possibility of effective 'smart regulation', *Social and Legal Studies*, 15, pp 534–51

11 Bevan, G and Hood, C (2006) What's measured is what matters: targets and gaming in the NHS, *Public Administration*, 84 (3) at eprints.lse.ac.uk/16211/

12 Miles, R (2014) *Conduct Risk: When Compliance Becomes a Game,* Thomson Reuters

13 Miles, R, Chapter 6: CROs' relationships with traders, in *From compliance to coping*, as above

14 Miles, R, as above

15 See, for example, conductcosts.ccpresearchfoundation.com/ conduct-costs-results

16 See *Trust Barometer* annual surveys at edelman.com

17 Miles, R, as above

18 The author welcomes correspondence, and particularly case examples, concerning encounters with 'compliance gaming', to: r@DrRMiles.com

19 *Chicago Tribune*, 3 September 2002: 'Ties to Enron blinded Andersen'

20 *The Guardian*, 24 February 2015: The Barings Collapse, 20 years on, at theguardian.com/business/from-the-archive-blog/

21 Sykes, G and Matza, D (1957) Techniques of neutralization: A theory of delinquency, *American Sociological Review*, December 1957

22 McGoey, L (2007) On the will to ignorance in bureaucracy, *Economy and Society*, **36** (2) at tandfonline.com/doi/abs/10.1080/ 03085140701254282

23 Miles, R (2014) *Games of Compliance*, Thomson Reuters, Risk Culture series

24 International Organization of Securities Commissions, at www.iosco.org

25 FCA and PRA fines against ATM providers: fca.org.uk/news/fca-fines-rbs-natwest-and-ulster-bank-ltd-42m-for-it-failures ; bankofengland. co.uk/publications/Pages/news/2015/093.aspx

26 publications.parliament.uk/pa/cm201415/cmselect/ cmtreasy/728/72808.htm

27 Sheedy, E, Griffin, B and Barbour, J (in press) A framework and measure for examining risk climate in financial institutions, *Journal of Business and Psychology*

28 Griffith-Jones, J (2015) *FCA chairman's speech to the Trust in Banking Conference,* 20 October 2015, at fca.org.uk/news/

29 Cox, L A (2008) What's wrong with risk matrices?, *Risk Analysis*, **28** (2)

30 Slovic, P, Finucane, S and others (2004) Risk as analysis and risk as feelings: Affect, reason, risk and rationality, *Risk Analysis*, **24** (2)

The 'behavioural lens', Part 1   08

Wide view

Introduction: Normal and not-normal

The phrase 'inappropriate behaviour' has now become the catch-all fashionable term to describe what your granny would just have called 'being naughty'. In workplaces, social spaces and (especially) halls of education around the world, lists of inappropriate activities are posted by people in authority who hope that everyone will note the points and then behave better. Should we expect this compliance strategy to work?

Example inappropriate behaviours

Extracts from a typical modern university campus list[1]:

- aggressive communications;
- unwanted attention;
- written material (exam topic, e-mail, etc) suggesting that a student may be unstable/mentally unwell;
- stalking (repeated attempts to impose unwanted communication or contact);
- threats of harm.

This is all about what we consider normal and expect in a given context. Yet, if you sniggered inwardly at the banality of that campus list, stop and think for a minute: has your firm, or a firm you know, perpetrated some of these things on customers, in the past? Over years of running a consumer helpline for a major trade association, I recall many instances of providers doing all five of these, and more. No, really: one major brand, for example (who shall remain nameless) used to maintain a file marked 'NUTTERS', where certain persistently complaining customers would be logged. Others' handling of both sales and complaints would fit the above definitions, as in 'repeated attempts to impose unwanted contact' (cold-calling, anyone?), and 'threats of harm' (saying you will impose a penalty charge on a customer who wants to leave a contract early).

Themes and concepts in this chapter

acceptable and expected behaviour – affective/affect – agency/power (loss of) – asymmetric incentives – asymmetric information – 'bank run' – behavioural lens – bounded rationality – bystanding – cognitive load/ overload – cognitive miser – constructive challenge – customer detriment – customer-centric – delayed harm – denial – disruption – dissonance – dread – dynamic sense-making – emerging markets – hidden harm – hostility triggers – imposition – inappropriate behaviour – insider dealing – loan-to-value – meritocratic – moral courage – mortgagor – negative equity – 'normal people' and social perception – overload – physical v existential dread – privileged treatment – procrastination – public goods – reifying/reification – relentlessly empirical – repossessed – risk appetite – risk (in)equity/fairness – risk-averse – 'rock star defence' – rogue trader – social labelling – social licence – socially defined – spotlight effect (bias) – stakeholders – sticky bias – 'tells'/tell signs – tipping point – tolerance v acceptance (of risk) – tragedy of the commons – transparency – trust and goodwill – untouchables – 'what actually happens' – whistleblowing

Acceptable and expected behaviour, then, are what makes the normal person's world go round, and we should not be arrogant in trying to hold our efforts at expert risk management aloof from this. In fact, as we have heard directly from the regulator's view in Chapter 7, mastering the art of seeing that normal person or customer-centric view is at the core of good conduct. As we have also seen, econometric measures of risk and corporate performance are of precisely no value at all in this task. What is needed is something new. What is needed is, in fact, what follows in this chapter.

Luckily, we already have most of the toolkit for doing this, in our heads, thanks to human evolution. Less fortunately, most people are not familiar with how to access and arrange this intuitive knowledge into a useable framework. Again, simply read on – over the next dozen pages, all the hard work, behavioural research and social science heavy-lifting has been done for you (and yes, it took 20 years, but that's the beauty of textbook publishing).

To begin at that common starting-point we all have: each one of us has a personal sense of appropriate behaviour. It is about what we consider normal, in the context, taking cues from all around us. Let's start with a couple of easy ones.

Normal?

- Drinking a bit too much, losing a few clothes and singing raunchy songs might be just the kind of behaviour that makes one the life and soul of a bachelor party (or indeed, let's be modern, bachelorette).

- Calling a competitor rude names, and even manhandling them some, is all part of the cut-and-thrust, if you're playing various types of field sports.

- Yet none of those forms of behaviour is likely to play well at, for example, a job interview.

It is clear from this – indeed, obvious to anyone with regular social skills – that appropriate behaviour is very much a matter of context.

Who, then, decides what's 'acceptable behaviour'? How do we work out what behaviour is expected of us, in various different contexts? And how do we relate any of that in a practical way to reduce our exposure to conduct risk?

In laying out the behavioural lens approach, this chapter presents new ways to ask and answer these questions. Along with these prompt-lines for research and definitions of five core factors, the chapter offers a range of ways to notice when rules differ from social norms, and how the activity of compliance checking differs from the real-world practice of acceptable behaviour.

The great social scientist, jazz pianist and octogenarian free-thinker, Howard Becker, nailed this important difference in his hugely readable study of musicians, drug-taking and social labelling, back in 1963. Becker notes a vital difference between formal rules and acceptable behaviour: that acceptable behaviour is socially defined. This means that most people are less concerned about what law enforcers eventually do with rule-breakers, and more about how other ordinary 'people like us' respond to the rule-breaking at the point where we see it happening. It is this social view, not the strict legal view that determines how 'acceptable' any particular form of misbehaviour is: 'Just because one has committed an infraction of a rule does not mean that others will respond as though this has happened... Formal rules ... may differ from those actually thought appropriate by most people.'[2]

With this in mind it is not hard to see, for example, why we tend to give a generous social licence to talented creative people. As we enjoy listening to a great song, the pleasure we get from it makes us ready to excuse the musician (a bit) for any non-standard behaviour. (A social norm famously seen in a *Times* editorial calling for the release of a young musician called Mick Jagger, imprisoned for a 'mild' case of drugs possession in 1967. The *Times* thundered: 'Who breaks a butterfly on a wheel?'[3].) We are, by the way, much less forgiving when other professions such as financial 'rogue traders' attempt to use the same 'rock star defence' (see Chapter 7).

Meanwhile the people who design laws, rules and risk control systems – including governments, regulators and risk managers – keep on seeing the world in a way that suits their purpose but which too often leads to failure for lack of realism. The classic rule-maker view is that when a rule is handed down to a regulated group, the group will simply (and collectively) recognize the logic and value of the rule and get on with obeying it. You may have spotted the obvious flaw here: many people simply don't do as they are told. And yet, many rule-makers persist in the convenient, self-comforting delusion that regulatees will respond positively when rules are imposed on them.

Ironically, seeing financial regulators' faces all over our news bulletins reminds us of this reality. Those news items show that providers are still breaking both the actual rules and the social rules of acceptable behaviour, by treating customers carelessly. Granted, we are in a transitional period as new rules are introduced, but to the normal people out there, all this looks suspiciously like old-school business as usual. The behavioural approach explained in this chapter helps us to understand why single cases of customer detriment can quickly become mainstream, popular causes and headline news. How is it that some topics resonate so strongly with public intuitions about lack of 'good behaviour'?

Tolerating isn't the same as accepting

To recap briefly: we saw earlier why behavioural economists like to observe how normal people think, as a reported output from their relentlessly empirical research into what actually happens. Now you know some behavioural science basics, it is time to apply these to creating a behavioural lens view of what goes on in regulated financial markets, and life in general.

We need first to overcome a big classical economics misconception that is deeply ingrained in the 'risk industry'. Amid all the talk of risk appetite, financial firms tend to assume that the human thought process leads to *accepting* a given and defined level of risk. The problem lies in that word, 'accept' – it is misleading, as it mis-describes the process of how the average, non-expert person appraises risk. So let us set this straight, before moving on.

People *tolerate* risk, they don't *accept* it. This is an important distinction. The general population consists very largely of those normal people, who normally don't like being made to take on extra risk in their lives. As the behavioural science makes clear: although people will take a mild risk for a very likely payoff, much beyond that basic proposition we are risk-averse animals[4], both in our boundedly rational outlook[5] on the world and in our intuited, affective outlook[6]. We are also extremely and even unreasonably picky in the way that we source information about risk, partly because of innate biases[7], partly because we are emotional and social creatures, rather than purely rational[8].

A quick example to illustrate that social dimension to risk-taking: true, some part of each of us has a selfish desire to make the most of an opportunity for profit. But at the same time, we also have an acute sense of the common good – call it natural justice, or public goods – which deters us from taking 'more than our fair share', and prompts us to criticize others who do. If, in any market, a few players selfishly seize 'more than their share', then 'the system of consumption becomes unsustainable, and in the long term, everybody loses'[9]; the so-called tragedy of the commons[10].

That point about a social dimension to risk introduces the next major insight, and a large step along the road to understanding and using the behavioural lens.

Two forms of licence

If you are in the business of asking a group of people to do anything – say a group of staff to do some compliance training, or customers to contract to buy a new product – probably without knowing it, what you need is *two* forms of licence. Sure, you already knew about one type of licence: the kind that any regulator issues to you to do a risk-controlled activity, whether it's a licence to drive a car, or to trade in complex derivatives. What interests us here is the other form of licence, which nobody will ever print out for you, but which you cannot function without: your social licence to operate.

If that sounds fanciful, stay with this. A cynic might well think at this point, 'There's my trading licence, printed, on the wall of my office. I don't know about this social licence thing, I can't ever see it, so why even consider it? Anyway, who'd ever take it away from me?' This would be shortsighted, and quite contrary to the regulator's recent thinking on conduct risk. It would also be disputing a very large volume of research[11], and at least one highly respected policy organization[12] focusing on social licence; as will the rest of this chapter. Besides, practically for the reader, having come this far, it would be a little contrary not to stay for the focal point of the present book.

What that large volume of research comes down to is essentially this – and please, consider it carefully: an organization of any kind will only exist for as long as the people around it believe it has a legitimate purpose. Now, recalling that people only ever *tolerate* a level of personal risk, but don't actively *accept* it, a similar principle applies for an organization: those people who directly interact with it (sometimes called its stakeholders) are not all actively supporting the organization. Indeed, none of them at all may be supporting it; as with the old high street banks, many customers may simply be put off leaving, as they contemplate the effort needed to change provider, and cannot discern a better alternative. That's not customer loyalty, it's apathy. Instead of actively supporting, what stakeholders more often do is passive: they withhold their disapproval. And that's the essence of the social licence to operate: people may tolerate how you behave, but don't assume that this means that they accept it, let alone welcome it.

We are now approaching the central premise for the behavioural lens; how it works, and why it is so useful.

From bystander to aggressive challenger: Noting the tipping point

Tolerance, then, is not acceptance and is not support. People prefer bystanding, or at least not being disturbed, rather than being forced to change their preferred outlook and patterns of behaviour. Habits can be comforting; change may feel inherently threatening. The behavioural lens takes account of these effects.

Many people, and especially company directors, hold a bias-informed belief that they are the centre of attention and general curiosity, wherever they go – call it spotlight effect[13] or simple self-consciousness. Studies of this bias suggest that in your own normal everyday life, other people are paying far less attention to you than you think they are. Thanks also to other biases of their own, such as stickiness, procrastination, and the bystander effect, most of your stakeholders, most of the time, are not thinking about your organization at all; or if they are, they are not actively worried about risk. Rather as, when I go to lecture in a new venue, I don't expend a lot of energy worrying about risks to the structural integrity of the building (as in, 'will the ceiling fall in before I finish giving the lecture?'). As thoughtful individuals we are cognitive misers[14]; simply put, we don't expend energy thinking or worrying about hazards that our experience says are unlikely to occur here and now, or unlikely to matter much to us in the way we live our lives.

Returning to the social licence, then, there are some types of core resource support that every organization needs to function at all. As a bare minimum these would probably include: access to resources of staff; the ability to produce goods or other content; access to some forum where goods (or ideas) can be exchanged; and some form of consumers (whether they're buying product, subscribing, voting support, or some other form of engagement with you). Withdraw any of these resources, and you might as well just go home. So here's where those social licence-givers cross paths with you:

When tolerance ends

When you do something – knowingly or carelessly – that disturbs those passively tolerant people from their preferred, quiet stance of withholding disapproval... they will change their stance to active, critical engagement. At that point, any of them may group together and withdraw your social licence in no time at all.

If that still all sounds a bit abstract, let's just recap: an organization only ever exists with the consent of its stakeholders; they give it its social licence by not obstructing it, and by continuing to trade/interact with it. Now comes the real, non-abstract outcome: organizations that are not 'legitimate', that people no longer want to see doing what they do, will hit a tipping point of social acceptance, then disappear. Over the years, or sometimes in a matter of days, entire business sectors have fallen from public acceptability – tobacco, fur, whaling, civil supersonic air travel – from a combination of, what exactly? Customers stopping buying? Aggressive regulation? New technology making the old ways redundant? Newer, better competitors? All of these and more, certainly, but what is the underlying pattern?

Behavioural science has invested great efforts in understanding the factors that inform this tipping point, and in particular why expert risk analysis differs from social (normal person) perceptions of risk.

The behavioural lens draws together a range of the research findings and theory structures to present a straightforward and useable account. Some of the main factors[15] that lead normal people to hold different views from experts are summarized in the box below.

How public perception of risk affects your social licence

Some factors that make normal people more anxious than risk analysts

Your activity will raise public alarm when:

1 It's an *imposed* load:
   - it's increasing;
   - they have no personal control over it, and/or can't stop it happening;
   - it's a manufactured risk, not a 'natural' one.
2 It's *unfamiliar*:
   - how/why it works isn't (yet) understood;
   - game-changing new information about it is just arriving (analysis/watchdog);
   - experts disagree about how risky it is;
   - it might disadvantage children/future generations.
3 It feels *scary*:
   - bad things could happen later on (delayed harm);
   - it threatens personal safety/security;
   - it disrupts an established way of life.
4 It feels *unfair*:
   - it's not clear who really benefits;
   - it implies a secret deal or 'cover-up';
   - the people most exposed to the risk aren't the ones who get the benefit.
5 It's *'not what people like me do'*:
   - identified 'normal people' ('people like me') have been badly affected;
   - your organization isn't trusted, already;
   - no 'normal people' will agree with, or defend, what you're doing.

To keep things tight, when placing factor groups 1–5 into the behavioural lens, I will use the following summary labels: LOAD, NEW, DREAD, FAIR and SOCIAL.

Time now to take a first look through the lens.

The behavioural lens

Thinking about those stakeholders and *your* organization now, there are two kinds of activities (by your staff) that the stakeholders vaguely care about, in that bystanding mode that we just looked at: the stuff that they *tolerate* you doing, and the other stuff that they *want* you to do. It can help to think of these as accepted and expected behaviour.

Then there's another set of activities the stakeholders also care about, but not in a good way: your misbehaviour, which includes any misconduct as formally identified by a regulator, as well as other forms of misconduct that customers and the regulator haven't yet got round to telling you they don't like. Remember, if you force a person to change their settled view of 'tolerable risk', and especially if you force them to change behaviour, they will resent and challenge you. To get ahead of this risk, with the regulator and with customers, the key to understanding is to know *what types of behaviour on your part will trigger this hostile response* (see box: How public perception of risk affects your social licence).

What kinds of event, activity and patterns of your behaviour will turn tolerant people into your fiercest critics? There are five broad types of provocation that account for the triggering of most hostile responses; these are the five factors that make up the behavioural lens. Having identified these, the behavioural lens now expands on them.

The five factors derive from some heavyweight research in social and cognitive science – all of which itself is incredibly interesting but would need a book of its own. (In fact, it already has hundreds of books of its own; at the end of each chapter, and in the annexes at the back of this book, some of the best appear on a recommended reading list.) Rather than get into all that detail here, wherever core points are underscored by 'keystone' theories, these are highlighted. The overlapping fields of behavioural science, decision theory and the political science of regulatory design have all earned their researchers global recognition, including several Nobel Prizes, with no doubt more in prospect as this fast-moving field continues to expand. My respected colleague, friend and editor at the *Behavioral Economics Guide*[16], Dr Alain Samson, produces an excellent and concise annual review and meta-analysis of the best new developments in these fields.

The beauty of the five-factor behavioural lens is how easily you can apply it to understand a wide range of enterprises and situations. It is especially useful for revealing hidden pressure points where people and organizations might be at risk of collapsing under stress. The lens is also predictive, helping to identify where a new regulatory 'clampdown' is imminent; where an industry sector is liable to collapse; where an elected body is about to lose voters' confidence; where conventional (economic) risk models fail; and where there will be public demands for review of, for example, safety standards. Underlying all of these and many other forms of threat to social licence, the lens looks dispassionately at changing attitudes to what constitutes acceptable and expected behaviour.

At the core of the tool is a simple premise, grounded in sound behavioural research: in engaging people in any new activity one is requiring them to tolerate involvement in it. But all too often their passive tolerance is mistaken for active acceptance. The reality is that we all tolerate the range of risks we engage with, but for each risk we will often review this tolerance – albeit infrequently, even randomly, and depending heavily on context. Catch our attention with some new spin on a familiar risk, for example, and we're on the case in a flash (example: what's road safety going to feel like to all of us, when cars start going driverless?). Each person's tolerance for risk may be upset by one or more of five sets of human-behavioural factors that *do not have a basis in rational judgement*, which is why they have resisted old-school economic analysis in the past.

From here, it is appropriate to look at the behavioural lens in a question-overview format (Figure 8.1).

As we review any incident where an enterprise is failing or public opinion is rejecting an initiative, the onset of one or more of these five factors will normally explain the failure. Designers of policy, rules, regulations and controls can use the behavioural lens to help overcome their expert bias, considering in advance the real risk perceptions and limits to acceptance among individuals and groups most affected by any proposed change.

Initially, the reader who is already familiar with behavioural economics and cognitive science might find the approach somewhat reductive of a complex set of cognitive theories and findings. Bear

Figure 8.1 Question-based overview of the five factors

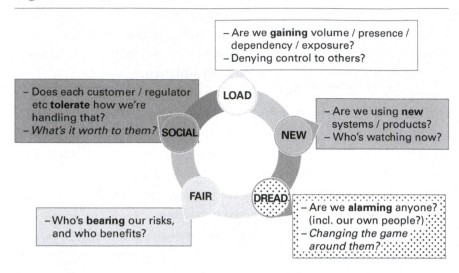

– Are we **gaining** volume / presence /
dependency / exposure?
– Denying control to others?

– Does each customer / regulator
etc **tolerate** how we're
handling that?
– *What's it worth to them?*

– Are we using **new**
systems / products?
– Who's watching now?

–Who's **bearing** our risks,
and who benefits?

– Are we **alarming** anyone?
(incl. our own people?)
– *Changing the game
around them?*

with this as meanwhile, for a reader who is new to the field, the
opposite might apply – that it is not reductive enough. To keep both
camps satisfied, the lens will be explained one component at a time,
before exploring further some of the background science, and multi-
layered applications (Figure 8.2). The first perspective, then, is at
entry level.

Figure 8.2 Five factors (overview)

Understanding how your behaviour turns tolerant people against you

These five factors explain why people who were formerly tolerant, will turn against you. Using them, we can now expand their outline points into more detailed questions and start to apply the lens to real-life situations. First, each of the five factors gets a full profile of its own (Figures 8.3–8.7).

For each of the five, I list first some situations (from the normal-person/customer point of view) where the factors apply. These include some financial service/customer care situation examples, although the latter part of Chapter 8, and all of Chapter 9, will detail further conduct-specific instances; the introductory set presents a general picture, showing how widely the lens can be applied across many situations where an organization's behaviour is in question. Then we have some of the tell signs (things you might hear people saying that show the factor is present). Then there's a selection of the formal labels that behavioural risk analysts might use to refer to the factor and its components. Finally, two sets of questions designed as prompts to help your own research: to identify where the factor is present, and to reflect on the best way to manage it.

Figure 8.3 Five factors – LOAD

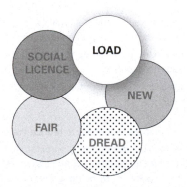

Table 8.1 LOAD types and examples

LOAD factors	Types and examples	
Common characteristics/real-life situations where LOAD is a lead factor	**Terms and Conditions**	You're handed a 100-page compliance statement to sign
	Hard-to-follow instructions	You can't use the gadget you just bought until you've assembled it, using a badly translated manual
	Harder work	You must work overtime, and no, it's not voluntary
	Cost	Without warning, your financial provider has raised the cost of your mortgage
	Displacing the effort	A provider making customers do everything for themselves (travel checking-in, form filling, supermarket checkouts…)
	Too much choice	You must choose between 72 different types of coffee in your local café
	Powerless	Without telling you, a provider makes a few small-looking but vital changes in your 20-paragraph Terms & Conditions statement
Things people say	'I'm spoiled for choice' 'There's just too much information, it makes my brain hurt' 'That's more than we can handle' 'This looks unstoppable' 'I just can't begin to make sense of it'	
Some types of load (labels)	• **System/process overload**: trying to take on too much with too little resource • **Cognitive** overload: too much information/choice/uncertainty • **Imposition**: no alternative, forcing change • Increased **affect**: see also DREAD, SOCIAL below; eg rising peer pressure	
Questions to help identify LOAD factors	▫ How much are we 'out there'? What extra activities are we taking on? (expanding sales, regional presence, public profile) ▫ Are we overextending resources, putting a strain on old systems, trying to do more with the same or fewer resources? ▫ How much are we dependent on others/exposed to external contractors?	
Questions to help manage LOAD factors	▫ Can we put in extra resources to reduce the strain? ▫ Can we reduce our dependency on external providers? Do we really need to get others (eg contractors/customers) to do the work or would we gain more goodwill by doing it ourselves? ▫ Are we talking constructively with the people affected?	

Figure 8.4 Five factors – NEW

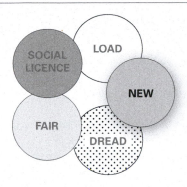

Table 8.2 NEW types and examples

NEWness factors	Types and examples	
Common characteristics/real-life situations where NEW is a lead factor	**New market opportunity**	You are about to launch a new product/business, or enter a new market
	Change of contract/product	You are being offered a change of contract, or to replace your favourite product with a new version
	New detection process, diagnostic or audit	A price comparison website reveals that your products are poor value
	New watchdog	Your regulator starts talking to the ombudsman about your history of customer complaints
	Change of working practices/rules	A new government/regulator compels you to produce new employment contracts
	New formula	You're invited to invest in a new type of complex derivative
	Secrets revealed	A wiki site publishes leaked details of your offshore transactions
	New indictable offences	You find you are now personally open to prosecution under the Senior Managers Regime
	New tech	In business, you find you are open to losses from a cyber 'social engineering' attack, high-speed trading, peer-to-peer, etc; or perhaps you're invited to try out a driverless car, or to fly a personal drone
	New image of a problem	A risk you used to find hard to focus on suddenly comes clear when disaster strikes in a familiar place

Table 8.2 *continued*

NEWness factors	Types and examples
Things people say	'Do we have to?' 'Now I know that, no thanks' 'Did you see…?' 'I never knew that; that's not good'
Some types of NEW (labels)	• **New threat**: any risk that nobody knew was there before; or just, you doing some new activity • **Disruption**, by new competitors, technologies, changing markets or social habits • **New focus**: increased media attention, including leaks or whistleblowing • **Insight**: having a new or alternative way to detect the presence of a risk • **Reification**: (see also end of chapter): when people realize that a previously abstract hazard (the thought of a risk) is a real and direct threat to them
Questions to help identify NEW factors	▫ What new enterprise activities are we getting into? (markets, technologies, delivery, partnerships, media) – are these activities untried, unproven? ▫ Are there newly visible ways to measure and account for what we do? – Is there a new public audit, regulation, risk diagnostic test or reporting standard, watchdog? ▫ Are we asking anyone (our staff/other) to take on or learn some new, unaccustomed activity? – Will they be forced to work with new or unfamiliar methods, technologies or people?
Questions to help manage NEW factors	▫ What steps are we taking to make people more comfortable with the change, to get used to the idea of doing things differently? (learning, trial running, reflexive listening, watching for 'near-miss' events) ▫ How constructively do we respond when someone makes a mistake with a new activity? ▫ How good are our answers to the new diagnostic/audit questions? Do we welcome discussion of the findings? ▫ How favourably do we compare with what our peer group is doing?

Figure 8.5 Five factors – DREAD

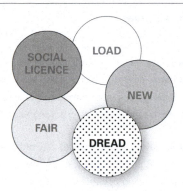

Table 8.3 DREAD types and examples

DREAD-inducing factors	Types and examples	
Common characteristics/real-life situations where DREAD is a lead factor	**Pain or discomfort**	Taking a family member to the Emergency Room, you're kept waiting
	Commitment	You must decide whether to fix the interest rate on your mortgage for the next three years
	Slippery slope	It turns out one of the high street banks was involved with money laundering; are the others implicated? Might we be 'guilty in hindsight'?
	Hidden harm	For years, your mortgage-linked savings product has been failing to keep pace with the loan it was supposed to pay off
	Future generations	Finding that your plans for safeguarding your children's financial future are in doubt
	Sense of security	Being forced to work by 'hot-desking' rather than from a known office
	Powerless	Having your loan foreclosed on; being the subject of a hostile takeover; markets seeming to turn against you
Things people say	'This is painful' 'I can't bear to think about it' 'What if this is just the beginning?' 'Can't I be treated as a person, rather than a problem?'	

Table 8.3 *continued*

DREAD-inducing factors	Types and examples
Some types of DREAD (labels)	• **Physical safety**: fear for the security of yourself and family • **Delayed harm**: sensing that it's going to get much worse later • **Denial**: unwillingness (sometimes pathological) to face consequences • **Dissonance**: clashing views (eg among experts, or expert-to-public) on the level of hazard • **Existential**: having your preferred way of life abruptly upset • **Affect**: dread of physical injury, or of threatening behaviour • **Lost agency**: feeling powerless to save yourself from oncoming harm; losing governance/control of the organization
Questions to help identify DREAD factors	□ Are we doing any activities that people can't fully control or predict? □ Is there a 'game-changing' situation happening, eg in markets we are in? □ Are we involved in taking away people's 'support systems'? □ Have any in our peer group had serious problems? Any cover-ups? □ Do we engage in high-risk and/or life-threatening activities? Any of these becoming more so? (slippery slope) □ Do our decisions have long-term impacts, especially on the daily lives of families and children? □ Are experts arguing about what is 'the right thing to do' in our sector?
Questions to help manage DREAD factors	□ Do we know how far people see us as carelessly causing harm? □ What's our record in managing high-risk activity? If good, can we point to it? If not, can we improve, then point to improvements? □ Can we reduce the primary source of stress on people affected? Can we also work to support people who have been stressed as a result of what we do? □ Can we improve clarity of understanding, to reduce dissonance?

Figure 8.6 Five factors – FAIR

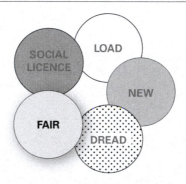

Table 8.4 FAIR types and examples

FAIRNESS factors	Types and examples	
Common characteristics/real-life situations where FAIR is a lead factor	**Not who I thought I was dealing with**	Finding that your bank has sold your mortgage or small business loan to a debt trader, without telling you
	Profits before people	Declaring big dividends just after a round of redundancies
	Privileged treatment	Banks bailed out by taxpayers
	'Untouchables'	Super-salespeople appear exempt from conduct rules as long as profits are strong
	Golden parachutes	Big payouts for departing directors, regardless of the state of the business
	You are your employer's banker	Zero-hours contracts for staff/delaying payments to suppliers
Things people say	'Can they do that?' 'Poor value' 'They have a case to answer (over…)' 'They're taking people (staff/customers/markets) for granted' 'They're giving rewards for failure' 'Who's the customer, here?' 'Time to clamp down on abuses' 'They're all just in it for themselves'	
Some types of UNFAIRNESS (labels)	• **Asymmetric information**: as when the seller (firm) knows something that the buyer doesn't; can include **insider dealing** or simple mis-selling • **Asymmetric incentives**: where typically the seller (firm) gets more profit from the transaction than the buyer (typically an unsuspecting consumer) • **Gaming**: such as, exploiting weaknesses in a risk reporting system, to conceal inconvenient truths in its 'gaps' • **Risk inequity**: where when two parties are contracting together, one takes more of the risk, and the other gets more of the reward • **Social injustice**: any situation where some people get privileged treatment or access, especially when others suffer and are excluded	
Questions to help identify FAIR factors	☐ Who gets the benefit, v who bears most of the risks, in our model? How does each stakeholder benefit (or suffer)? ☐ Are there 'untouchable' individuals or groups in the organization, or among its major stakeholders? ☐ Have we had social or news media comment on 'rewards for failure', 'unfair' practices, 'poor value', 'a case to answer'?	

Table 8.4 *continued*

FAIRNESS factors	Types and examples
Questions to help manage FAIR factors	☐ Are our incentives fairly balancing risk-taking and reward? (between management and staff; sponsors, employees and customers) ☐ Ask outsiders for their view: is there a 'case to answer'? ☐ Can we redesign our reward systems to value good conduct observed (ie customers' perception of benefit), not just how much effort we make? ☐ Could this activity *look* like a stitch-up? ☐ Do people talk about 'the way we do things around here', as if it's good to exclude any outside scrutiny?

Figure 8.7 Five factors – SOCIAL LICENCE

Table 8.5 SOCIAL LICENCE types and examples

SOCIAL LICENCE factors	Types and examples	
Common characteristics/real-life situations where SOCIAL LICENCE is a lead factor	**Now a socially unacceptable activity**	If you were planning to trade sub-prime debt (or fur, tobacco, whale meat, or ivory) you'll find it harder nowadays; the world has moved on
	Not being transparent	Engaging in money laundering, trading with proscribed states/organizations
	Paying for privilege	Corruptly paying for access, eg forceful lobbying, paying foreign officials for market access
	Deference	Being too respectful of legacy activities and processes
	Whistleblowing	Misconduct is forced into the open when an insider reveals all
	Inequality, hidden preferences	Maintaining a 'glass ceiling'; narrow social sourcing of Board members

Table 8.5 *continued*

SOCIAL LICENCE factors	Types and examples
Things people say	'They just don't "get it"' 'Too much groupthink' 'It's still an old boys' club' 'We can't accept their unaccountability' 'I don't trust this lot' 'Time for a change – let's vote them out' 'I'm sure I'm not the only one who…'
Some components of SOCIAL LICENCE (labels)	• **Trust** and **goodwill**: acceptance that you are valued by the effort you put into your relationships with stakeholders, including hearing their views • **Meritocratic culture**: equal opportunities for every social origin, race, gender and sexuality • **Transparency**: democratic process and accountability • **Openness to challenge**: how far you welcome alternative points of view • **Moral courage** (including long-termism and deferred gratification): leaders make decisions, knowing that short-term hardship may be necessary to improve long-term value and quality • **Dynamic sense-making**: how good at interpreting fast-moving events and incomplete information?
Questions to help identify SOCIAL factors	▫ Is the sector as a whole seen as 'well-behaved'? – Admired for best practice and innovation? – Any points especially admired? ▫ Have other providers suffered revolts (by customers, shareholders, even peer providers)? What were their fatal mistakes? ▫ Do we hear social and news media comment that our sector is 'out of step' with changing times, and/or allows 'unacceptable' practices? ▫ Is there a political 'crackdown' on sector practices, with new rules coming? ▫ How early in our product design process do we involve risk assessment? (If early, good; if late or never, not good.)
Questions to help manage SOCIAL factors	▫ Do we read (and commission) research on 'most admired' enterprises, and analyse the differences between them and us? ▫ How far are people happy with 'our way' of doing what we do? If happy, point to this; if not, find out why, fix it, then point to it. ▫ Do we actively research why people trust or distrust us? Do we focus on and work to remedy those points where customer trust is low?

Viewing real-world behaviour through the lens

Having looked at the first five component parts of the lens, and the behavioural questions that they prompt, there now follow two real-life examples of misconduct.

The first is at industry level: the early 2000s mis-selling of household mortgages and associated derivative contracts. The other is at firm level: the self-destruction of a revered British bank. The two cases show how the five factors of the behavioural lens sometimes work in sequence, as it were clockwise; sometimes in a less linear way (see Figure 8.9); but always ending up with loss of social licence.

Figure 8.8   The mortgage crisis, 2000s

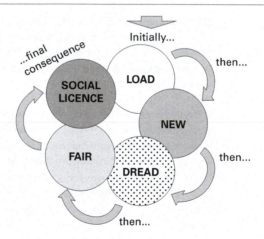

Example 1: The mortgage crisis, mid-2000s

First, then, the five factors may act *in sequence*, as described below.

In the early 2000s, the financial services industry had been deregulated, encouraging providers to launch wider ranges of mortgage products (cognitive LOAD: more choice), with looser controls on the risk posed to customers (hazard LOAD: more customer risk), as politicians also loosened tax restrictions on the housing market (social LOAD: more incentive to buy) and house prices were rising (monetary LOAD: more cash cost and affective LOAD: more sense of urgency to buy before prices climb out of reach).

Many of the mortgage contracts offered unprecedented loan-to-value risk (NEW hazard to the borrower and lender). Many providers underwrote the funding of their mortgage offers by using repackaging of debt (through NEW derivative financial instruments). Some providers bundled together their repackaged mortgage contracts and resold them en masse to third parties whom the mortgagors (householders) had never met, exposing the homeowners to NEW (unfamiliar) owners of debt, some of whom abruptly demanded the house keys back. When house prices subsequently fell, homeowners found themselves in the NEW situation of owning an asset with negative equity, for which there was no provider advice available, and also facing a NEW situation that they had never had to contemplate: handing their house keys to a stranger who had foreclosed on the debt and repossessed the property.

When originally taking on the mortgage, the new homeowner had faced and tried to ignore the usual anxiety (DREAD: denial of consequence – optimism bias and short-termism) about whether they would be able to keep up the mortgage payments. When the original provider had sold the mortgage on to the secondary debt trader mortgagor, the householder may have been aware of this, and experienced some anxiety about not really understanding what reselling of a mortgage really meant (DREAD: fear/approach avoidance); or may only have discovered the resale when the new contract owner called to take repossession (DREAD of the unknown; existential dread; fear of dispossession/homelessness; depression over losing one's symbol of social status/domestic security).

Subsequently, many homeowners discovered that the very providers who had evicted them were now being bailed out with public (that is, taxpayers') money. The dispossessed homeowners felt that the providers had an UNFAIR advantage, and that it was UNFAIR as a citizen to have 'paid twice', yet lost everything. Which brought the final phase…

A public opinion and political review of the SOCIAL LICENCE of the entire industry of mortgage providers. When the directors of some providers also received large performance bonuses, not only dispossessed homeowners, but many still-comfortable citizens, felt that the balance between risk-taking and social benefit was UNFAIR (risk inequity). As securities markets collapsed and national economies slowed to a halt, voters in many countries affected felt that their governments, who had presided over the crash, no longer deserved support. In the United Kingdom, United States, and many other countries where general elections followed soon after the 2008 crash, the presiding government lost its mandate.

In countries and regions whose whole investment banking sector had collapsed, the withdrawal of SOCIAL LICENCE at the ballot box was even more extreme: Iceland, Spain, Greece and the Republic of Ireland not only experienced political turmoil but saw mass street protests, some violent, and criminal prosecutions of leading bankers. A decade on, some countries' new conduct rules reflect voters' newly reduced tolerance for financial providers' old behaviours: the SOCIAL LICENCE as expressed by Australia's conduct regulator, ASIC, includes automatically pressing for criminal charges against financial mis-sellers.

This brief review of the 2000s mortgage crisis through a behavioural lens shows a standard sequence of events, running through LOAD, NEW and DREAD, into FAIR and ending in collapse of SOCIAL LICENCE.

Other sudden shocks to public confidence may follow a less standard sequence, as we will see next.

Example 2: The Barings Bank crash

The initial or main driving factor may not always be LOAD. When we apply a behavioural lens to the Barings Bank crash of 1995, a different sequence of factors is evident (see Figure 8.9).

The directors of Barings, a venerable British bank (founded 1762), in the early 1990s thought they saw a double opportunity for NEW sources of profit in the Far East: in NEWly emerging markets and in a type of product that was NEW (at least to them), derivatives. Vesting a large amount of faith and credit into a single remote operation, they LOADed up their risk, advancing cash and trading funds to a promising young trader at the Simex market, the Singapore Mercantile

Figure 8.9 The Barings Bank crash, 1995

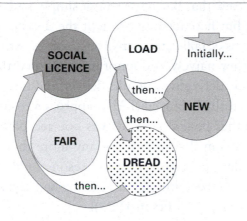

Exchange (securities trading floor) where many of Asia's derivatives were traded. Barings' board thus took primarily a NEW risk: entering a NEW (untried, unfamiliar) market and with a NEW (unfamiliar) set of financial instruments, they then compounded this by LOADing all their financial risk into a narrow play.

The trader running their Simex team, one Nick Leeson, soon realized that he was out of his depth but feared telling his superiors about how large a hole he had created – a DREAD of consequence and accountability. (There is some suggestion that his bosses, half a world away in London, were also blindly optimistic, suppressing their own DREAD of consequence and liability by not properly asking what risks were being run, preferring just to bank the profits and keep potential losses 'out of sight, out of mind'.) One fateful night in February 1995, Leeson took an unlicensed market position – essentially, a gamble – greater than the entire capital value of the bank, lost the bet, and fled.

Back in London, the directors of Barings petitioned for help from their fellow British establishment bankers and the Bank of England. To their horror, they found that the other banks withdrew the customary support. Up until then, the SOCIAL LICENCE of the sector held that respected banking firms helped each other out of trouble. With that social pact gone, any prospect of a bailout went with it. Soon afterwards, the bank was taken over – sold for just £1.

What led the other bankers to reverse generations of supportive habit was their view that Barings had not simply had a little bad luck in the markets, but had actively brought the disaster on themselves. By taking undue risks, failing to control and oversee extreme and remote risk-taking, as they naïvely and ignorantly pursued the super-profits they thought that derivatives would deliver, the directors had upset the bank's historically balanced (FAIR) approach to commercial risk-taking. In the other banks' view, it was not acceptable or expected to bail out Barings in this situation – any more than it was a FAIR expectation by Barings' directors that Leeson could single-handedly keep the bank profitable (although his trading had, freakishly, delivered 10 per cent of Barings' profits in 1993).

Reification: When a half-imagined risk 'turns real'

One of the defining processes of social perception of risk is when a hazard that people only vaguely knew about suddenly comes into sharp focus in the public mind. Behavioural researchers sometimes call this effect reification. When a group of people faces a new, unfamiliar form of risk, it can be tempting for them to play down the risk, to avoid having to worry about it on the grounds of 'out of sight, out of mind'.

There is a part of us that tends to fear the discovery of new information about a risk. This is why men of a certain age avoid visiting the doctor when they are feeling unwell: as at least one physician has said, 'Many [adult] men go to the doctor for the first time in their 40s — on a stretcher with a heart attack'[17]. For many people (and especially for middle-aged men, it seems), admitting that a present risk is, well, present would somehow change what felt like a vague possibility of hazard into a 'real thing' in their minds. The same effect is true for all of us: once we have a clear mental picture of the risk, it is harder to dismiss it as something unreal.

That earlier state of apathy, or unreality, may be challenged by one of two types of event. Either a crisis will occur in the real world, focusing general public attention; or someone might publish information that places normal people squarely in the frame of being directly exposed to the risk.

This may be best explained with two simple examples from recent history.

Reality of missiles strikes home: The Cuba crisis

In October 1962, US spotter planes discovered that Soviet Russia had seemingly begun to install nuclear missiles on the communist-friendly island of Cuba, 90 miles from the coast of the United States. At first, the move was thought to be a Cold War bluff. But then a newspaper published an infographic showing how Russia's Cuban-based missiles could strike US citizens' homes, right across the United States, in less than four minutes (Figure 8.10).

Figure 8.10 The Cuban missile crisis brought home to US citizens, 1962

The same day, US public anxiety ran wild and many citizens started to prepare for World War III.

What had changed? The infographic reified what had previously been a loosely imagined threat, by showing ordinary citizens that their homes were just four minutes away from being destroyed by a nuclear attack. By converting a strategic (political and military) risk into a personal threat to the home of every US citizen, the news-paper's infographic image[18] transformed the level of public concern.

Panic makes savers' risk even more real

Financial crises can also become reified in the public imagination. Northern Rock was a UK mortgage bank that had pursued an aggressive growth strategy but whose wholesale market supporters refused to extend their credit in August 2007.

Figure 8.11 The Northern Rock bank run crisis 2007, reified

Although the Bank of England stepped in with emergency lending to bail it out, some customers who had deposited their life savings with Northern Rock decided they would rather withdraw their cash. Within days, news images of savers queuing outside Northern Rock branches encouraged other savers to do the same – sparking an old-fashioned 'run on the bank' (Figure 8.11). The news pictures had made the risk real, giving social proof that withdrawing deposits was the 'right' thing for customers to do.

Conclusion

This chapter has introduced the behavioural lens, besides examining several important supporting concepts: apathetic tolerance for risk; reification; and the five core factor sets that trigger a hostile public response (overload, the shock of the new, dread, risk equity and review of social licence). The lens is a useful tool for generating questions, both to help identify oncoming behavioural (misconduct) risks, and to set narrow conduct issues within their necessary wider context of good governance and organizations' collective social responsibility.

This analysis shows how, contrary to classical economic and risk models, the 'irrationality' of people's reaction to our conduct is more predictable than we thought. People may reject what we thought would be a good proposition, whether a product, service, or some other form of intervention that was intended to help them. The explanation for their hostility lies not in mathematical proof but in the behavioural lens with its more finessed reading of cognitive and emotional states. The lens is designed to be an easy tool to use, pulling together, as far as possible in plain language, complex and diverse elements of neural and behavioural science. By viewing through this lens any existing or proposed initiative or activity, managers can benefit their organization by helping understand how a breakdown in social licence may occur, and what measures might be put into place to prevent this.

The successful commercial risk-taker, like the successful public-sector guardian, understands that we achieve change by empathizing with other people's circumstances and expectations, then seeking to identify a common direction of travel on which all can agree. Politicians might call this 'framing the narrative'; I prefer to think of it as using good science to identify common points of humanity. Humans like to feel they are part of a group with shared values and expectations. Organizations (including governments) who take some action that carelessly puts this expectation in doubt should not be surprised when this provokes a violent reaction. The behavioural lens offers a simple method to predict where such barriers to acceptance may arise.

Think of it as a 'structured common sense' guide to considering how people out there are likely to respond to various forms of conduct, on your part.

The next chapter applies the behavioural lens to a series of topical challenges for conduct risk managers. It also shows how to apply the lens in greater detail to produce a range of different perspectives on risk-taking, from an everyday 'layman's' view, to the boardroom, to the regulator, to the behavioural analyst. With this approach, you build reserves of social goodwill to help protect value in a business and constructively question others' assumptions, including some of the lazy orthodoxies of past control regimes. In time, all manner of groups with an interest in risk governance may come to use the lens to compare the acceptability of their own agendas with others', and among more scientifically minded analysts of risk perception, to reappraise and make new sense of their own aims and experiences.

Notes

1 University of Adelaide (2015) *Examples of Inappropriate Student Behaviour*, at adelaide.edu.au/student/behaviour/examples/

2 Becker, H S (1963) *Outsiders: Studies in the sociology of deviance*, Simon & Schuster, New York

3 Rees-Mogg, W, Who breaks a butterfly on a wheel? in *The Times* Leader editorial, 1 July 1967

4 Kahneman, D (2011) *Thinking, Fast and Slow*, Allen Lane

5 Simon, H A (1982) *Models of Bounded Rationality*, MIT Press, Cambridge

6 Slovic, P, Finucane, M, Peters, E and MacGregor, D (2004) Risk as analysis and risk as feelings: Some thoughts about affect, reason, risk and rationality', *Risk Analysis* **24** (2)

7 Dobelli, R (2013) *The Art of Thinking Clearly*, Sceptre

8 Ariely, D (2008) *Predictably Irrational*, HarperCollins

9 Ariely, as above

10 Lloyd, W F (1833) *Two Lectures on the Checks to Population*, Oxford University Press

11 Grayson, D (2012) *Business-Led Corporate Responsibility Coalitions*, Harvard University, John F Kennedy School of Government with Cranfield University, at hks.harvard.edu/m-rcbg/CSRI/publications/report_26

12 The Good Governance Forum, at Tomorrow's Company: www. tomorrowscompany.com

13 Gilovich, T, Medvec, V H and Savitsky, K (2009) The spotlight effect in social judgment: An egocentric bias in estimates of the salience of one's own actions and appearance, *Journal of Personality and Social Psychology*, 78 (2); meta-reviewed in McRaney, D (2012) *You Are Not So Smart*, Oneworld

14 Samson, A (Ed) with Miles, R (2016) *The Behavioral Economics Guide*, London School of Economics, at behavioraleconomics.com

15 With acknowledgement to Kasperson, R and Stallen, P (1991) *Communicating Risks to the Public*, Kluwer

16 Samson and Miles, as above

17 NBC, 14 November 2012: *Too tough to get sick; Why men won't go to the doctor*, at nbcnews.com/id/49794785/ns/health-mens_health/t/

18 For original infographic see: CORBIS/British Library

The 'behavioural lens', Part 2   09

Staying ahead of the regulator

Introduction

In Chapter 8, we saw how applying a behavioural lens to any risk-control situation can help to reveal the human tensions that might cause the controls to fail. Two examples of control failure, the 2008 domestic mortgage and bank liquidity crisis, and the Barings crash of 1995, showed how to use the lens to produce an alternative, behaviour-based take on events.

In this chapter, we will look through the behavioural lens at a range of regulated conduct topics. The lens also yields some tips and techniques for improving an organization's wider communication about risk with customers and other stakeholders.

Themes and concepts in this chapter

affective shock – asymmetry/asymmetric information – attestation – bias effects – cognition of risk – customer due diligence – customer-centric – defunct assumptions – dissonance – fathering – fit and proper person – goodwill – grey areas – lines of sight – loss-aversion – precautionary – procrastinating – reifying – Relevant Authorized Persons – risk–risk trade-off – sanctions – sense-making – significant influence – slippery slope – social licence – social proof – 'tells' – trust – unproven innovations – whistleblowing – wilful ignorance

As seen from the growth of conduct regulation described earlier in this book, financial firms now face a growing list of topical challenges to their management of this new category of risk. As regulators' remit expands, both on their own account and through regulatory alliances, practitioners need to raise their own game. This means not just being aware of and complying with the latest regulations, but actively considering where the next pressure for behaviour change is going to come from. To help you with this task of anticipation, Chapter 9 adds an extra perspective that the behavioural lens can use to capture three further outlooks on each risk-taking situation. These outlooks are: the everyday, lay person's view; the risk governance specialist's (corporate, political or regulatory) view; and finally the view taken by a behavioural scientist, emphasizing processes of risk cognition (how people mentally make sense of what's happening). As with the overall behavioural lens in the previous chapter, the analytical components of these three perspectives are first laid out then applied to example topics.

As a prelude to all that, a few words about the nature and significance of trust; and a simple way to alert yourself to when colleagues are subverting your plans for change. First, trust and goodwill.

Bank your goodwill, build your trust

Is your organization trustworthy? You'd probably say yes, one would hope.

But now let's rephrase that question, slightly, to consider more carefully the meaning of that word, trustworthy: Is your organization worthy of trust? Does it keep on earning, continuously from everyone, the right to be trusted?

As touched on at the end of the previous chapter, to keep your social licence intact you need to sustain at least a basic level of public trust. There are clear causal links between trust and goodwill, and between trust and cognition. The more that people trust you, the more they are willing to deal with you, and the more they listen to (and remember) what you have to say[1]. As a starting point for maintaining general confidence in its risk-taking, your organization needs to acknowledge this. To start with, it might be helpful to think of goodwill as an organizational resource called, perhaps, 'social capital'. Later, if challenged about your conduct and good intentions, you can make use of this resource to help safeguard your social licence.

There is one particular image of trust and goodwill that I have found speaks powerfully to many different organizations: imagine that your goodwill is a form of currency that you can pay into a savings account. Day to day, you need to be able to draw a little on your reserve of goodwill for your organization to function as it must: you have to, say, ask that member of staff to do a favour, or this supplier to rush an order through. Sometimes you need to make bigger withdrawals: say, to get this community to accept your application for a trading licence; or to ask that regulator whether they see your firm as well behaved. As any mature human knows, if you are asking someone for something that benefits your own interests, the other person is likely to expect some reciprocal benefit – if not now, later; but at some point, and never not at all. Building goodwill is the skill of 'paying it forward'. Without it, your request for help would come across as a random demand falling from a clear blue sky[2].

Trust matters because it is a precondition for having any kind of social licence – financial services in particular are, in plain language, all about being trustworthy. In which case, trust is a vital precondition for any conversation you might want to have with customers, and regulators, about how you manage your firm's risk-taking. Ask yourself, in all honesty: 'Are we credible? When we speak, do people listen?'

It is partly because of this cognitive effect that trust is seen by behavioural economics as a form of public goods. It promotes general wellbeing, easing social contact, and also cooperation in any form of enterprise, for example by keeping costs down when cooperators can 'take on trust' each other's commitments to help.

Returning then to the idea of your goodwill as occupying a bank account, consider for a minute: it's a savings account. Obviously it doesn't allow an overdraft, as that would break the social rules of reciprocity, like asking a complete stranger for a favour. You therefore need to make some deposits into the account first; only then can you begin to draw on any of the goodwill you need to get other people to cooperate with you. Now, as that may all sound a bit abstract, here are a few concrete examples of actions you can take that bank some goodwill into your (still imaginary) account.

Actions that bank goodwill for you

- You build relationships.
- You get to know your local people, and what issues they care about.
- You engage with your critics and understand why they think as they do.
- You are truthful and informative, offering objectively confirmed facts.
- When there is any dispute, you are consistent and fair.
- You do what you say you will to help.
- You are known for getting results when dealing with people's problems.
- You communicate in a civil manner.

All being well, having deposited goodwill thanks to any of these actions then makes it easier for you to ask for more help, and expect more cooperation, from people you are working with.

In case that was getting a bit too simple, though, beware that there is a powerful reverse effect to all this. Keeping the behavioural lens factors in mind – imposing overload; too much newness; inducing dread; acting unfairly; losing social licence – here are some actions you might take that will drain goodwill out of your account. (Of course, no one really benefits from these, least of all you, assuming you cared at all about your social licence.)

Actions that waste your goodwill

- You are remote and apparently not listening to valid concerns.

- To settle disputed points, you invoke process and systems.

- You deny extant and known problems, maintaining that 'our systems are good', whatever the evidence otherwise.

- You miss chances to engage and improve.

- You tell staff to 'do as I say, not as I do'.

- Your conversational style is patronizing and aloof.

- You react 'uncaringly' to news that other people find distressing.

As you might expect, behavioural economists are a bit more analytical about the cognitive aspect of all this, but they sum it up quite straight-forwardly: trust is 'an important public resource', a form of 'public good, like clean air and water'[3], smoothing and simplifying all kinds of human activities in organized and family life. Problems arise because trust is slow to build and relatively easy to damage or destroy – just 'a few bad players in the market can spoil it for everyone else'[4]. It is clear from this why the conduct regulator sees a linkage between individual good conduct and the headline regulatory responsibility to 'maintain orderly markets'.

While we are looking at goodwill, or lack of it, as you institute conduct-based changes most people will tell you to your face that they want to cooperate and do the right thing; but some of course will not mean it, and will ignore or pretend to forget what they had agreed to do, in the hope that they can carry on as before without changing their behaviour. Now is a good time to mention a feature of human behaviour that helps us to recognize and deal with this problem of, let's call it, moral non-compliance, or failure of follow-through: the tell.

Reading the 'tells'

In the list of ways to waste your goodwill, just above, was one point about 'invoking systems'. As seen in discussion of systems thinking throughout the book, many risk managers cling to the comforting but mistaken thought that prescribing in detail how staff must interact with customers is the best way to keep the firm out of trouble with the regulator. Wrong. As we have seen, humans being the contrary animals they are, applying this kind of systems thinking not only fails on its own terms but also may foster staff subcultures of rebellion as they 'resist the identities imposed on them'[5]. It is more motivating for a member of your staff, and a happier experience for the customer, to let the two of them interact as human beings; as normal people rather than part of your system. Look twice when you find anyone turning down a request on grounds that it's 'not our policy' (what, it's not your policy to be helpful?), or 'going by the book'. Do you, maybe, farm some types of customer out to a poor-quality subcontracted call centre? Is those customers' experience of you that the 'computer says no'[6]? When did you last check on that?

This is part of a wider pattern of moving towards more customer-centric conduct, just as the conduct regulator wishes. Cultivate the habit of listening intelligently and critically to your firm's conversations with the outside world; try to hear yourselves as they do. There are opportunities to try this internally, too – one of which is listening for signs of cognitive gaps. Behavioural science calls the effect 'leakage'; poker players call it a 'tell'. Whatever *you* call it, a tell is a change in a person's behaviour that provides a clue about some form of cognitive gap. This is a useful form of personal risk radar, if you have ever been puzzled as to why someone, or a team, is not dealing straightforwardly with you.

Unconsciously, everyone from time to time gives off a tell, a sign that reveals a gap or inconsistency in their understanding, or intent to comply: for our purposes here, it's a gap between a stated intention and not actually intending to do anything; or between receiving an instruction and being unable or unwilling to process it in a useful way. Many a request for compliance is challenged by 'wilful ignorance', which itself needs challenging. Now you can be the challenger, if you will.

For our purposes, the tells we are interested in are the signs that the people we are speaking with either do not see the significance of what they have been asked to do, or are perhaps concealing some form of continued 'gaming' rejection of your request to engage in an activity. (For poker players, in case you were wondering, a tell can be a useful sign that the other player holds a strong or weak hand of cards).

Without getting into a detailed briefing on body language, other non-verbal signals and unobvious indicators, here is just a quick list of verbal tells that this author has noted in observing boardroom conversations between executive rule-breakers and risk governance leaders. The easy way to use this as a tool is as follows: look down the list and, if you have ever been in a meeting where someone at the table said one of these things, that's someone who needs to sit with you for a serious chat about conduct risk.

Blanking the risk: things people say

Others' verbal 'tells' alerting you to take the initiative and look harder:

- 'We've done all this work, let's not have to change it now.'
- 'This process is based on a system/assumption that everyone subscribes to.'
- 'This [objection] has never been an issue before.'
- 'That just isn't what's happening here.'
- 'Of course, this is outside your expert field, I appreciate.'
- 'You have no authority here, it's down to my team what we do.'
- 'That one? It's just a blip, or a modelling error, an outlier – don't count it.'
- 'If it isn't in the plan, it isn't a problem.'
- 'Nobody raised that point when we first discussed this.'
- 'How could we have known?'
- 'It's too early to say if that's significant at all.'

In the previous chapter, the behavioural lens showed how to spot when your organization is in danger of ignoring the need for change, especially a need to focus more on customers' needs. (In this way the lens helps you to be more 'customer-centric', as the regulator wants.)

Now we will move on to meet the second set of dimensions for the behavioural lens.

Points of view: The behavioural lens, second aspect

After applying the core five factors to some real case examples in Chapter 8, now we can apply them using three alternative points of view: see Table 9.1. By adopting three alternative viewpoints, we can better question our own preconceptions and locate the latest boundaries of acceptable and expected behaviour.

First, to define the three viewpoints:

The three viewpoints

Level 1: Popular, everyday ('Street')

On this first level, the five factors of the behavioural lens are presented as the kind of everyday questions that might be raised by a passer-by, or by family members between one another, or by unskilled employees in an organization, or by citizens wanting explanations from their government.

Level 2: Corporate and political risk governance ('Safeguards')

At the next level, the same questions are reframed in the manner that groups professionally responsible for risk governance tend to address them.

Level 3: Risk-cognitive interpretation ('Science')

Finally at the 'behavioural and cognitive' level, the five factors attach to salient strands of academic theory and applied research. This includes known bias and behavioural effects, which can offer valuable alerts, for example to a widening social demarcation of 'unacceptable behaviour'.

Overlaying these three perspectives on our original five factors of risk cognition produces a 3×5 factor grid (Table 9.1):

Table 9.1 Five factors, three viewpoints

	Street (lay view: citizen, passer-by, family member, new customer)	Safeguards (governance view: a provider's board; the regulator; policy-makers)	Science (risk-perception analytical view: behavioural economists; academic researchers and observers)
Load	What extra activity are you forcing me to take on? Are you forcing me to take on more than I can handle, or am I capable of? Is there just too much choice? Is there too much pressure (generally) to do something I'm not comfortable doing? Do I understand what I'm supposed to do?	Are we trying (too hard) to make our existing process produce more? Are we overextending our people, processes and supply systems? Are we testing the limits of what the rules allow (or seem to mean)?	Is there cognitive overload (too much information), forcing people into excessive 'sense-making'? Are people being forced to take on more than they can (physically or emotionally) cope with? Is this about to stress-test people's current limit of tolerance? At what point will people's tolerance break?
New	This is all too new; isn't it just change for change's sake? Am I having to learn, or get accustomed to, something new? Are you forcing me to work with unfamiliar methods, technology, or people? Can I now see clearly something I didn't know about you before? Can I make sense of these new instructions? Why should I change my habits?	Is it imperative that we bring in new methods, products, ways of talking about them? Is it possible to introduce this change without anyone being concerned about it? Are our new activities untried/unproven? Are we newly visible as we do this? Is this too much of a break with what people are used to? Are there new investigations/risk reports/rules that reveal what we are doing?	Is there dissonance? Are they forcing people to abandon anchor points, reframe perception, abandon comfortable assumptions, change behaviour? Are people willing/able to accommodate those changes? Are new data sets available that expose defunct assumptions?

Table 9.1 continued

	Street (lay view: citizen, passer-by, family member, new customer)	Safeguards (governance view: a provider's board; the regulator; policy-makers)	Science (risk-perception analytical view: behavioural economists; academic researchers and observers)
Dread	It's scary, must I face up to this? What if I can't? Is this a total game-changer? Could it be less painful? Does it seem that you're harming people I care about?	Are we (or is anyone in our supply chain) alarming anyone – including our own people? Are we concerned enough about people's anxieties? Is this activity 'lawful but awful'?	Is there visceral fear of injury, deferred or vicarious harm? Is this threatening people's sense of self/habitual comforts? Is this denying people control/jeopardizing the future? (How fearful *might* people be as they learn more about what's going wrong?) Is this inducing existential dread? Are you reifying (making real) a threat that was only abstract before?
(Un)Fair	Really, is that fair? Can they do that? Who's taking the risks, who gets the benefit? What do my friends and family think about that?	Does a lack of complaints mean that all is well? Are customers' legitimate concerns noted and acted upon?	Is there equitable distribution of risk-taking and benefit? Is there an apparent skew (asymmetry), acting against some of those involved? Is this exhausting a limited supply of a social good (tragedy of the commons)?
Social	Are we okay with that? Is that what we'd expect and accept, as 'doing the right thing'? Do I like the way you're handling things? Why should I put up with this? Don't they know that times have changed? Is this really for me, now?	Was our 'Conduct/CSR compliant' stance enough? Have people's expectations and tolerances changed? Are we seen as well behaved/'best in sector'? And how's our sector itself seen?	Are we seeing a change in the legitimacy of this activity? Are the 'norming' processes of establishing social proof themselves changing? Is 'social proof' changing as a result of clearer knowledge, or persistent bias effects? (hindsight, herding, 'moral panic'?) Where is the 'friends and family test' being applied?

Applying the three levels

Time now to apply the 3×5 multi-viewpoint version of the behavioural lens to a couple of case examples, putting the questions into practice.

Example 1: Emma's endless mortgage

Now we will apply those three perspectives to a regulated financial service topic: keeping mortgage borrowers informed about costs of the loan, and the need for repayment.

Fifteen years ago Emma Chizett, then 45 years old, took out an interest-only mortgage to buy a house. Property seemed expensive and as her income was limited, she could only afford to pay the interest on the loan, not to repay any of the principal that would begin to make her (rather than her lender) the owner of the house. That lender, Humungous Loans Ltd, had sold her an interest-only mortgage for 100 per cent of the value of the house, without asking Emma about her plans to repay the principal of the loan.

As the years passed, two things happened: first, whenever interest rates began to rise, Emma's income stayed more or less the same, meaning that she could only just afford to keep paying her monthly interest instalments to Humongous, but nothing more. Second, house prices started to fall a bit. (Yes, this does happen – it happened in 1990–93 and again in 2007–09[7].) Emma now has no equity in her home. Meanwhile, she is nearing retirement, has been enjoying her steady job, and has been looking forward to living in her own house in her later years.

As retirement approaches, Emma wonders what to do. Humungous hasn't bothered to contact her, apart from sending an annual statement, since she first took out the loan.

What does the behavioural lens make of all this?: see Table 9.2.

Emma Chizett herself is fictitious, but based on real cases, and a dangerous underlying source of market fragility right now[8].

Table 9.2 A 3×5 viewpoint behavioural lens for Emma's mortgage

	Street (that's Emma)	Safeguards (that's Humungous, and the regulator)	Science (that's us, observing)
Load	I have this big load of debt, plus the anxiety of not knowing if Humungous will let me stay in the house that I think of as my own home.	Emma is looking increasingly like a bad debt. Although she's on the books as a long-term loyal customer and good regular payer, this can't continue. Throwing her out of her home is clearly detrimental in one way, but so is selling her an interest-only mortgage and rolling it on for 15 years with no plan to pay off the loan. Which is the worse conduct?	Emma probably found it hard to reify the amount of the debt. She allowed her paying of regular interest to feed her short-term bias; she displaced having to think about the more burdensome question of repaying the loan.
New	(Nothing new; it simply bothers me that there is something I should know, but don't. Retirement will be something new, of course, but I can't think clearly about that just yet.)	We are going to have to tell her, soon, which will come as unwelcome news. Maybe there's a chance of just keeping everything as it is for a bit longer…	The affective shock, coming soon, of facing eviction will certainly be new. Meanwhile, it's a *lack* of novelty that's the problem here; no one has raised a question that should have challenged both parties' complacency long ago.

Dread	I just can't think about the future, or how big the debt is, or how the house isn't mine.	Nobody wants to tell Emma; also nobody wants to disturb a long-term contract that appears to have worked perfectly well for 15 years – except that it's about to stop working, of course.	Emma has an existential dread of losing her familiar support systems – both a loss of material comforts, and the ultimate threat of homelessness. Also straightforward loss-aversion.
(Un)Fair	How could they have sold me a promise of owning a home, and not warned me or explained? – It's all their fault I'm stuck now.	By not warning Emma, it looks as if we have made things worse; but if we had warned her she would have been upset for longer. Isn't it just as unfair to expect a provider not to repossess a house that's legally theirs?	Emma is averse to inequity, as everybody is. But she has also been suppressing her dissonance about the true situation: deep down, she probably knows that she (and her provider) have procrastinated – they've avoided facing up to the plain fact that she has no ownership of the house.
Social	There must be lots of people in my position, and something should be done about it.	There are many people in Emma's position, many years into interest-only mortgages. Although it's a form of customer detriment, it is also storing up future bad debts for providers; the regulator has yet to tackle this.	As more and more late-middle-aged people overcome their dissonance and face up to the knowledge that interest-only mortgages may make them homeless, society will have to acknowledge (reify) the problem. At that tipping point, this will become a political hot topic, forcing regulatory change.

The next example is also based on a real and notorious case, but is presented in an anonymized way as it is not intended to express any direct judgement on the specifics of one case. Once again, the underlying problem is more general.

Example 2: Bill's resold small business loan

William Stickers (Bill, to his friends) is a family man and professionally a self-employed jobbing carpenter. As his business has been thriving, with a bulging order book, two years ago he took out a small business loan with First Foxy Bank to expand his business. He used the loan to help take on two apprentices, lease a bigger van and buy some new tools. As Bill has kept up his loan repayments and kept his current account at Foxy in credit for two years, everything has seemed fine.

Meanwhile though, unknown to Bill, First Foxy has been negotiating to sell its entire portfolio of small business loans to Badger Credit, a company that isn't a bank at all – it doesn't even have a banking licence – instead, Badger is a wholesale specialist in buying and selling other businesses' debts. Badger is not interested in having any kind of relationship with any of Foxy's former creditors. Rather, Badger's business model looks at getting as much cash in as quickly as possible by whatever means, and these means include, one day, knocking at the door of Bill's lockup and forcibly taking possession of his van, complete with tools.

Deprived of his means of earning a livelihood, Bill is now forced to lay off his apprentices, and his business folds. Three people are now unemployed and numerous customers left with unfinished work, all because Badger preferred a quick cash collection to a more socially useful, long-term commitment to an entrepreneur.

Foxy has done nothing illegal, but what about the acceptability of its conduct, and the state of its social contract with its former customers? See Table 9.3.

Table 9.3 A 3×5 viewpoint behavioural lens for Bill's resold loan

	Street (that's Bill)	Safeguards (that's the Boards of Foxy, and Badger; and the regulator)	Science (that's us, observing)
Load	When I took out Foxy's business loan I didn't expect a hidden ambush by Badger – that's more than I bargained for.	Foxy sees it as simply unloading (de-risking) a portfolio of higher-risk debts.	Foxy has widened the dissonance gap between Bill's (prosocial) view of a small business lender and Badger's (pure 'systems thinking') view of Bill as simply a debt to be collected.
New	I didn't know they could do that – never heard of it happening before. This completely changes my view of what banks *can* do – and *actually* do.	Reselling small business loans is a new(ish) and still unusual commercial development. Should a bank have a right to exercise this (legal) option to trade a debt, without informing the customer?	Foxy has dumped a cognitive shock on Bill by changing the rules of engagement; Badger has 'moved the goalposts'; knowledge is now clearly asymmetrical, where it wasn't before.
Dread	A company I'd never heard of, and know nothing about, Badger suddenly seem to have total power over me, my family and my business; now I'm losing everything.	It's hard not to conclude that this is plainly 'customer detriment', as there is no customer benefit whatever – unless we interpret Foxy as a customer of Badger, which is a perverse reading of it!	Foxy's action has created an existential (and practical) crisis for Bill; and raises a wider 'slippery slope' anxiety for all small business borrowers.
(Un)Fair	I contracted with a bank, not a debt collector. I wouldn't have borrowed from a loan shark, how come Foxy seems to have turned into one?	As a small business lender, Foxy surely has a duty to stand by its customers, more than to lay off its doubtful debts; Badger's presence is not at all customer-centric.	Just because it's technically possible, and 'good business' for Foxy to lay off the debt, doesn't make it good practice: 'lawful but awful' exploitation of asymmetric knowledge.
Social	Can they do that? I mean, can they just shut me down for no reason? Aren't there laws against that? Anyone else feel as I do about this?	(See also NEW above.) The first social function of banks is support business enterprise, not to get into financial engineering to turn a fast profit.	Badger doesn't see the social licence view at all, has drawn a false distinction between debt and support for enterprise.

A behavioural take on Senior Managers Regime and 'grey areas'

Since March 2016, the British conduct and prudential regulators (FCA and PRA) have enforced their initiative for making identified senior managers personally responsible for risk control[9]. Commonly referred to as 'SMR' (for Senior Managers Regime), it includes rules for certifying responsibility (Senior Managers & Certification Regime, or 'SM&CR'), and specific rules for insurers, whose businesses fall within the conduct regime from 2017 (Senior Insurance Managers Regime, or 'SIMR'). Other conduct regulators, notably Australia's ASIC, have been looking to adopt and extend similar principles.

This book has a different but complementary aim: to raise intelligent questions to inform the board's approach to conduct risk. Using the behavioural lens provides a competitive edge from closer understanding of the regulator's view of what customer-centric thinking should include. (The aim here is not to provide detailed technical compliance listings – there are already in any case many professional advisor firms' initiatives doing just that, while the FCA's website www.fca.org.uk remains the authoritative source for up-to-the-minute briefing on this still developing initiative.) For our purpose here, it is appropriate to include some pointers on key behavioural aspects of SMR, consistent with the regulator's stated purpose to 'improve genuine accountability in firms… not [with] a tick-box approach, but genuine engagement'. Although that purpose includes a technical requirement of defining 'far greater precision about individual responsibilities', the outcome of that review of responsibilities, and of wider thinking about 'appropriate' conduct, is to create a new licensed 'basis for upholding individuals' standards of behaviour'[10]. Through this initiative, the regulator is explicitly linking board roles and good conduct, holding individual senior managers personally accountable for any misconduct in their firm, for recognizing what is 'appropriate' conduct, and for promoting this throughout the firm. It is this wider purpose – let's call it engaging intelligently – that is our common aim here. The regulator recognizes that decisions may be *affective*, on both sides (vendor and customer), as much as rational.

> ## What's 'affective'?
>
> 'Affect' is a cognitive science term for emotion swaying your rational judgement. More specifically, how your mood or feelings at a given moment may lead you to filter information that you use for decision-making.
>
> So, as you are approaching a supermarket checkout, it is not rational to buy chocolate. But affect reminds you that you feel tired and want a 'reward' for all that pushing a trolley around, and you find yourself picking up a bar of chocolate that is conveniently next to where you're standing in line.
>
> The supermarket's owners, of course, know all about affect.

The detailed compliance requirements include rules on accountability (identifying your function, certifying you are both a 'fit and proper' person, and competent to do it); remuneration (aligning risk and reward); and protection for individuals who report misconduct (whistleblowing rules to 'promote a culture where people can speak up'). Financial firms, including banks, investment firms, building societies, credit unions and (from early 2017) insurers are all subject to conduct rules. Senior managers must be pre-approved by the regulator and annually reassessed by the firm, including producing 'fit and proper' (for example, criminal record) checks and signed Statements of Responsibility backed by an attestation of competence.

Senior manager roles affected include all executive board directors and executive directors of international firms' UK branches, together with certain non-executives ('NEDs'): the chairman of the board and the chairs of the risk, audit, remuneration and nomination committees. A summary list of key regulator-defined Senior Management Functions, with their designated regulatory code identity numbers, is supplied at the end of this chapter as an appendix. Some identity numbers are broader than others; for example, the responsibilities of SMF6 and SMF7 senior managers, as Heads of Key Business areas and Group Senior Entities respectively, are defined by their authority over earnings (over more than 20 per cent of gross revenue) or significant influence over other Relevant Authorized Persons (RAP).

When attesting to responsibility and competence, most firms will by now be familiar with producing a management responsibility map, which ensures that there are 'no overlaps and no white spaces'[11] in setting out who is personally accountable for each business activity and process. The map includes not only this allocation ('apportionment') of responsibilities, and their reporting lines, but also broader arrangements for management and governance. The FCA's conduct rules are enforceable over UK bank employees regardless of where (overseas) they may be working, and over non-UK firms at any point where they are active in the FCA's jurisdiction. For example, the rules apply to a New York-based chair of a risk committee of a UK subsidiary of a US retail bank.

Although that may sound like a higher level of technical complexity than this book aims to address, this all ties back into a simple underlying point about good behaviour: The certification regime is the regulator's newest method for trying to prevent your employees posing 'a significant risk of harm' to anyone – not just to customers, but also to colleagues. While firms have some discretion about certifying who can do what tasks, the conduct regulator may challenge any decision to certify a 'material risk taker', wherever he or she is working.

As seen in Chapter 3, the rules governing conduct are broadly defined but may be more narrowly applied where the regulator feels that a practitioner's or firm's behaviour is contrary to the spirit of good conduct – so-called 'lawful but awful'[12]. A recap summary appears below.

Summary 'good conduct' rules-in-principle – based on FCA/FCA + PRA, 2016[13]

All individuals

rule#

CR1 – Act with integrity.

CR2 – Act with skill, care and diligence.

CR3 – Be open and cooperative with regulators.

CR4 – Pay due regard to the interests of customers and treat them fairly.

CR5 – Observe proper standards of market conduct.

Senior Managers (SMR)

rule#

SM1 – Make sure your firm's business is controlled effectively.

SM2 – Make sure your firm complies with the regulator's requirements and standards.

SM3 – Only ever delegate your responsibilities to an appropriate person, and oversee this carefully.

SM4 – Disclose to the regulator any information of which they would reasonably expect to have notice.

As discussed throughout this book, these rules combine pointing to specifics ('the regulator's requirements and standards') with a broader appeal to exercise good judgement and intuition where this is the right thing to (as with 'open', 'fairly' and 'proper'). The behavioural lens offers guidance as to how the regulator frames their thinking about what the 'right thing' is, from time to time and in various evolving contexts.

Applying the lens to 'grey areas'

Having said all that, naturally enough providers remain anxious that a regulator's change of heart on any given topic might expose them to a retrospective enforcement action – punishment by hindsight, as it were – and this aspect of the 'rules' remains vexed.

On one hand, it is reasonable for providers to be concerned that if, say, the market turns against a product they have previously sold, this is not their fault, even if the customer loses money; the provider would defend the sale on the basis that it was the best possible advice at the time.

On the other hand, there have historically been many providers who were all too ready to make a quick hit-and-run profit on selling financial products to a naïve client, knowing full well that the market could turn. This is amply confirmed by evidence from the crash of 2008, with such activities brilliantly documented, as classic social history in the making, in particular by Michael Lewis[14] and John Lanchester[15]. Let's keep in mind that customer detriment is not just about mis-selling personal finance products to consumers. Taking just one example: Lewis describes how the entire nation of Iceland became naively captivated by the promise of easy money, creating 'the most rapid expansion of a banking system in the history of mankind... the value of the Icelandic stock market multiplied nine times between 2003 and 2007'; yet this was all based on a 'handful' of 'lightweight' bankers, operating locally in Iceland, who with 'no experience in finance [were] taking out tens of billions of dollars in short-term loans from abroad', buying into 'sucker' opportunities that were readily unloaded by cannier investment bankers in other more experienced markets.

Clearly, there is scope for providers (and indeed the regulator) to have reasonable doubts about the extent to which financial advice can or should hold itself out to be 'future-proof'. As the above example showed, after a customer has bought into a product or position, markets may turn against them but this may or may not be an outcome that the provider foresaw – and it can be incredibly hard for a regulator to prove how much the seller knew about, or suspected, such a turn of events occurring. At one end of the spectrum lies the utterly cynical 'pump and dump' activity of securities traders who hype a stock to create, for example, either a quick price-rise sale opportunity, or a future opportunity to profit from short-selling; they may be helped in this by unscrupulous analysts on their home team, who are willing to publish reports that give credence to their position; meanwhile bona fide investors are duped into buying or selling at the wrong end of the price movement. At the other end of the spectrum are simple changes in market sentiment around one particular company stock, which might leave a long-term small shareholder hanging on in the hope of recovering some value in the investment, but which are not attributable to any kind of skulduggery on the part of the professional traders.

For this reason, an important future direction for conduct risk research is to work collaboratively with practitioners to establish points of common agreement – and difference – around some of these conduct exposures that might be termed 'judgement calls'. Nobody wants to run the risk of being prosecuted for honestly making a bad call, yet in theory a customer could accuse a provider of detriment for this, and the regulator might take the customer's side in any subsequent dispute. That's why a research team including this author is studying conduct risk 'grey areas', collecting providers' views and experiences of what may be seen as a defensible judgement call. To be clear: the grey areas are not seen as situations that the regulator might exploit opportunistically for political gain (see Chapter 6). Rather, they are conduct risk exposure hotspots, where regulatory guidance is wanted but is unlikely to be forthcoming, as the regulator wants to reserve the right to prosecute where it appears that detriment was caused by a provider's careless or deliberate action.

From this author's own conversations with providers, it is generally accepted that consumer financial products now enjoy a higher degree of certainty as to their conduct exposure, in part because the regulator appears predisposed to focus on high-profile consumer brands, as a political expedient (see Chapter 6), although this at least established some precedents as to what is acceptable or unacceptable. Conversely, there is greater uncertainty in the commercial banking and insurance markets, where professional-to-professional judgement calls are the more normal order of the day. While it is relatively easy to show, as a prosecutor, that a consumer is ignorant of the consequences of a badly advised decision, the same cannot so easily be said of a professional investor buying from an experienced vendor of wholesale products. Absent other proof, however, where a customer of whatever capacity or experience suffers some form of detriment after striking the contract with the vendor, it simply seems more likely that the regulator's suspicion will fall on the vendor. One can understand why vendors are concerned to protect themselves, such as by sponsoring one of the world's leading universities to study 'acceptable behaviour' around the sales process.

Some relevant 'grey area' situations are listed below, with behavioural lens comments added from the author's own observations.

These examples are significant because they point to where there are wide variations in confidence among providers as to whether they are *applying* the best possible conduct risk preparations and attestations across the many different types and lines of business affected. By observing providers' concerns and noting related behavioural effects, we can better anticipate regulators' concerns on behalf of customers, and use this insight to improve future allocation of compliance resources.

Example 'grey area' points of conduct risk exposure[16]

Circumventing sanctions or other controls (anti-money laundering [AML] etc): *Questions this raises:* Has there been 'creative compliance' or simple ignorance in applying the controls? *Behavioural lens view:* Is this just because NEW controls are unfamiliar, or an unFAIR attempt to exploit regulatory uncertainty?

Quality of **attestations**, clear **lines of sight** and **apportionment** of responsibility under SMR: *Qs raised:* What objective proof is there of senior managers' claims to fitness and competence? *B-lens:* Are senior managers seeking to exploit others' deference because they take their SOCIAL LICENCE for granted?

Customer due diligence to establish beneficial ownership (who is the ultimate owner of a given investment): *Qs raised:* Where a provider has been caught out as non-compliant following a shift in a 'compliance threshold', was this influenced by market pressures and peer expectations? *B-lens:* Was the provider overLOADed with NEW compliance information, and genuinely believed that it was maintaining best practice?

Tax advice: Sometimes an item of 'tax planning' advice, sold to customers as a benefit, is caught in a change in the law so that it becomes illegal. *Qs raised:* Using the new law in retrospect, this may mean that the provider has been enabling tax avoidance, a criminal activity; as this might in turn make the customer a criminal, there is clear 'customer detriment'. *B-lens:* Providers always DREAD the implications of uncertainty over whether a regulator might enforce with hindsight, and regard such 'moving the goalposts' as not FAIR to them – never mind the customer.

In-house analyst reports/advice on share values: Many investment banks have a team of in-house analysts who publish research and estimates on the value of various securities. *Qs raised:* Where these securities include the shares of a company that the bank is launching onto the stock market (a so-called IPO) or other public market event, there is a risk of conflict of interest or customer detriment. *B-lens:* Customers are right to DREAD hidden influences. The regulator is suspicious that providers are making unFAIR and antiSOCIAL abuse of insider knowledge – their asymmetric information.

Unsuitable product sales: Various types of financial product sold have, over time, been found to be 'unsuitable' for the buyer. *Qs raised:* In future the regulator looks willing to apply the test of 'suitability' more widely. Products previously ruled unsuitable include credit insurance and interest rate swaps. *B-lens:* Again, providers stand potentially accused of exploiting unFAIR advantage, customers' ignorance of NEW contracts and cognitive overLOAD when these are explained.

Business loans resulting in borrower detriment; where a provider has resold a loan to a third party debt trader, the customer may not be aware of this. *Qs raised:* Especially if the third party then calls in the loan, the customer suffers detriment but may have no recourse against the original provider. The conduct prosecutor is more likely in future to investigate the provider in this situation, for increasing the customer's exposure to detriment. *B-lens:* We might expect the loan customer to experience DREAD on learning that the loan has been called in, but also rage at the unFAIRness of this, and questioning of the provider's betrayal of SOCIAL LICENCE. This latter question (in the form of 'Can they *do* that?') would in turn get a sympathetic hearing from the regulator.

Rate changes: Where a provider reduces interest payable on a customer's savings, or increases interest due on a customer's loan, they must always give fair notice of this. *Qs raised:* The circumstances of 'fair' may be subject to local interpretation. *B-lens:* Simply unFAIR and contrary to SOCIAL LICENCE.

Preferential rates: Many providers offer 'special rates' of interest exclusively to new customers, to attract them in. *Qs raised:* The regulator stands ready to accuse providers of causing detriment to existing customers who were excluded from getting the benefit of the special rate; providers also have a habit of reducing the preferential rate at the end of the introductory offer period, again, without necessarily telling the customer about this. *B-lens:* Is it fundamentally unFAIR to offer 'sweeteners' to attract new customers? Providers (in many sectors besides financial services) would argue not. But existing customers may perceive it as unFAIR, LOADing extra administrative costs on them, and contrary to SOCIAL LICENCE.

'Fathering' of dirty money: Where, for example, a UK-regulated firm acquires an overseas financial business including a list of wealthy customers, then finds that the acquired firm has never checked these customers' identities or the origin of their funds. *Qs raised:* The firm must retrospectively check to see if it can bring the new customers into line with control standards on identity verification, anti-money laundering and compliance with sanctions. It may choose to 'de-risk' the acquired business by inviting potentially awkward customers to leave; but many of the customers concerned might be perfectly innocent, and complain that they have suffered detriment if their accounts are cancelled. Is 'de-risking' detrimental? *B-lens:* The firm is seeking the right risk–risk trade-off here: is it better to avoid the DREAD uncertainty of finding that a customer is a criminal; or to be accused of unFAIRness by closing accounts on a precautionary basis?

'Unfairness' in demand-driven pricing: Many products – including mortgages, airline tickets, Uber taxis and music downloads – are now priced on a 'demand' or 'surge' pricing basis. (That is, the asking price may rise at times of peak demand). *Qs raised:* While demand pricing makes commercial sense in terms of classical economics, regulators may regard it as detrimental to customers. The pricing policy relies on hidden information (only the provider has all the demand-level data), presumes that customers may be treated unequally, and denies the customer a degree of control. *B-lens:* Demand pricing appears unFAIR as it exploits hidden information (the demand level); it also causes existential DREAD over lack of agency, as the customer feels they have no control over the price. (As identified in a 'misbehaviour' science study: when iTunes raised the price of downloads of Whitney Houston's music, following the singer's death, consumers were 'outraged' at this 'unfair' exploitation'[17].)

International 'safe harbour' agreements: May not withstand changes in data security standards between the jurisdictions at either end of them. *Qs raised:* Providers are concerned that where the United Kingdom and/or another jurisdiction changes its standards for data security, the conduct regulator might hold that there has been negligence in exposing customers to unreliable systems. *B-lens:* Providers have a primary DREAD of a cyber security breach, of course; but they also DREAD uncertainty around a regulator's change of mind regarding what is a FAIR exposure to a risk; again, 'moving the goalposts' is seen as an unFAIR imposition (compliance LOAD) on the provider.

Conclusion: Personal and organizational conduct

Conduct regulators are increasingly interested in exposing providers whose (often legacy) business strategies make life unduly difficult for consumers, or which compromise market integrity, or frustrate competition[18]. For providers, the key lies in striking the balance between 'big picture' and individual employee experience.

Those big-picture concerns include the wider economic and social factors you would expect, such as: the state of inflation and interest rates; regulatory change, in particular pressures for greater transparency; and the impact of changing technology on firms' resilience and self-knowledge, and consumers' habits. Some of these factors have a close bearing on how the regulator defines detriment, as when increasing technology and transparency raise customers' expectations and open the way for disruptive new 'challenger' providers. Technology is an especially multi-headed risk, with new opportunities often coming hand-in-hand with new threat vectors, as when sharp rises in connectivity, and the Internet of Things, increase exposure to cybercrime.

At the level of organizational good conduct, as a minimum the regulator expects firms to keep a clear forward view and show they can respond to change, as new combinations of risks emerge: such as the potential 'perfect storm' compound risks posed by an ageing population with unsustainable mortgages (as we saw with Emma in Table 9.2), or pensions being newly encashable just as markets turn highly volatile (as happened in midsummer 2016).

While managing the firm's overall conduct in this wider environment – which the behavioural lens can help with, as we have seen in the 'grey area' examples – boards also need to stay focused on individual employees' behaviour. The key here is to introduce all staff to a behaviourally aware approach, using tools such as the behavioural lens to alert each individual to make greater use of their own, generally reliable intuitions about 'doing the right thing'. Any business and operational risk has the potential to become a conduct risk, if systems thinking is carelessly applied (as we revealed with a behavioural rethink of Foxy's treatment of Bill, in Table 9.3). The root cause of a conduct risk, as in Bill's case, may be a business-driven decision, but it is the impact on the customer, and how the firm reacts to this, that bring it to the conduct enforcer's attention.

As another brief example, cyber risk may at first seem like a pure operational risk concern. But consider, then, the detrimental effect of a mass failure of a bank ATM network following a hacker intrusion. Several banks have experienced this, and subsequently been caught off guard when the conduct regulator's first concern has been to protect customers, who were unable to access their own deposited cash; banks whose ATMs failed were then fined. Think of this as a changing point of view – and use the behavioural lens to anticipate it.

In a well-behaved organization...

- Everyone cares about customers' interests and market integrity.
- Senior managers are highly capable, with clearly defined roles and accountability.
- Business is sustainable – in every way.
- Profits are 'quality profits', not just 'profit at any cost'.
- Customers are regularly asked what they think, and evince high levels of trust.

The key is to involve individual employees, using their own local understanding and experience to support the firm's management of larger, corporate-level risks, as well as it informing their day-to-day interactions with customers and each other. A risk-aware culture promotes a sense of security and trust, encouraging individual employees to feel comfortable calling out a risk issue as they see it arise, while still in step with the firm's operational risk framework.

Well-behaved employees...

- help each other (and managers) to understand complex topics and technologies;
- are alert to when 'something's not quite right', giving earlier warnings to spot and prevent fraud and cyber threats;
- think about how to prevent things going wrong, rather than just fixing things afterwards;
- consider how each decision supports customers' interests;
- understand that good conduct sustains good-quality commercial business;
- appreciate that their instincts and judgement are valued;
- respond positively to rewards for good customer outcomes.

In the final chapter, besides a round-up of key ideas from throughout the book, we will look at creating a risk-aware culture using behavioural insight gained in the past two chapters; and look ahead to see how the technique can help to address the changing priorities of conduct regulators around the world.

Appendix

Designated Senior Management Functions under SMR (FCA/PRA approved)

SMF number: role

1 Chief Executive

2 Chief Finance Officer

3 Executive Director

4 Chief Risk Officer

5 Head of Internal Audit

6 Head of Key Business Area

7 Group Entity Senior Manager

8 Credit Union Senior Manager

9 Chair

10 Chair of Risk Committee

11 Chair of Audit Committee

12 Chair of Remuneration Committee

13 Chair of Nominations Committee

14 Senior Independent Director

16 Compliance Oversight

17 Money Laundering Reporting

18 Other Overall Responsibility

19 Head of Overseas Branch

21 EEA Branch Senior Manager

22 Other Local Responsibility

PRA-designated roles: 1, 2, 4–12, 14, 19
FCA-designated roles: 3, 13, 16–19, 21, 22 (Numbers 15, 20 not listed)

Notes

1 Ariely, D (2008) The cycle of distrust, in *Predictably Irrational,* Harper Collins

2 Cialdini, R B (2014) Reciprocation, in *Influence: Science and Practice,* Pearson

3 Ariely, as above

4 Ariely, as above

5 Leidner, R (1993) *Fast Food, Fast Talk: Service work and the routinization of everyday life*, University of California, Berkeley Press

6 With acknowledgement to *Little Britain*, BBC

7 UK data from Nationwide, at economicshelp.org/blog/5709/housing/

8 Miles, R and Moroney, T (2016) *Mortgage Customers: How to square a vicious circle*, Berkeley Research Group, at thinkbrg.com/media/publication/

9 Financial Conduct Authority at www.fca.org.uk/: see *Strengthening accountability in banking*, CP14/13; and *Strengthening accountability in banking and insurance*, PS16/5

10 Financial Conduct Authority briefing pack (2016) *Strengthening Accountability in Banking*, accessed at www.fca.org.uk

11 Miles, R and Jones, T (2016) *Getting Conduct Risk Right First Time*, British Bankers' Association at www.bba.org.uk

12 McCormick, R and Stears, C at conductcosts.ccpresearchfoundation.com/conduct-costs-results

13 FCA 2016 briefing pack, as above, at www.fca.org.uk

14 Lewis, M (2011) Wall Street on the Tundra, in *Boomerang*, Allen Lane; and (2012) *The Big Short: Inside the Doomsday Machine*, Penguin

15 Lanchester, J (2010) *Whoops!: Why everyone owes everyone and no one can pay*, Penguin

16 Cambridge University, Judge Business School/Conduct Risk Insights team, work in progress

17 Thaler, R (2015) *Misbehaving: The making of behavioural economics*, Allen Lane

18 Financial Conduct Authority (2015) *Risk Outlook 2015/16*, at www.fca.org.uk

Looking back, looking ahead

10

Introduction

Over the course of nine chapters, several themes have contributed to building a new picture of how to create business value through an unconventional, behaviour-led approach to managing regulatory risk. This final chapter will recap key learning points; offer a forward view of conduct regulators' upcoming points of concern; and look to the future with the greater understanding now gained.

The first section of the book, assuming little knowledge as a starting point, traced the origins of financial conduct regulation, from its roots in behavioural science through the political pressure following the banking crisis of 2007–08. The early success of the political project of conduct control quickly took the new regime to a different place on the landscape of public governance. More recently this has led to the export of a conduct regulatory template to many other jurisdictions around the world.

The middle section of the book probed the dilemmas that regulators must resolve as they approach the task of controlling risk-taking and 'bad behaviour', not least the readiness of regulatees to subvert a regulator's attempts at new forms of control. It considered some structural challenges that are unique to regulators in the financial sector. Highlighting a series of inherent weaknesses that regulatory agencies must overcome, we looked at why financial firms are especially resistant to regulation (their economic strength, longevity, and so on), and challenged some of the earlier regulators' failed assumptions, which had made a fresh approach necessary.

Also shared were some original research findings on the origin of misconduct in organizations generally, such as the tendency of informal groups to ignore and subvert the management structures that firms have formally labelled (such as formal lines of reporting responsibility). The new generation of financial conduct regulators seems to have scored some early successes in overcoming these challenges to their legitimacy and traction over wayward providers. Enforcers may now be looking to the future with greater confidence, although we should expect that reform, both of controls and the ingrained bad attitudes they address, will continue to be a long-term project. The focus on both providers' own behaviour, and the customer experience on the receiving end of it, is emerging as an appropriate and fruitful strategy for the new enforcers.

That said, it is also right to question sceptically whether the oncoming wave of criminal enforcements is consistent with the original good intent of the behavioural scientists whose work informed it. An alternative reading is that the worldwide rush into conduct regulation is just a political expedient, as a 'fig-leaf' that allows insecure governments to mount populist prosecutions against token senior managers in an already distrusted sector.

The global expansion of conduct regulation at least brings one clear benefit to regulatees: we can now discern points of commonality, in the intent and application of rules, among the various regulators. These allow us to begin to assemble patterns that inform a global taxonomy of 'conduct enforcement risk'. Over time, this will allow for ever more accurate prediction of where the next enforcements will strike, by territory and by product type. This insight will in future be hugely helpful, in the short term to relieve strain on resource-stretched risk managers and their boards. In the longer term, it will significantly shape how boards allocate future spending on compliance and training programmes.

In the final third of the book, we approached the vexed question, which regulators (fairly enough) refuse to prescribe: 'What does 'good conduct' look like?' By reviewing a range of directly researched[1] bad behaviour, the so-called 'games of compliance', and contrasting these with activities that regulators have privately admitted they would wish to see more of, the reader has been able to see the regulators' approach to setting their agenda. This identifies good practices and behaviour patterns that regulators will like and support. Knowing these factors, firms are equipped to be more resilient and future-proof against later extensions of conduct regulation and the new wave of inter-agency alliances between regulators.

To this, the next chapters then added a tool that specifically gets the job started: the behavioural lens. This allows organizations that may have been put off by prescriptive, mechanistic and uninvolving earlier plans for conduct 'frameworks' to enliven these with an approach that involves all staff in recognizing their own everyday contribution to 'working risk-aware'. After explaining the behavioural lens tool with simple and topical examples, it was shown predicting and preventing conduct risk exposure by applying it to grey areas where no clear practice of good conduct has yet been established to the regulator's satisfaction.

By looking at conduct in a purely behavioural (not legalistic) way, we have seen how its fresh, direct and unconventional view offers firms a new way to identify and overcome misconduct in many forms. Beyond the directly identified current dilemmas of conduct, it is then possible and helpful to apply the lens to a wider range of risk governance concerns. Taking the 'three viewpoints' approach, in particular, helps to identify the distinct concerns of customers, regulators and boards, while also keeping an eye on the point of view of the behavioural researcher, which itself continues to inform the regulator's future agenda. The section also showed how applying all of these techniques, together with an informed awareness of the impact of trust-building, will surely help to build and protect value in your enterprise. By focusing the behavioural lens on a range of current conduct risk challenges, it was possible to align responses with the latest personal accountability requirements on directors, under the Senior Managers Regime.

Equipped with the behavioural lens, you are also now better placed to foresee regulators' future preoccupations and avoid the expense of finding yourself unexpectedly in a prosecution 'hotspot'. Having this greater confidence in turn enables anyone whose business involves making risk-based decisions to reduce strain on capital (and shareholders' patience), to serve customers' interests without detriment, and to anticipate in a more risk-aware way future market needs and expectations.

Chapter 10 will now look at additional sources to use to inform your self-knowledge of good conduct; offer summary 'best practice' guidance; compare pre-FCA and current attitudes to regulation, highlighting the change during the time since conduct rules were introduced; suggest questions that newly behaviour-aware boards should be asking themselves; note a couple of imminent sources of disruption, knowledge of which will help your resilience; and consider what the future holds for the control of conduct, between regulators and regulated.

Future-facing (1): Other new approaches to being 'conduct compliant'

While the behavioural lens is perhaps the most powerful tool for change, there are of course several other worthy initiatives in this field, some of which I have also been directly involved with. Four of the best are briefly summarized here.

The global conduct taxonomy, described above and in preceding chapters, itself rests on the unglamorous but vital activity of tracking of conduct enforcements around the world. Various organizations that employ political and legal analysts (unsurprisingly, data handlers, research groups, consultancies and law firms) now keep databases that record wherever a conduct enforcement has occurred. It is important to note, however, that logging the simple fact of a completed prosecution, even including details such as the offence and fine paid, is not sufficient to build up a global taxonomy picture; this requires a level of insight into jurisprudence, regulatory design and behavioural psychology that the raw data alone will not give. Having had some involvement with these projects, I am happy to confirm objectively that the best of them deserve the premium that they ask their clients for. There is a world of difference between simply looking at a mass of data and understanding what it means, as the best analysts do; they are worth seeking out, as opposed to the less thoughtful species of number-cruncher. There are sadly too many of the latter and not enough of the former. If you want to sort the good from the poor, I suggest asking them to explain their taxonomy and methods for triangulating (validating) their findings. Any who either don't understand those questions, or are unable or unwilling to do you the simple courtesy of explaining it in language you will understand, avoid. Any who are passionate but also able to articulate their intelligent interest at any level that satisfies you, hire. You won't find a shortage of pitches for this service, at any rate.

As we have seen by using the behavioural lens, there are also analysts who can help you to shape a newly informed view of what constitutes 'acceptable', 'unacceptable' and 'expected' behaviour, as seen by your customers (or the public, or the regulator, politicians, etc; and your position relative to your industry peer group). These range from conventional market research firms, through specialist quasi-academic and academic-attached research groups, to news media analysts, social media and network analysts, and various other sub-specializations. Again, if any of these is pitching to you, be wary of snake-oil salespeople. There are many excellent research specialists; there are also many stinkers. As a general rule, mistrust any researcher whom you feel intuitively is telling you what you want to hear. There is little point in paying for a research view that sheds no fresh light on your organization's self-knowledge. (Some game-playing research firms will, of course, make a contrarian point of saying something to shock you. Again, trust your intuition.) Also, question their methodology. Along with some distinguished colleagues[2], I am cynical about the use of bald statistics, as in a '22 per cent net customer approval rating'. Reductive figures of this kind are similar to the binary models of compliance that we saw discredited earlier in the book; they offer no scalar detail. In the case of the 22 per cent net approval rating, for example, this may be disguising the fact that 39 per cent of your customers loathe you – the maths is simple. A more nuanced, scalar reading of the same information might take the trouble to identify *why* and *on what issues* you had a problem with the sizeable minority. Don't engage any researcher who is not interested in getting at the root causes of a behavioural problem that your customers present. Oh, and don't hire a researcher who tells you that all your customers love you – that can no more be 100 per cent true than your own claims to be '100 per cent ethical' or '100 per cent compliant' (see box).

Why saying you're '100 per cent compliant' is untrue, unhelpful and misaligned

In saying you can never be 100 per cent compliant, my point is not to accuse you of being unethical or game-playing, but rather that it is *impossible* to be either fully 100 per cent compliant, or even certain that you are compliant. Four good reasons why: staff come; staff leave; new products are trialled; regulations change. As each of these occurs, there is a period of transition when those people or products concerned are not fully up to speed with current training or rules. That's perfectly normal.

But, think about that: for all these reasons and more, your compliance is always quite legitimately a work in progress. So let's stop pretending to ourselves, and to regulators, that full compliance is a daily reality.

Conduct regulators say privately – and the industry should be willing to test this – that firms who are truthful and transparent on this point are better aligned with the 'conduct project' (that is, behavioural thinking) and consequently will earn greater respect with the regulator than those who bluff. The positive way to present this is to talk about how your firm is progressing along a path of learning and embedding conduct risk. Some people are beginning to call this your *conduct risk maturity*, which is a good name for it.

Most of the advice above on behavioural research agencies also applies to suppliers of customer experience surveys. These are an excellent technique – I especially recommend 'mystery shopping' surveys where a pretend-customer tries out the sales experience and reports back to you on their perceptions of staff conduct. There are, though, two much simpler and often overlooked techniques you can use yourself with little or no outside help or cost. First, try going 'back to the shop floor': that is, along with your fellow directors, go and take a personal, unannounced and as far as possible anonymous sample of a service your firm provides. In a big firm, where front-line staff don't tend to recognize directors, this tends to be easier than you might imagine. In any size of firm, another simple technique is for directors to listen directly to customer complaints; this can be done either by sitting in the call centre, or by sitting in the office where front-line service managers deal with things – you can disguise your presence by saying that you're there as an auditor (which is true, if you think about it). Listening directly to customers, and indeed to junior staff as they deal with customers, can provide a sudden dose of reality that no amount of statistical reports in board meetings can equal. Farming out this task to an external research agency may give you a greater level of penetration than the directors can achieve as a relatively small group, but you will lose much of the immediacy. And again consider: getting directors personally involved in this shows a strong commitment to 'customer-centric' thinking, which the regulator will love you for doing.

Finally, there are rapidly developing new techniques for aggregating and meta-analysing firms' internal management information and transaction data. These make for some striking behavioural inferences about the nature of risk communications – and risk culture – in a firm. Some risk managers find this a little too Orwellian, as this is all about assembling patterns of behaviour out of sets of real-world observations that the staff may be unaware of. In many banks, though, it is already standard security and compliance practice to meta-analyse telephone and e-mail traffic, for example, and increasingly social media traffic too, for the perfectly legitimate purpose of crime detection and prevention. 'Meta-analysis' means not just simple analysis of content (as in, what subject was discussed in a certain phone call or e-mail), but the analysis of how a given individual item (call or e-mail) fits into a wider pattern of behaviour – as in: Does this sales-person spend a lot of time in contact with people who are neither clients nor prospects? Or in giving preferential treatment to some for no apparent reason? and so on.

On the same point, if you are a corporate risk manager, do give serious thought to co-opting your colleagues in human resources, who should in any case be able to bring some behavioural expertise, to look at this with you. One quick example[3]: A team head of trading in a bank, widely respected for their team's sales figures, was found to have achieved those figures by means of aggressive hiring-and-firing, which ultimately could only be described as abusive. But here's the tricky bit: this individual had co-opted the HR department into the 'game', coercing HR colleagues into disguising the personnel records of people who had been summarily fired, and issuing legal restraints ('gagging orders') against the dismissed employees. Eventually this individual's comet-trail of abuse came to light when a group of ex-employees compared experiences, realized for themselves the pattern of bad behaviour that had happened, and successfully took their collective case to the authorities. That is one of the points of conduct risk: misconduct takes many forms, and ultimately the customer's suffering (by being force-sold a product) may also be reflected in destructive patterns of behaviour within the firm. Good behaviour, and bad, ripple out in many directions, but the customer experience is undoubtedly a good place to start.

'Hot topics': Using the lens to inform a wider corporate view

When you apply the lens to a specific set of conduct topics, as we have seen in Chapters 8 and 9, it produces focused results that you can feed directly into your programmes of conduct risk development. But applying it more widely also pays dividends for general resilience, improved risk governance, and even sales, as its many current users have found.

Where the behavioural lens came from

Although the behavioural lens is a great tool for analysing your sensitivity to conduct risk issues, and reviewing the related state of your customer care, I first conceived and developed it over many years' applied research as an easy way for complex organizations to improve their general capacity for risk-sensing.

After developing the lens initially for a military academy's postgraduate 'risk-sensing' workshops, I tested it as a tool for analysing the 'what actually happens' gap in other sectors, including higher education, international law firms, sector advocacy groups (trade associations) and professional services marketing. It worked well, right across this range of corporate applications, so I brought the modified version that you see in this book to some financial services firms who were receptive to it, and it has proved very popular indeed with them as a ready way to start 'risk-aware working'. That phrase, risk-aware working, I coined to describe and embrace several aspects of board perception of and engagement with risk. These include the related ideas of 'dynamic sensing'[4], cognitive capacity, applied intuition, 'friends and family' tests of social appropriateness, delusion (Dunning-Kruger) testing, and situational awareness generally.

I have also found that describing the lens as a way to 'see beyond the risk register' strikes a universal chord with risk managers. Many of these have learned, too often the hard way, to be wary of the blind spots that risk registers create around social licence concerns.

The lens incorporates at a deeper level layers of insight from leading researchers in behavioural, cognitive and political science, some of whose work is cited in the reading list at the end of this book – though only a fraction of it. For a more thorough technical account, or if you have trouble sleeping, you are welcome to dive into my professional and academic research[5].

While there is now a steadily growing list of financial firms using the lens in bespoke versions that I have designed for them, the generic version in this book is useable in its own right. The generic tool also functions at corporate affairs level, as a 'hot topic' discussion generator. This broader function, producing clearer insights into strategic uncertainty and identifying undetected threats to 'social licence', is now described. Where the lens has been introduced to many organizations for this purpose, including commercial firms, the public sector and NGOs, they are still happily using it.

Any board directors wishing to improve their broader risk governance – not simply conduct risk management – are very welcome to train the behavioural lens on a wider horizon of strategic concerns. One of the pleasures of the behavioural approach is how widely it can be applied, and the lens tool makes this easy, painless and even pleasant (although it often also has a habit of highlighting a few uncomfortable truths). Some further uses of the lens are summarized here.

The lens can provide early warning of a rising tide of public hostility, as where there is increasing anger among a group of people who feel powerless to prevent a hazard encroaching on their lives, and hence are feeling disenfranchised by those responsible for their risk governance. This is the kind of oversight that may cost boards of directors their seats, and ultimately control of the enterprise. In the wider world, it can abruptly cost political leaders their majority in elections; and may occasionally even lead a large group to self-exclude from regional involvement (as with 'Brexit').

It can suggest where there is a cognitive gap (where a 'reality check' is needed) anywhere that you may have blindly imposed controls that are not effective. Knowing this, offers you a chance to re-engage with those concerned. For example, you might use this knowledge to improve risk governance and relations with investors and local communities who might otherwise resent you imposing your plans without asking.

It can provide more realistic, grounded reporting of progress when you are assessing compliance risk and operational risk. This will support you when you want to take steps to make your risk management more proactive.

For conduct regulators, who themselves now like to work 'risk-aware' using the same principles, the lens helps to discern points where uncooperative regulatees will resist attempts at control. Just like corporate organizations, regulators may also use the lens to scan for oncoming threats that may disrupt their own legitimacy.

It can also help firms to connect regulatory and compliance concerns with other risk disciplines, and their associated risk management frameworks.

For boards of all kinds who may be subject to sudden and disruptive intervention by regulators, the lens helps to identify and predict changes in external pressure, both through direct regulatory change and through the changes in public opinion which, via the politicians, inform the regulator's own agendas. Day to day, down among the unglamorous details of compliance and risk management, it also makes risk and compliance functions more proactive and visible. On this last point, above all, it helps risk specialists to demonstrate their value to the firm, protecting licences, capital, and the right of the board to keep on determining the strategic direction of the business.

Finally, when considering 'hot topics', it is worth always keeping in mind, as we have seen, that regulators themselves acquire knowledge and intelligence from a wide range of sources. Informing how you apply the lens, you might want to include in your sources of insight consumer groups (including your own customer complaints handlers) and ombudsmen, and researchers compiling benchmark and comparison studies of acceptable behaviour.

Future disruptions

Up to this point we have used the lens to focus largely on *internal*, self-made conduct risks to the firm – the risk that your own staff's careless behaviour may lead to the organization 'shooting itself in the foot', in that delightful old English phrase. There are also, of course, many *external* sources of disruption; the way that your organization responds to these is also a measure of its conduct risk-awareness, and the regulator will look for customer-centric values here too. It may be a little consoling to note that many of these external factors are as threatening to the stability of conduct regulators as they are to providers. A few of the 'rising tide' risk issues are noted here.

We may as well start these with the threats to the stability of regulation itself. A number of regulated financial service activities present various forms of slow-burning threat that may turn critical without regulatory intervention (which may not be forthcoming until it is too late). These systemic time-bombs for the regulator include the group of products known as 'equity release', besides generic problems with encashment of pensions; overlong mortgage dependency, as we saw with Emma in Chapter 9; and the proliferation of unregulated 'grey markets' that attract customers without offering protection. Any one of these hazards might, in time, reach a tipping-point in public confidence where the regulator is seen to have lost control, and hence public legitimacy.

Then there is the changing demographic shape of the financial services market, as this interacts with new technologies. In plain terms, as time passes, young millennials will begin to outnumber older customers until at some future point the millennials, who by and large are used to communicating only digitally via smartphones, will start to question the value of (for example) an antique, branch-based banking system. Why, they will ask, do financial providers keep on providing expensive analogue-world artefacts such as branches, plastic cards and messages printed on paper, when it's so easy to do everything virtually? They will then migrate en masse to whatever next-generation financial providers are around, if they haven't already done so. (As the lens sees this, a critical-mass shift in Social Licence.)

Hand in hand with new technologies comes the dark-side risk from those same developments, in the form of cyber threats. On recent evidence, showing an increasing range of cyber criminal actors and threat types, we may assume that cyber hazards and their consequential costs will continue to grow inexorably. We may expect some of the resulting incidents will trigger crises of public trust as big brands falter. (On the behavioural lens point about asymmetry of resources, I would just note a lawyer colleague's remark that financial criminals have 'unlimited commitment to self-education'.)

On the wider point of applying behaviour science to reveal where organizational crises might occur, in the past few years humanity has become very much better at identifying the human ingredients of being 'predictably irrational' – with the emphasis on prediction. With behavioural research, as with research seeking to model any kind of phenomenon, early findings get to a fair approximation of 'what actually happens'; later, if research goes well, the clarity of the analysis builds up, layer by layer, until there is a model that has not just *descriptive* but *predictive* power. That said, the history of science of all kinds (notably economics) shows models being created that are then proved invalid when real-world events upset them.

Before and after the 'conduct project'

Talking of the real-world effect of risk interventions, this is a good point at which to look back to see how far the climate surrounding conduct regulation has changed in the years since it was introduced. Some of these perspectives may surprise you, as we live in the brave new world of customer-centric compliance.

Back in the heady days before the crash of 2008, I was in the midst of a study of bank CROs and the rule-breaking staff that they had encountered. At that point, although there was clearly a fracture between claimed ethics and practice, few practitioners anticipated what would happen within a year of making these comments (the global market meltdown following a liquidity crisis and the widespread overtrading of credit derivatives based on oversold mortgages).

The comments of 'old school' practitioners stand in stark contrast to the comments of similar practitioner groups nearly a decade on, in the summer of 2016. This subsection offers the 'before and after' comments from my research interviews, with little analysis needed as the attitudes speak for themselves. Because the first concern of behavioural research is 'what actually happens', these comments offer an unmediated insight into some drivers of the original conduct problem, and into the new view of good conduct that has begun to emerge since the crisis.

Example attitudes 'before'[6]

- 'Many risk officers thought their job was to find a way around regulation as opposed to implementing.'

- 'After a while people just get conditioned; it's like ignoring the fire alarm when it goes off. So you think: "Everyone else is doing this so it must be all right. This is obviously normal behaviour… everyone else is in this product, so we've got to be. And anyway I'll miss out on my bonus if I don't."'

- 'Principle-based regulation is all very well, but there are parts of the market which aren't very principled.'

- 'Banks' biggest problem has been our belief in risk assessment systems … this comforting myth that you can just stick a "risk probe" into any project, like checking a turkey in the oven.'

- 'The way that we work is that the real profit is made out of instruments that are brand new, before they become commoditized. So by definition they are developed before other people, including regulators, can understand them.'

- 'There's a fundamental failure to recognize that a 700-page compliance report is absolutely useless to anybody… (it) encourages people to hide behind words… it hasn't created greater transparency.'

Example attitudes 'after'[7]

- 'Despite the UK regulator cancelling its much-heralded investigation into banks' risk culture, in 2016, the back story at any regulatory briefing remains that we are working to fix the culture.'

- 'Risk governance, risk culture and incentives are inextricable – indeed, interchangeable – factors in indicating and determining conduct.'

- 'Through new lenses, we need to reassess attitudes towards sanctions and compliance.'

- 'Bank chief risk officers' (CROs') number one anxiety now is misconduct, including financial crime, as an existential threat to their business.'

- 'Failure of learning from past mistakes, or even to maintain "institutional memory" at all as people come and go, continues to be a big problem for financial organizations.'

- 'The new behavioural regulators (since 2012) focus on individual behaviour; that is, people's personal agency for ethical norms, standards and values; and how corporate risk governance can improve the "legitimacy" of the financial services industry. We now talk about "risk culture" and mean by this a system of values and behavioural norms.'

- 'The purpose of regulators intervening in banks is clear: to find effective ways to prevent misconduct. Regulators see now something that wasn't so clear to them before, that banks' misbehaviour can have a systemic impact – it harms not just the commercial prospects for the bank concerned, but the reputation of the whole jurisdiction where the bank operates.'

- 'The old rules were mainly concerned to protect capital adequacy. Since 2016, the leading "meta-regulator" [the Basel Committee on Banking Supervision] has identified misconduct as a form of systemic risk, to be controlled as a key point of resilience.'

Questions for board members

A technique that many boards find useful when adapting to change is to ask each other the 'questions that we'd least like to hear'. Conduct risk presents plenty of these; a sample selection is included here to help get you started. The behavioural lens will readily generate many more.

- Do you personally know what's meant by, and can distinguish between: behavioural risk and conduct risk; bias and behaviour; risk and uncertainty?

- Are you clear as to your personal, and our collective, responsibilities under conduct risk and the latest Senior Managers regulations? Have you clearly defined ('apportioned') the responsibilities that are exclusively yours? When you attested to these, how confident were you of the claims to competence and skill that you were making?

- Which of us on the board has direct overall authority for responding to customer complaints? How have we recently exercised that control, to keep customers happy? How does the firm use rewards and restraints to promote good customer experiences?

- What actions have any of us taken to shut down persistent 'rule-gamers' on our staff?

- How do we, as a board, maintain up-to-date definitions of 'acceptable and expected' behaviour in the organization? How are our personal expectations of staff behaviour and attitudes changing? What methods do we use to track changes in other people's expectations of us?

- What forms of regular analysis do we commission to validate objectively our claims to good conduct? (customer feedback, trends in enforcement, peer-provider comparison, benchmarking, other?)

- In what practical ways does our firm put customers at the heart of its business?

The value of the behavioural approach

'What's the financial value of all this?' boards are justified in asking. There are at least three forms of saving.

First, making your firm a less conspicuous object attracting the regulator's attention through old patterns of careless misconduct and ignorance of how to define appropriate behaviour.

Second, predisposing the regulator to trust and engage positively with you because you don't simply comply, but have shown you can take the initiative – including by reading this book – to find out more about what the regulators' interests are, that inform their behavioural agenda.

Third, you will be starting to use these new insights to modify and reset your budget priorities for resourcing compliance, staff learning and customer experience research.

Getting that resource balance right is key for a number of reasons, some less obvious than others. Straightforward compliance with the rules will help everyone to avoid the, often, large costs of fines and of fixing the dysfunctional parts of the business after a prosecution. Doing your part to support market stability helps to minimize strain on your regulatory capital (and indeed working capital) and on shareholders' patience. Good conduct is simply good for business (in terms of stronger cashflow and market goodwill); by 'paying it forward' when you keep customers well served you will avoid causing them detriment, which would annoy the regulator, but more importantly for building goodwill, you are anticipating future needs and expectations.

By knowing what good conduct consists of – as defined by your customers' concerns, rather than some regulator's prescription – you will also secure the far broader goodwill needed to protect your social licence. If everyone who deals with your organization finds that you are, in practice, well behaved, responsive and humane where there are any concerns, and attuned to the regulator's outlook, you should have nothing to fear from conduct risk. How confident can you be that this is the case?

If your aim is to be able to budget more precisely for costs of compliance, that's a perfectly reasonable aim, but it needs to be informed by a thorough awareness of your behavioural risk exposure, including other people's rating of your conduct. As you think about those compliance costs, do also weigh them against the three types of cost of *non*-compliance – of which many people only ever consider the first two. It's worth explicitly running through these with your board, to focus everyone's attention. Misconduct incurs cost in various forms, as any alert board will appreciate; any non-compliance will return to haunt you as one or more of three kinds of enterprise costs, as follows.

The first cost, as everyone knows, is to cashflow. If cashflow is already tight, and sales have fallen because your brand is in trouble, it can be hard to find ready money to cover the sudden extra costs of fines to be paid, recovery plans after a scandal, and the effects of staff displacement during a clear-up period.

The second form of cost impact of non-compliance is the effect on an organization's capital. Recent fines against non-compliant banks took out a large chunk of their freshly raised capital, undermining banks' claims that they were in a fit financial state to restart lending to small businesses. Damage to capital takes other forms too: falling share price; increased cost of corporate borrowing, following a rating agency downgrade; potential loss of market access and goodwill, as established counterparties withdraw; and the impact on human capital, meaning that when your reputation is poor, you will find it harder to hire and keep good people.

Which raises the third, and least recognized, type of cost. While worrying about falling cashflow and share price, boards may be overlooking the biggest cost of all, the cost of losing control of the business. This may arise in the form of a regulator withdrawing a licence to trade, or, harder to foresee (without a behavioural lens), the gradual loss of social licence as stakeholders of all kinds back away from you. In the end, there is a direct cost to board strategy, as commercial and compliance failure exacts the ultimate price, and the firm falls victim to a hostile takeover.

In case these interpretations of cost feel a little esoteric for ordinary staff, there is another way to consider the issue. You should make employees consciously and constantly aware that it is better business, meaning better cost control in the long run, to behave well than to be non-compliant. Any perceived short-term 'benefits' of cutting corners and bending rules will always in the end be outweighed, in the conduct regime, by the now far larger costs of punitive fines and remediation – even before taking into account the catastrophic effect on goodwill.

The alternative to these costs, so much preferable, is to promote good conduct by each employee taking a measure of personal involvement in it. Encourage everyone to welcome, and pay regular attention to, wider sources of 'conduct awareness', such as dialogue with customers and consumer watchdogs, and practising regular 'friends and family'-level explanations between staff at all levels.

At board level, as we have seen, there is plenty of scope for more sophisticated and thought-provoking questions about what 'good behaviour' will need to consist of in future. If you are not already doing this, check what planned new rules the regulators have in the pipeline – any half-decent corporate law firm should be able to help with this. Plug in the results of those 'taxonomies of enforcement' that we looked at above, to help inform your training and compliance budget for the coming year. By all means talk to a specialist behavioural risk analyst about, for example: the causal roots of recent prosecutions against practitioners in your field; 'near-miss' events that you may have experienced directly; and your highest-exposure products, activities and jurisdictions, according to the analyst's 'heat map' of topical behavioural exposures.

In case all of this sounds too defensive, as we approach the end of the book let's keep in mind a more positive aim that the conduct regulators themselves have – even if they don't mention this much in public. If you ask them, many of the new regulators will admit that they would rather spend more time congratulating practitioners for good behaviour, than pursuing enforcement actions for misconduct. With that uplifting intention in mind, let's look at some sure ways to put a smile on the regulator's face.

Seven steps to conduct risk happiness

... or at least, preparedness

With many firms' conduct risk management frameworks already some years into operation, the following recommendations are less about the mechanics of setting up a control framework and more about the prevailing attitudes that will see your conduct compliance efforts rewarded by the regulator leaving you alone – and possibly even congratulating you on taking the initiative.

First and least glamorously, just press on with the business of observing and reporting on practical compliance. Under SMR, board and senior managers have to have hands-on control, with their responsibilities clearly set out and divided up ('apportioned'). When they certify that they are competent, fit and proper, it is probably a good idea to get at least one objective second opinion on this.

Next, as we have seen somewhat relentlessly in getting to know the behavioural lens, get an independent and rolling-update view of what kinds of behaviour customers accept and expect from you. A 'big data' analysis may contribute to this, but most importantly form your own view of it by observing those 'normal people' the behavioural economists talked about in the middle section of this book. Don't settle for mediated reporting; find out as directly as you can. Try doing it yourself, even.

Also keep yourself informed about the regulator's view. What books and studies are the regulators currently reading, do you know? Find out (again, a tame behavioural researcher may be useful here), get your own copies and read them. As you may by now have worked out, conduct regulators have a big appetite for reading stuff about behavioural risk (including bias effects and rule-gaming); fresh research on customer-end experiences (including in the form of ombudsman data and consumer attitudes research); and any news from fellow regulators about the global spread of the conduct regulation project (such as other regulators' manifestos, research and enforcement news).

The next point should hardly come as radical advice, yet many firms don't think much about it. When designing new products, think first and hardest about the real benefit to the *customer*, not just the profit margin for the provider. Consider the entire lifecycle of the product, including the declining years of a long-contract product such as a 20-year mortgage, or life assurance. Involve risk managers early on in the product design process – this is one of the strongest signs to the regulator that you take your customer-facing responsibilities seriously. Firms that don't do this tend to be worse behaved than those who do. The regulator knows this, and will use it as a ready reckoner to judge your attitude to conduct risk in general.

Again, when designing your packages of incentives, whether for salespeople, directors, or anybody else, think first about rewarding anyone who does right by *customers*. If everyone does this, profit should take care of itself as customers reward good service with loyalty and onward recommendations. It's the opposite of the old-style hit-and-run approach to selling.

When hiring staff, get the best quality people you can, and look after them. Don't simply hire worker drones; get thoughtful people and ask them for their views. At the sharp end of the business, where everyone is directly customer facing, people's intuitive sense of when there's a problem is generally better than yours is in the boardroom. Welcome that prompting, and listen to it.

Finally, inform your own forward view of where future behavioural risks might arise. Invest in new tools such as the behavioural lens, horizon scans and causal analyses of recent enforcement actions against misconduct. Most of all, keep your behavioural radar tuned. Which brings us, sadly, to a concluding look ahead.

Is the future behavioural – or something else?

A decade back, as the mortgage-driven financial crisis unfolded, the recently appointed first generation of chief risk officers found themselves caught in the crossfire of an unmanageable brief. With few exceptions, they couldn't exert the control they needed to have, to persuade often-reluctant boards to take seriously the threat of business collapse that followed from a long-standing casual attitude towards relations with regulators, and in many cases customers too. Fast forward to the present, and we have seen a sea change, with firms appointing senior risk governance specialists who are, as one distinguished commentator notes, 'some of the most intelligent, thoughtful and multi-disciplinary educated individuals we've ever seen in the financial system'[8]. The business of managing risk, and of reflecting on the role of conduct as a component of organizational risk, has made huge strides.

But we must not be complacent. Just as there is a new generation of more enlightened, polymathic risk managers, so too the rising generation of comparison-conscious millennials, who are not at all sentimental about historic brands, stands ready to explode a sector that is still notably 'sticky' in its attitudes to embracing changing technology and social outlooks. Within the next few years – making no predictions as to exactly when – the old, taken-for-granted business model of financial services will come to an abrupt end. This will be a reflection, not just on slowness to adapt in the face of changing patterns of social engagement with service providers, but also the pay-off from a long-standing unwillingness by providers to really get to know the needs, concerns and anxieties of customers. Those providers who are most behaviourally aware will not only survive the regulator's scrutiny, but also the threat of cynical deselection by a largely disillusioned public.

One might ask, as the financial service business model changes (all too slowly) in the face of new service media, to what extent providers' change of outlook has been informed by deeper understanding of behavioural factors, either as compelled by conduct regulation, or as a matter of intelligently applying foresight. My personal view is that conduct regulation has thus far simply coexisted with financial business, rather than informing a deep change in product provision; but this may be the bias effect of historical exposure (as a researcher) to a whole lot of practitioner abuses speaking. Let's not underestimate that.

To leave on an altogether more positive note: behavioural science continues, thrillingly, to provide ever more dimensions of insight. We have not just the technology for observing the real-time functioning of electrical surges in the brain and the shifting balance of neurotransmitter chemicals inside your head; we can now also apply taxonomies of the new behavioural risks to look forward and predict who is most likely to do what next, whether good things or bad. Best of all, if your role is to make sense of the seemingly irrational behaviour of board colleagues, we now understand how and why 'motivated reasoning' derails the cognitive processes of an otherwise articulate and intelligent group.

For now, hang onto your behavioural lens and use it well. We may be sure that there are exciting times ahead.

Notes

1 R Miles, 2014, Thomson Reuters

2 For example, Tony Cox (2008) What's wrong with risk matrices?, *Risk Analysis* **28** (2) and Brian Toft (1996) 'Limits to the mathematical modelling of disasters' in *Accident and Design: contemporary debates in risk management*, UCL/Routledge

3 Author's private research archive on 'rule-gamers'; research sponsored by King's College London, 2007–09

4 See Dekker, S on 'dynamic fault management' in *Understanding Human Error* (2006) Ashgate

5 See more than 200 sources cited in Miles, R (2012) *From Compliance to Coping,* King's College London

6 Extracts from R Miles, briefing on CRO attitudes research project, 2006–08 (King's College London), as debriefed to the Institute of Operational Risk, Glasgow Caledonian University, 28 October 2011

7 Extracts from R Miles, private CRO research groups (2012–16) for Thomson Reuters and Cambridge University, Judge Business School

8 Cambridge University, anonymized, senior risk analyst forum, summer 2016

GLOSSARY

abstraction Making a market in products that exist only in virtual, not physical form; or that simply can't be seen by casual onlookers, as with many financial contracts and services; for the provider, not having to rely on physical presence in order to trade.

acceptable and expected conduct / behaviour – *see* **norms**

action bias The way we often believe it's better to 'do something, anything' rather than do nothing. We act on a powerful (and often wrong) assumption that it must be better to take action – and be seen to take action – than to wait and see. This bias produces many misguided interventions, especially by politicians keen to impress an electorate.

affect Jargon word for 'emotion', in a decision context. Many people naturally use an affective ('feelings-driven') mode of decision-making. *Normal people*, as opposed to economists, are not much good at weighing up risks and benefits rationally; and they don't like having to wade through the details of hard decisions. At times when we absolutely *have* to make an immediate decision, we're much more likely to decide based on how we feel, at that moment, about the likely outcome.

affective shock A moment when your rational judgement is impaired because your feelings (anger, arousal, anxiety, etc) overwhelm it.

agency / power (loss of) The extent to which a person has control over a situation they find themselves in. Thus where there is 'limited agency', the person can't much effect any change in their circumstances.

amoral calculator Person who coldly weighs up the 'benefits' of misbehaving (such as cash dishonestly gained) against the 'risks' to their dishonest enterprise (such as getting caught and disbarred), ignoring the ethical dimension. An amoral calculator might, for example, consider the profit from mis-selling a product (P) against the possibility of being caught (C), and the cost of any fines if so (F). Using this sum, if P exceeds C × F, an amoral salesperson may continue to mis-sell their product. This is why it's important for a regulator to impose punitive fines and maintain high rates of detection.

anchoring / 'sticky bias' Unwillingness to change one's mind after an initial decision or review of the facts. Form of *priming* effect whereby initial exposure to a single fact serves as a reference point and influences subsequent judgements about value. If you're told that a pair of shoes was priced at £100 but is now in the sale at £50, you think you're getting a bargain – even though the shoes cost £5 to make.

apportioned responsibility Under the UK Senior Managers regulatory regime: the requirement for senior managers to divide up among themselves who is personally (and solely) responsible for the various functions of their business – and for this division of responsibilities to have 'no white spaces and no overlaps'. The regulator's aim, in theory, is to prevent, for example, a board of directors from blurring the issue of which one of them is ultimately responsible for control of each aspect of the business.

asymmetric incentives Where the rewards to the salesperson for selling (or mis-selling) a product are out of scale with the product's benefit to the customer, either in amount or in timescale, or otherwise don't reflect the nature of the contract sold. For example, a 20-year mortgage contract, sold by a salesperson who is rewarded in full and in cash during Year 1 of the contract, does not encourage the provider to think about the customer's long-term needs.

asymmetric information Where one party (typically the consumer) has less access to information about the product than the other (typically the seller). At the extreme, dishonest sellers may conceal product information from naïve buyers, in order to secure a (misconducted) sale. A dishonest used-car salesperson who puts sawdust in the gearbox of an old banger to conceal its rattling is wilfully creating asymmetry of information – the gearbox fault will not make itself known to the buyer until some time after the sale.

asymmetry Where two or more aspects of a transaction (knowledge, rewards, pricing) are badly out of balance. As when a customer's knowledge of a product is very much less than the salesperson's – *see* **asymmetric information**.

attestation The formal process of each senior manager assuring the regulator, in a signed personal statement, that they are competent to perform the job function they hold.

audit ritual / ritual compliance How, after a while, executives tend to 'go through the motions' of checking information, as a form of comfort-seeking, without pausing to question underlying assumptions[1].

Bayesian A form of maths calculation of probable risk, enabling analysts to factor in numerous, and newly arriving, items of evidence to infer the most likely outcome. First published by Rev Bayes in 1763[2], then largely ignored until the arrival in the 1990s of computers with enough heft to put its predictive power to good commercial use – marketing credit cards, for example.

behavioural / behaviour-based regulation / conduct regulation A set of new disciplinary rules and sanctions focused on *detriment* to customers. Devised by regulators borrowing concepts from cognitive and *behavioural science*, such as *biases* and *asymmetric* perception of risk.

behavioural economics How understandings from *behavioural science* help us to see and predict patterns in people's decision-making, especially when they're trading (buying, pricing, selling).

behavioural lens / view Easy-to-use tool to analyse the risk of people being unable or unwilling to engage with a given activity (such as joining in a new enterprise, changing their behaviour, or complying with regulations). Although the tool itself is simple to use, it incorporates multiple layers of expert behavioural insight.

behavioural risk / conduct risk The potential cost resulting from any things that your staff do (especially around customers) that cause *detriment* to customers, and/or undermine trust or value in your business. Conduct risk, as a subset of behavioural risk, is the potential cost resulting from any of your employees or suppliers committing any of the newly regulated conduct offences.

behavioural science At core the study of 'what actually happens' as humans interact and respond to events. It often focuses on observing real human behaviour and questioning why people's behaviour does not conform to rational expectations, as humans behave *irrationally* much of the time. Increasingly, as this research uncovers our biases and social influences, our irrational behaviour is found to have certain patterns – we're *predictably irrational*.

benchmarks Standard indicators agreed for use across a sector as set point 'norms', for example for the level of daily prices struck in a given marketplace. One of the most famous benchmarks, the London Interbank Offered Rate (LIBOR), indicates each day the average interest rate that leading banks will charge to lend money to each other; this affects the price of many other products down the line, such as how much interest you must pay for your home loan (mortgage).

bias effects What happens after various systematic (non-random) errors in our thinking start to upset any attempt to make a logical, well-informed decision. Some biases are self-serving (such as *optimism*, which helps keep us alive). Others flow from evolutionary kinks in the ways that our brains deal with incoming information (*see* **cognitive bias**).

binary v scalar (view of compliance) A binary question has only two possible answers, such as 'yes' or 'no'. This set-up forces a respondent to choose between two, perhaps over-simplified options. Real-life choice situations are more nuanced, evidently. So if asked: 'Are all your staff trained in the latest compliance standards, answer yes or no?', in most cases the truthful answer would be 'no', because at any given time some people won't have completed their training. Yet most respondents will answer (untruthfully) 'yes'. Compliance procedures relying on a series of such binary questions will produce a perverse consequence: the respondent quickly concludes that 1) since neither response option is 'true', both are meaningless, and so 2) that the compliance process itself doesn't matter. By contrast, scalar questions ('on a scale of 1 to 10, to what extent do you agree that…') work far better to capture people's real view of a situation.

biteback A form of unwanted consequence, often from new technology; finding that an innovation brings new forms of harm, alongside its expected benefits[3]. For example: the invention of motor transport also brought more intense forms of road accident; the 9-11 terrorists 'repurposed' civil airliners as flying bombs; social media have transformed human communications, and even helped to bring down corrupt regimes, yet also ushered in new forms of antisocial behaviour such as trolling, cyberstalking and 'twitter shaming'.

'black-letter law' Commercial lawyers' jargon for a situation that they prefer: where the rules governing acceptable behaviour are not ambiguous in any way. For example, when a certain type of contract is explicitly permitted, or forbidden. The opposite (arguably) is 'principle-based' rules or guidelines; these suggest broad types of activity that the regulator might prefer you to do (or not do), but stop short of allowing or forbidding any specific contract.

Black-Scholes An economic model (formula) for calculating the varying price over time of a marketed asset, based on observed behaviour in the market. Useful for pricing various forms of *derivative*, whose value may otherwise be set according to how the buyer or seller happens to feel about it at a given moment in time.

blame-shifting Organizing your reports of management information in such a way that anything going wrong is 'not your fault' but someone else's. Blame-shift manoeuvres are routinely seen in regulated markets, in public life, and in the criminal courts (where *denial* has its own branch of behavioural criminology[4]). We also see blame-shifts when sports are played: such as when a soccer defence player 'dives' to sabotage an opponent's legitimate attack. *See also* **constructed ignorance**.

bounded rationality A leading theory of human perception and decision-making, showing how we are 'blind to the limitations of our own understanding'[5]. Our human ability to make fully rational decisions is limited ('bounded') by our capacity for thinking, and by our not using all the available information. For example, when limited time is available, we simply skip past the practical realities of trying to acquire good information, and make a decision based on any knowledge that's on hand (*availability bias*).

box-ticking Approaching a management task (such as compliance) as an unthinking routine to be completed, rather than series of real questions that need to be thought about intelligently. Also refers to a form of *creative compliance* where the employees being audited believe that 'making a mark on a piece of paper' (ticking a box) means that nobody then has to change anything in the real world (such as their own bad behaviour).

business culture The attitudes and beliefs that shape how employees of a commercial firm go about their work from day to day; in regulators' view, having a business model and practices rooted in the fair treatment of customers, and market integrity.

bystanding Not intervening to fix a problem, because you believe – perhaps sincerely – that someone else will shortly be coming forward to fix it. In a notorious behavioural case study[6], a young woman was murdered despite the nearby presence of many witnesses (between 12 and 46 of them; accounts vary), none of whom raised the alarm. In a modern variant of bystanding, people often take photos or 'selfies' of some form of catastrophe unfolding in front of them – seemingly blind to its risk to them, or to the more pressing need to contact the emergency services.

capital adequacy / 'regulatory capital' A form of cash buffer against business collapse, that banks are required by regulators to maintain. It is the minimum fraction of a bank's business value that the bank must hold ready on its own account (in 'liquid form') in order to be able to pay off its market obligations.

careless record-keeping The conduct offence of failing to keep close track and note of where (particularly clients') money actually is, around your organization.

catastrophe-driven regulation The way that new rules always seem to be made in the aftermath of a disaster, allowing the political risk governance community to say that 'lessons were learned'. If you think about it, all regulation is a by-product of disaster; it's a political reflex action against the event of embarrassment after having failed to control the thing that went wrong.

cherry-picking Of a regulated organization responding to a regulator: selective reporting of favourable information. Commonly, running far more than the prescribed number of tests, then selecting and editing together a set of results that is skewed in favour of the conclusion sought. Also known in British government circles as 'policy-based evidence gathering' (as a wry comment on *gaming* against 'evidence-based policymaking' – itself a perfectly sound principle).

choice architecture / 'nudging' The regulatory design practice of influencing choice by changing the manner in which options are presented to people. For example, when presented with the option to opt *in* to donating their organs to hospitals after death, few people choose this; when presented with the same choice as an *opt out*, most people accept it. Popularized by a book called *Nudge*[7].

citizen mobilization A way for *normal people* to challenge abuses by powerful organizations' *vested interests*. As pioneered by social activist movements, including socialism itself, and (from the 1960s onwards) consumer activism and 'Rules for Radicals'[8]: It's about drawing together large numbers of people who have been adversely affected by, for example, the outcome of a public policy, or the presence of a 'dirty' industry, or an unsafe or mis-sold product. When people gather, focus on a single clearly defined issue and petition government about it in large enough numbers, reforms follow – change of government, even. This is perhaps the purest expression of the *social acceptance* factor in the *behavioural lens* model.

classical economics / neoclassical economics (as distinct from *behavioural economics*) Field of study which asserts that human decisions can be fully explained by logical analysis and by an assumed human preference for 'resource maximizing' (such as making money and accumulating property). Classical economists typically invoke *econometrics* to support this point of view. Behavioural economists disagree, on the grounds that *normal people* often don't do as classical models predict.

client assets Money, contracts and other valuables held in clients' names by financial providers. The point is that a client's money is not the provider's own. Despite strict rules about handling and accounting for

client money, many misbehaving providers continue to treat it as
their own.

cognitive bias Any systematic (non-random) error in thinking, that
regularly makes our judgement deviate from what would be considered
desirable as accepted norms, or correct in terms of formal logic.

cognitive failure Being unable mentally to process new information or
sensory stimuli, as a result of physical or mental damage sustained, or
overload (see below).

cognitive gap The difference between what we perceive as happening, and
what's actually happening. Often it's a gap in our understanding, when
we're ignorant of how to engage with something unfamiliar to us, or
unable to make sense of the available information. *See also* **dissonance**.

cognitive load (and **overload**) How much of your brain's processing
capacity is taken up with handling new information or sensory stimuli.
Overload occurs when your brain stops being able to make sense of all
the incoming information; like a processing chip in a computer, our
brains have *bounded* capacity to organize high volumes and concurrent
multiple strands of information. For example, it is now known that we
can't, in fact, multitask; rather, we switch rapidly and serially between
cognitive 'channels' – although after too long spent doing this, our
brains stop cooperating.

cognitive miser We ration our use of brain resources, just as we conserve
our bodily energy, though this is mostly done unconsciously. So, for
example, we may be inclined to think of other people in terms of
stereotypes, rather than seeing their true personalities; and we tend to
use *heuristics* (mental shortcuts) to lighten the *cognitive load* that a
decision needs, such as only making use of information that is close at
hand (an 'availability' heuristic).

command-and-control An outmoded form of risk control policy which
wrongly presumes that the best way to get people to do things is to tell
them, then force them, to comply. The opposite of *nudge*. An alarming
side-effect of command and control has been its proponents' insistence
that this approach works, despite much evidence that well-informed
populations respond adversely to it.

common goods The objective of many public policies of risk control:
to promote activities that make life better for people.

conduct costs All the money that you have to budget and spend, as a
conduct regulated provider organization, to comply with the new
rules; and possibly also to spend on recovering after a prosecution
for misconduct.

conduct regulation The (rapidly) increasing body of rules prescribing acceptable and expected behaviour by commercial providers of financial services, and setting out specific 'customer detriment' that providers must prevent.

conduct risk (*see also* **behavioural risk**) Any behaviour by your staff (especially towards customers) that undermines trust or value in your business, and that a regulator says creates *detriment* to customers or a 'disorderly market'. Includes managers' *inaction*, in the form of failure to anticipate and overcome customers' own biases or ignorance during the product creation and sales processes. Under these rules, for the first time senior managers are personally liable for any misconduct in the business they manage.

confirmation bias / hindsight bias Seeking out or evaluating information in a way that fits with existing beliefs (for example, looking for reasons to stay loyal to a brand rather than considering making an informed choice to change).

conflict of interest Where, for example, an organization's business loyalties might prevent it from making a decision objectively; or when a member of staff may derive personal benefit from a task they are doing in an official capacity.

confusion marketing A salesperson using 'too much information', taking advantage of a customer's cognitive limits, ignorance or biases to sell a product that may be inappropriate; exploiting *asymmetries* of knowledge and information between customer and provider.

constructed ignorance Where the people who design risk controls (such as board risk committees, regulators and governments) deliberately include some 'deniable space'[9] within the controls, so that if anything goes wrong they cannot ultimately be held accountable. This is an invidious and sophisticated form of regulatory *gaming*.

constructed preferences A form of selective memory: we will tend to recall most readily facts that are supportive of a point of view we hold, or for a course of action we'd intuitively prefer to take.

constructive challenge Questioning why things are as they are, but in a way that encourages a search for better alternatives. For example, not saying 'Our IT system is failing under the pressure of socially engineered hack attacks', but instead saying 'How can we improve our resilience to social engineering attacks? Perhaps by training staff to increase their *situational awareness* of human factor risk?'

corporate social responsibility (CSR) A once voluntary, but now largely formalized, code of good behaviour to which organizations publicly subscribe. Commitments typically include good conduct in the organization's own activities (environmental awareness and sustainability, fair rewards and trading) and voluntary support for neighbouring communities, charities and socially disadvantaged groups.

cost-benefit analysis Quantifying, in terms of money, the expected benefits of a course of action, and then subtracting the expected costs, to produce a notional 'net benefit' (or net cost).

creative compliance When a practitioner, to avoid an unwanted control, manipulates a rule so as to turn its impact away from the intentions of the legislators or enforcers, and towards the practitioner's own interests.

credit crunch In financial markets, a point in time where lenders realize that they may have taken on more business than they can manage, so they panic and stop extending credit to each other. It's a largely *behavioural* effect, which is why few *classical economists* saw it coming in 2008, when it induced a general standstill in world financial markets.

cultural cognition – *see* **motivated reasoning**

customer-centric An approach to doing business (and to respecting conduct rules) that focuses firmly on the customer's needs.

customer detriment – *see* **detriment**

customer due diligence Taking steps to identify who your customer really is and that he or she is who they say they are, such as by checking their passport and business credentials.

'dark side' research Approaching the investigation of 'good conduct' by first studying how and why people *mis*behave; talking directly to mis-sellers and conduct rule-breakers about what they do and how they justify their actions.

data fallacy The myth, popular among regulators, government ministers and business risk managers, that 'the more information we have, the better decisions we will (automatically) make'. This ignores the common risk of 'information overload', aka 'can't see the wood for the trees'.

death of deference Why senior people and public figures can no longer expect to hide behind a veil of assumed respectability; in the modern age of social media and (perceived) meritocracy, it is no longer assumed that anyone should respect anyone else simply because they have senior status in an institution.

de-biasing / bias-correction Requirement by conduct regulators that providers take, and prove, all reasonable steps to prevent customers from buying products as a result of their own *cognitive biases* (such as *anchoring* or *over-optimism*), or the seller's biased presentation of choice (such as *prominent features* or *asymmetric information*).

decision science Fields of academic study that examine how human beings take decisions; including neurology, cybernetics and social psychology, besides most of behavioural economics (within which notably: Game Theory, *Prospect Theory*, and *bias effects*).

delayed harm A significant *dread* factor: likelihood that an activity engaged in today will result in damage to you, or others close to you, at a later date. Historically there have been many notable cases of delayed harm caused by various industries, such as: asbestosis; over-use of antibiotics; human-made climate change; and the marketing of unaffordable loans.

delusion (of adequacy), **delusional** – *see* **Dunning-Kruger effect**

denial A *bias* state of being unwilling or unable to acknowledge the presence of an imminent threat to wellbeing, or the consequences of one's own bad behaviour.

denied agency Taking away a person's power to make decisions or to exercise control over their own life.

de-risking Some commercial firms' crude response to a regulator's demand for better management of risk: typically, by identifying any customers whose risk profiles are 'inconvenient' and asking them to leave; or by ceasing trading in a product that's about to face new regulations.

derivatives A financial contract whose main value is realized if and when an expected event happens, such as needing a market price index to reach a certain level.

detriment, detrimental Conduct regulators' term used to describe any harm suffered by customers as a result of their buying financial products. This includes where providers are (or seem to be) working for their own benefit and against the best interests of a customer – so-called *mis-selling*. A provider who causes or allows customer detriment is liable to be prosecuted by the conduct enforcer. Conduct regulators use the notion of 'customer detriment' as a broad critique of the financial sector's service failings, and give the highest priority to the customer's point of view. Enforcers see themselves as having a duty to support any consumers who see themselves as having been sold 'the wrong product', or having suffered from any other 'failings or misconduct' by providers. (FCA's phrases.)

disruptors The latest wave of financial service providers who use new technologies ('fintech') to change business models and methods of service delivery. For example, a loan provider with no presence on the high street, who sells exclusively using a smartphone app.

dissonance In cognitive science, the gap between the reality of what's happening and how you explain to yourself what's happening, as you may prefer to interpret it; a discomforting clash that you might experience between your own thoughts, beliefs or attitudes, and a contrasting reality – although often you'll try to kid yourself that your own misjudged view of things is the 'right' one.

dread Deep anxiety, as triggered by one of a defined group of 'dread risk' factors; these include *delayed harms*; hazards that are human-made (as opposed to naturally occurring); threats to our immediate physical safety, or to the safety of children and future generations; and any hazard seen to be approaching 'unstoppably'.

drivers of risk Any factor in the way you do business (or go about your daily life) that increases the impact or likelihood your being affected by some form of risk. This term is rather loosely used by many risk analysts to encompass all forms of *operational risk*, for example.

due skill and care Legal test of the basic standard of acceptable behaviour in customer service; now rather overshadowed by the tougher test of not causing *detriment*.

Dunning-Kruger effect When objectively measuring someone's (professional) ability and skill, a finding that they're unduly confident yet at the same time unaware that they lack the necessary skill. It is possible to test a person for this as a behavioural factor, showing on an indicator scale how self-deluded they are.

dynamic sensing of risk, **dynamic sense-making** The (rare) human intuitive faculty of being able to pinpoint a significant source of risk from among a mass of assorted incoming information. As highlighted by behavioural research[10], a skill commonly found in certain professions (such as aircraft test pilots, renal surgeons, self-made billionaire entrepreneurs, and submarine commanders) but alarmingly absent among most commercial board directors – however much they may claim otherwise.

econometrics, econometric measures / models Highly formalized decision tools, usually derived from mathematical modelling of probability, used to calculate risk in financial products. This approach seeks to justify a certain course of action by collecting information in the form of numbers, and arranging these into logical structures. It mistakenly assumes that 1) numbers and 2) money are effective *proxy indicators* for human behaviour – which they're not, of course. This is a major reason why the world needed *behavioural economics* as a better basis for appraising human conduct.

economic benefit Getting more money as a result of doing something.

'Econs v Humans' debate The academic argument between old-school 'neoclassical' economists ('Econs'), whose *econometric* view of the world relies on statistics and logic, and the new wave of behavioural economists who believe that we can understand ordinary human experience ('Humans') rather better if we take note of people's emotions (*affect*) and *biases*. Neoclassical economists in the past have tended to ignore how the vast majority of human 'normal people' perceive the world[11].

efficient frontier In simple terms, a curve drawn on a risk analysis chart that shows the best trade-off between taking a risk and achieving a decent level of return. Anything below the frontier is 'sub-optimal' (under-achieving, in the analyst's view); anything above it is taking 'excessive' risk.

emerging markets Financial trading in a developing country that has not yet instituted the risk control standards common in developed markets; a setting where investment carries greater risk, but with potential for higher returns.

empathy-deficient Having difficulty in understanding what other people may be thinking or needing. A familiar impairment in people with autistic spectrum disorders[12], but also sometimes found as a form of sociopathic disorder in senior managers.

endowment effect A form of *bias*. For the customer: valuing a thing more the minute that you own it (and maybe because you spent so much on it in the first place); defending your purchase of something expensive. For salespeople: encouraging the customer to buy the most expensive option 'because it must be worth the extra cost'.

enforced self-regulation / enforcement self-regulation A previously fashionable mode of regulatory control, commonly used before the arrival of *conduct regulation*, but discredited by the control failures of 2008. Under this regime, regulated organizations were required to self-report on their own levels of compliance, with the regulator occasionally stepping in to prosecute where non-compliance was found or suspected. The 2008 crash exposed the control fallacy of assuming that profit-motivated businesses could be expected to report objectively on their own probity.

enforcement against inaction Where a prosecutor takes action against a provider for *not* instituting a required risk control, such as for failing to set up a mandated framework for managing conduct risk.

existential dread Fear for one's future, typically after the recent removal of familiar safeguards or disruption of customary patterns of behaviour.

expert bias / expert problem Excessive faith in one's own talents, knowledge, or skills, or in those of an expert who has been drafted in to give topical advice. (*See also* **delusion of adequacy / Dunning-Kruger effect**.) Commonly, someone who may or may not have expert knowledge in one field comes to believe that this qualifies them to have an expert opinion on other topics. This form of bias is alarmingly common in corporate boardrooms, and should be challenged by any manager with conduct risk responsibilities.

external trust The extent to which people who *don't* work for you are willing to believe what you say.

fair outcomes What conduct regulators expect providers to achieve for customers; the opposite of *detriment*.

fantasy documents Typically, formal management plans for crisis recovery, or other forms of disaster management guides that are heavy on theory and advice, but with procedures that are too inflexible to be of practical value when a real catastrophe strikes[13].

fathering When regulations are found to apply to other parts of your organization; often as an unforeseen risk after acquiring another organization that didn't apply your (high) standards of compliance to its business. Occurring when, for example, after taking over a wealth management firm, you find that some of their clients fail your standards for identity checking, meaning that they are technically under suspicion of money laundering – and so are you, now.

financial capability The limits on a customer's access to information, or their 'literacy' in understanding your financial product jargon.

fit and proper person One type of personal quality that financial regulators require your senior officers to possess; in this case, not that the manager is competent, but that he or she is free from suspicion on ethical grounds – no criminal record, nor court judgements for personal debt, for example.

formal v informal organization A social theory highlighting the difference between how organizations claim they operate (with published forms of structured hierarchy, organizational charts, lines of reporting, and so on), as against 'what actually happens' thanks to the hidden influence of private, personal social links and values. As one example: Power in the boardroom is rarely as simple as stating that 'the chairman is in charge'; it is common in financial firms for the head of sales to have a stronger influence than many other board members, because the sales function has power as the most significant source of corporate earnings – that's the difference between the formal power structure (as shown in the Annual Report) and the real dynamic of behaviour in the room.

framing How you choose to acknowledge and describe a given risk or other phenomenon. Also, how you arrange the wording or illustration of any related choices to manage it, in such a way as to alter the 'natural' balance of attractiveness of each choice. (A creative complier will attempt to redefine rules in terms of local meanings: standard-form compliance is 'not how we do things,' as the pro forma approach 'doesn't apply to us.') The business of politics and regulation has been described as 'a framing contest'[14]; leaders compete to 'capture the narrative', and whoever succeeds wins public support for their proposed policy.

'friends and family test' – *see* **'what actually happens'**

fundamental attribution error The *bias* mistake of assuming that there is a simple cause, such as a single person's actions, responsible for creating a particular state of affairs. Such as: 'the bank's failure was entirely the fault of the Chief Executive'. This form of bias is closely related to what lawyers call the *ad hominem* fallacy, or 'scapegoating' – taking the over-simple course of attacking a person rather than searching for more complex explanations in the wider external circumstances. Public prosecutors, popular news media and internet trolls are often all too ready to employ this style of thinking to 'nail' senior individuals.

gaming (of rules / compliance) An attitude of misconduct that sees rules and compliance obligations as a chance for creative 'rule-bending'. In particular, exploiting weakly defined rules, to reinterpret them in a way that favours the practitioner's needs. (Not to be confused with Game Theory, a branch of probability-based *behavioural economics*.)

Gaussian copula Science jargon name for what most commercial people know as the graphic curve shape of 'standard distribution' – that is, a chart showing the normal frequency of events occurring in a given population. Fairly intuitively, it shows that the 'average' members or events in a given set of data tend to appear as a bulge in the middle, while 'outliers' tail off on either side.

generalizeability A desirable quality of a good piece of research: that its results point to broader conclusions that the world will find useful. For example, Kahneman and Tversky's (Nobel Prize winning) research[15] identified how people engage with various game simulations of probability and chance, but this insight informs a far wider understanding of why human beings take or avoid risks.

global financial crisis Although there have been several of these, most people now use this phrase to refer to the sharp downturn that hit financial markets worldwide in 2007–09. This followed the overheating and collapse of US and other markets in domestic mortgage lending, and various associated contracts such as *derivatives* and insurance.

global taxonomy (of conduct risk / enforcements) Ongoing academic research project that is showing how conduct regulators around the world are increasingly replicating each others' rule designs.

goodwill That element of the value of a business that is not accounted for by its physical assets alone; it's an extra element of value (or 'share premium') that reflects customers' preference to buy the brand, the firm's general reputation, and maybe an illustrious corporate history, strong current market prospects, shareholder confidence in the current board, and so on.

granular regulation Rules that are very detailed. The catch is, the more detailed the rules, the more there may be 'loopholes' in between the details – so granular isn't necessarily better.

'grey areas' Aspects of firms' regulated activities that are not yet clearly defined by new regulations; such as what 'good behaviour' means in practice, in certain areas where profit and ethics diverge.

groupthink Where an unexpected outcome arises after a group of (often senior, often expert, often highly intelligent) individuals makes an ill-judged collective decision. Groupthink is more likely when there is strong internal social pressure, with strict hierarchy, and the group is facing new forms of external threat. Group members may use *motivated reasoning* and follow private assumptions about what the expected outcome should be.

'heads on spikes' (informal phrase for) Practitioners' accusation that conduct enforcers are mostly interested in making populist attacks on high-profile senior financial managers, rather than prosecuting technical offences.

herding Justifying that you're doing what other people are doing, because they're doing it – a form of *social proof*.

heuristics – *see* **rules-of-thumb**

hostility trigger / hot button issue – *see* **hot topic**

hot topic Circumstances and/or event drawing sudden wider attention to an underlying problem that an organization is having; typically one of the 'five factors' highlighted by the *behavioural lens* in Chapters 8 and 9. When public concerns are left unanswered, any of the factors is liable to trigger hostility, as a 'hot button' focus for any related veins of social discontent.

hysteresis In cognitive science: time-lag between something happening and people realizing that it's happened, and starting to react. Adopted from physical science, where it refers to an object's tendency to exhibit a delayed reaction when forces are exerted on it.

illusion of certainty Belief that an event or outcome is perfectly certain, or a process error-free, even though it is not; suppressing the knowledge that an element of risk is present. See also *optimism bias*.

illusory correlation We are attracted to the idea that some actions and events are connected, or dependent on one another, when in fact they aren't. As part of this, we search for meaning in places where there isn't any. This form of bias is so ingrained in humans that entire industries (such as horoscope publishing) rely on it.

imposing, imposition Compelling someone to do as you want (such as changing their behaviour), rather than inviting them to see why change may be desirable.

inappropriate behaviour Doing something that is seen to violate one or more elements of the 'five factors' in the *behavioural lens* (see Chapters 8 and 9).

indicator Anything that points to, shows or suggests the state or level of something. In neoclassical economics: a statistic used to point out trends in markets and nations' economies.

inertia (bias) (*see also* **sticky bias**) Human tendency not to want to change one's existing position or beliefs.

information asymmetry A 'knowledge skew': the compromising effect on decision-making and balance of power, where one party has more or better information than the other. Financial service providers have far better information resources, and access to those resources, than either their customers or their regulators. Conduct regulators suspect that providers set up these conditions to exploit customers.

in-group A (typically small) group of people with a shared interest or identity, who use this identity as a way to exclude others – the 'out-group'.

inherent risk The probability of loss arising out of circumstances or existing in an environment in the absence of any action to control or modify the risk; in financial statements specifically, the risk of an error or omission due to some factor other than a failure of control – such as having complex business relationships with multiple parties.

input measure, not outcome measure (*see also* **indicator**) When describing a project, listing all the resources that you put into it (time, money, knowhow) as a way to evade talking about what the project actually achieved. A favourite ploy of politicians, who will talk at length about how much funding they have put into a policy initiative, but not so much about whether the initiative has succeeded in delivering real benefits to the public, such as an enduring shift towards more *pro-social* behaviour.

insider dealing Illegally exploiting access to unpublished information to make unfair profit when trading in securities, typically in publicly listed company shares.

irrational behaviour Our human tendency to do things and make decisions without logically evaluating the choices available, or even using all the available information (*bounded rationality*). Rather, we too often prefer to go for pain-free, rapid gratification; to avoid any loss; and to use expedient short-cuts (*rules of thumb*). Irrational behaviour is not random, though – it contains many *predictable* patterns that excite the interest of behavioural economists.

joined-up thinking / problem-solving Where one team or department (of an organization, such as government) talks to others, to use collective knowledge to help solve problems. Much discussed in principle, rare in practice, as local *tribal* loyalties tend to prevent it.

juniorizing, juniorization A game of human resources, in two possible forms: 1) Under the *Senior Managers Regime* of conduct regulation: to try to avoid liability for prosecution, a senior manager rewrites their own job description and job title, omitting 'senior sounding' words; 2) realizing that older staff tend to have more expensive salaries than younger staff, a department fires its most experienced staff, leaving the most inexperienced staff in charge – with sometimes catastrophic results.

knowledge certainty One of the two key factors in testing for *Dunning-Kruger* bias: how far you are comfortable that you *really* know a certain fact. When you claim to know that fact, are you 100 per cent sure? 90 per cent? Maybe less than 50 per cent? One group of people who score badly on the Dunning-Kruger test are those who are 100 per cent certain of what they know, but who actually have the facts wrong – in other words, they're *delusional*.

legitimacy Where a rule-maker or controller has a fair claim to popular support from the general public, and/or regulatees. It is this widespread support that gives the rule-maker their legitimacy or 'popular mandate' in the first place.

legitimizing / legitimated Where regular misbehaviour by line managers encourages junior staff to conclude that it is normal to ignore the rules – *see* **normalizing**. Not to be confused with *legitimacy* (see above).

limit of agency The point at which you stop doing something, as you accept that you alone don't have the power to change whatever it is you want to change; or in practice, when a group of people trying to change something decides to give up their campaign as 'un-winnable'.

lines of sight In compliance: managers having clearly defined responsibilities for overseeing certain aspects of the business; and for managers to see one another's responsibilities in the context of the whole enterprise.

liquidity (freeze, squeeze) In order to trade, financial firms need to be able to exchange cash with other financial firms. If the others don't trust you, they will stop letting you have their cash. Without access to others' cash, you soon run out of your own and, pretty soon, your trading activity grinds to a halt. *See also* **credit crunch**.

loan-to-value A factor that a lender assesses when deciding whether to give a customer a mortgage: what proportion of the value of the property (for example, house) to be mortgaged will the loan represent? The higher the proportion of loan-to-value, the bigger the risk for the lender; the maximum of 100 per cent loan-to-value would mean that the provider is lending the customer cash to the whole (current) value of the property.

loss-aversion The human feeling that you'd rather avoid the chance of a possible loss, than take a slightly less probable punt on a possible gain. Another key component of *Prospect Theory*[16].

manipulation / 'rigging' Deliberate attempt by a person or informal group to interfere with the free and fair operation of a financial market by introducing misleading information.

market abuse (*see also* **insider dealing** and **manipulation**) Using unpublished or unverified information to distort the price-setting mechanism of financial instruments.

mental accounting People think of their own money as divided into 'different bits', according to where it came from, what they plan to spend it on, and what method of payment they use.

micromort A one-in-a-million chance of dying as a result of engaging in a given activity. This is an all-purpose standard unit for measuring risk[17]. Helps any non-expert to judge how likely it is that doing any particular activity might kill them, and so not to worry unduly about it. A half-day session of hang-gliding carries a risk of 8 micromorts (that's a 0.0008 per cent risk of death); an overnight stay in a British public hospital, 75 micromorts (0.0075 per cent), which is itself the same risk as riding a motorbike 420 miles (from London to Edinburgh, say). Put it another way, 13,332 people should be able to motorcycle from London to Edinburgh on any given day, or to stay over in hospital, without worrying that they're about to die. Many people find this view reassuring.

mirroring behaviour The way that we learn to get on with other people by copying what they are doing. Our brain structure includes mirroring at a cell level (mirror neurons), supporting this basic survival skill that we begin to use from the moment we're born: one of the first things a baby learns is the benign effect of *reciprocating* (mirroring) a parent's smile.

mis-selling, misselling Where a financial provider profits from selling a product to a customer who gains little or no practical benefit from the purchase.

mission creep Where a public policy, campaign, or control intervention gradually increases its remit, attempting to widen its influence over a community.

models-based Of a risk control or regulation: relying on numerical data and *econometric* assumptions, rather than observed behaviour.

moral courage The intuitive human quality of 'doing what's right', even in the face of strong opposition from *vested interests*. Notably, this human resilience factor never appears in anyone's risk register, even though it's one of the most valuable human qualities of all.

moral value (theory) The idea that a decision will produce an 'expected utility' that may *feel* different from its financial value, as objectively measured. Originally hit on in 1738 by a mathematician[18] who realized that a £10,000 lottery win couldn't make him 'ten times happier' than a £1,000 win. *See also* **affect, Prospect Theory.**

mortgagor Someone who has borrowed from a lender, against the value of an asset such as a house.

motivated reasoning / cultural cognition Where having a personal motivation and/or professional interest in the outcome of a decision interferes with your attempt to analyse objectively the choice to be made. For example, turkeys would be unlikely to argue in favour of Christmas (even if they had the means to do so).

Murphy's Law An informal 'law' of research observation, and many other fields of human activity, that 'anything that can go wrong, will go wrong; often at the worst possible moment'.

mystery shopping Commissioning research agents to pretend to be customers, to report back to management on their experience of service received.

negative equity Owing a debt against an asset that is now worth less than the amount you borrowed to pay for it. A common customer experience in falling markets, as among *mortgagors* when the value of houses crashed.

neurochemical reward Types of chemicals produced in your brain, that make you feel good when you do certain activities. The levels of various chemicals such as endorphin and dopamine rise in response to, for example, you going for a run, so that you feel good both as you do it, and generally at the prospect of taking exercise.

Newtonian (rationale, assumptions) Following the principles of classical physics set out by Sir Isaac Newton, such as that for every action there is an equal and opposite reaction. Designing risk controls based on the laws of physics isn't a good idea, as it ignores the effect of human *behavioural* factors such as *affect* and *biases*.

normalizing (of misconduct) Typically, creating working conditions/risk culture where non-standard behaviour becomes seen as acceptable (such as by rewarding overly aggressive selling).

'normal people' / social perception Behavioural scientists' term for how non-expert people perceive the world around them, and in particular the risks in it[19]. So, 'normal people' don't stop to do full evaluations of risk; they just pause, take a quick intuitive view of whether they'll tolerate the risk, then press on with their lives. Social perception describes the same process in a group of people, across society as a whole, as in: 'Do we, in the modern world, accept that it's OK to…?'. A key part of the social component in the *behavioural lens* (fifth factor).

norms (current); **norming** The level of pro-social, 'good' behaviour that most of the population require; the resetting of these levels from time to time. Not to be confused with *normalizing* (see above).

'nudging' – *see* **choice architecture**

ombudsman A government-appointed independent mediator who helps resolve disputes between customers and service providers in a given business sector.

operational risk The prospect of loss resulting from inadequate or failed procedures, employee activities, systems or policies. So-called 'oprisks' include errors made by employees, frauds, hacking, and other forms of disruption to business.

optimism (bias) (*see also* **illusion of certainty**) The way we tend to overestimate how likely a good thing is to happen, and underestimate the chances of a bad experience.

overconfidence A *bias* effect: where your subjective confidence in your own judgements is greater than it should be, if you checked against an objective analysis of the situation. As in: 'Don't stop me, I know what I'm doing.'

over-extrapolating Justifying making a long-term commitment on the basis only of short-term information. For example, taking out a 20-year mortgage because you've just received a pay rise.

over-leveraged / over-geared In a business, to have borrowed more (for example, through loan stock) than you can safely repay on the basis of your current assets and earnings.

overload / cognitive overload To have imposed too much of a burden (such as of work to do). With cognitive overload, the burden is of too much information to have to understand; *see* **cognitive load**.

overselling Selling a product in quantities such that most buyers won't benefit from buying it.

oversight failure Not noticing that something's gone wrong.

perception of risk How our brains make sense of risky events, or of information about a risk, and how that conditions the way we respond to the risk. Often it's less about rationally weighing up a risk, more about how the risk makes us feel.

performative (compliance), **performativity** In simple terms: looking busy. Such as: creating a 'risk management initiative' that entails lots of activities designed to distract the regulator's attention away from a lack of any real progress on improving risk culture, or on reducing sales abuses, or on improving customer care and outcomes. A more common ploy than perhaps outsiders realize.

personal liability (SMR) Where under the Senior Managers conduct regulations, each senior person is responsible in law, him- or herself, for the consequences of a control failure in any business activity they manage.

perverse effects When what actually happens is the opposite of what the control measure was designed to achieve. For example, when in UK law various abusive individuals and corporations issued 'super-injunctions' to try to prevent journalists from publishing details about their misconduct; Freedom of Information campaigners only challenged even more vigorously, until the legal restraints gave way, exposing the 'super-injunction' issuers to far greater embarrassment. *See also* **Streisand effect.**

perverse incentives The conduct problem that management systems of risk and reward (well-intended or otherwise) may promote various forms of bad behaviour. For example: immediate cash bonuses, high commission payments on poor-value products, aggressive target-setting, and imposing unrealistically tight deadlines, all encourage mis-selling as a short cut towards 'making the numbers'.

physical dread Anxiety for one's physical (bodily) safety.

point of reference In social psychology, the people we privately look to, whom we regard as examples of 'how to behave properly'.

policy design Choosing which tools to use when trying to put a policy objective into practice – such as by 'nudges', incentives or enforcement. Should include thinking about what outcome it is practicable to try to achieve; and some regard to *perverse effects*.

political theatre Public servants, including regulators, doing something for the impression it makes in the news media, rather than for sound ethical reasons. *See also* **'heads on spikes'.**

post-rationalizing After the event, making up an explanation for why you did what you did. (If during the event anyone had asked you why you were behaving as you did, you wouldn't have had an answer.)

precautionary In risk management, the precautionary principle is a strategy that advises you to cope with a possible risk by treating it as if it's an actual, present risk. Applying this principle leads to all kinds of organizational paralysis, and public ridicule of over-zealous 'health and safety' rulings.

predictably irrational An aspect of being human. We don't always act logically; but that doesn't mean that our illogical behaviour is random – quite the opposite – our non-logical (intuitive) mind drives many patterns of behaviour. Many of these patterns are consistent and so can be predicted.

predictive power When a present phenomenon is tested scientifically, and the test is often repeated until it becomes highly reliable, the test of what *has* happened may begin to be used to suggest what's *going to* happen next. A test that is believed to show reliably what will happen next is said to have strong predictive power. Of course, when underlying conditions change, even the most 'reliable' predictors will tend to fail.

preferences and beliefs Categories of bias, which lead consumers to choose a product that may not suit their real needs. Salespeople should challenge these.

pre-notified inspections A form of compliance *gaming*; a regulator and a regulatee agree in advance when the inspectors will visit the firm, so that no 'unwelcome' findings are made during the inspection. Both parties agree that this (corrupt) arrangement maintains the appearance that all is well, and reduces their compliance workloads. Also known as a 'control bargain', it's a creative variation on *performative* compliance.

present bias / availability / recency Tending to give stronger weight to payoffs that are closer to 'now'. The 'availability' version of the bias encourages us to make a decision using only the information that comes to hand. For example, if we asked for three product brochures and only two arrived the next day, we might decide between the first two and not wait for the third. 'Recency' uses only the information we can remember as arriving most recently; this is why the final contestant on a TV talent show often gets the largest vote – the audience simply recalls their performance more vividly.

priming If we have in mind (even subconsciously) something that recently made us happy, we're more likely to agree to make a purchase. Salespeople know this, and so go out of their way to make us feel unusually cheerful at the exact point where we're about to decide to make a purchase.

projection bias The idea that the future will bring 'more of the same' that we've just experienced, and that our own tastes and preferences will remain the same in future.

pro-social Doing things for the public benefit. The opposite of antisocial.

Prospect Theory A cornerstone of *behavioural economics*[20]. This tool predicts, far more accurately than classical economics, how people will decide between alternatives that involve risk and uncertainty. Among other breakthroughs, it showed how people think in terms of 'expected utility' above or below a reference point, rather than in terms of absolute value, and are *loss-averse*.

providers For the purposes of this book: any organization providing financial services and having this activity subject to regulation.

proxy indicator / 'proxy' An indirect measure that its users claim is representative of 'what's happening', where there is no direct measure. For example, the manager of a change programme may cite as a proxy indicator the amount of money that has been spent on the programme, rather than reporting how much the programme has actually served to change real-world behaviour. Indeed, the only true measure of many programmes' outcomes is observed change in behaviour; other indicators are merely 'input measures'.

public goods Activities, products or services that benefit the wellbeing of the general public, typically without profit to whoever is providing them.

'quants' Business analysts who rely on quantitative measuring tools; people who prefer to use numerical and financial data to support decisions, rather than consulting qualitative data on behaviour, social attitudes, or other 'soft' factors.

rational actor The imaginary person at the centre of classical economists' assumptions: someone who is assumed to value profit and personal gain above all other considerations. This person is a useful imaginary friend for classical economists (who focus on measuring profit and organizational gains), but is a chimera. The idea of a rational actor misses the point that *'normal people'* out there don't think like this; real people tend to possess qualities such as altruism, emotional sensitivity and empathy, none of which the rationalist 'paradigm' can handle. *See also* **rationality assumption**.

rational compliance / rational compliers Obeying the rules because this appears to offer a quieter life than risking breaking them.

rational non-compliers / rational calculators People who work out that it might be more profitable (and/or fun for them) to break a rule than to obey it. The opposite of *rational compliers*; *see also* **amoral calculator**.

rationality assumption The basis of *classical economics* for most of its existence in the latter 20th century. Says that all human beings in market-orientated societies ('homo economicus') behave in certain ways, such as: making rational decisions; the self-interested seeking of wealth; and being mainly interested in the utility (value to themselves) of goods, services and relationships. It fails to address at least two big issues: that humans exercise their emotions when making decisions (*see* **affect**); and that even a world full of supposedly rational individuals is unable to take a rational view of long-term social challenges – hence we often over-consume resources (*see* **tragedy of the commons**). *Behavioural economics* has reminded economists everywhere that humans are irrational, and not necessarily in a bad way either.

'real people' – *see* **'normal people'**

rear-view regulation Writing new rules that refer only to failures that have happened in the past, rather than taking account of imminent and future changes in the market that's being regulated.

reason v intuition Two types of mental process for dealing with incoming information (about a risk, for example). Roughly corresponding to the two levels of brain 'System' described by Prof Daniel Kahneman[21]: his System I is the 'fast thinking' part of the brain, that instantly suggests a course of action at an instinctive level; System II is our rational brain, which takes more time to weigh the odds to produce a more informed basis for a decision.

reciprocity A form of 'social rule' that urges people to give back (reciprocate) any goodwill or kindness they have received from someone else; one effect is that, after someone has done something for you, you feel obligated to return the favour to them. Marketing practice exploits this sense of obligation, using gift coupons and 'free offers'.

reference-dependence The lazy, or self-comforting, assumption that 'future performance will be a continuation of the past'. May entail underestimating gains or trying to suppress an undue fear of losses.

reframing A technique used in cognitive therapy, and also in organizational communications: creating a different way of looking at a situation, by describing it differently and so seeking to change its 'meaning' for anyone who has been finding the experience discomforting.

regret Unwelcome emotional response in a person who has bought something, then finds the purchase has not satisfied them as they had expected it to. Also known as 'buyer's remorse'.

regulatees Any sector or group within it bound in common by a set of regulations.

regulatory assumptions Things that the people who design regulations would like to think are true, but which often are not – such as that management 'tone at the top' can dictate behaviour across an entire workforce.

regulatory capital – *see* **capital adequacy**

regulatory capture Where the organizations in a regulated industry are able to exert sufficient political and/or economic power to dictate what they want regulators to do. Powerful interests may co-opt the regulator's agents (seeking to make 'control bargains'), then marginalize them.

'regulatory dance' In political theory, an informal three-way agreement that persists between governments, regulators and regulatees, under which no one party may unduly upset either of the other two[22]. If any one of the three breaches this tacit understanding (through heavy-handed intervention, scandal, etc) the dance is deemed to have ended, to be replaced by a period of political reprisals, hard renegotiation, or even a whole new regulatory structure.

regulatory design How governments and regulatory agencies set about *framing* their instruments of control, including which forms of human behaviour and other factors they deem most important to acknowledge, accept or reject, and seek to influence. *See also* **policy design**.

reifying / reification The painful mental process of coming to realize that a notional threat or abstract worry is now real and physically present in your life.

relativistic risk-view Not giving a (potentially) serious risk the management attention it deserves, on the basis that there are many other serious risks out there.

relentlessly empirical What behavioural academics say they are: always looking for real-world proof of 'what actually happens', rather than defending theoretical models of how the world might work.

Relevant Authorized Persons A regulatory term describing a group of significant senior decision-takers on risk governance.

resource asymmetry Where one party, such as a *provider* (*regulatee*), has better resources – such as research capacity, access to legal advice, human resources or cash – than the other party (typically the *regulator*). The better-resourced party may exploit its advantage to 'push back' against attempted controls.

response effects The way that people taking a questionnaire tend to offer the answer that they think the questioner expects. Famously a problem for opinion polls, which have called wrong results in several national elections, after 'shy' voters' avoided telling the truth about whom they actually voted for.

responsible person A manager formally designated by the regulator as responsible for running a business function and/or its compliance with the rules.

risk appetite At its simplest, the amount and type of risk that an organization is willing to take in order to meet its strategic objectives. Soon gets a lot more complex when boards start to evaluate it in terms of numbers and acceptable cut-off points.

risk cognition How people perceive risk and consider engaging with it; including how they form subjective impressions rather than making rational evaluations.

risk culture A phrase now used by various *behavioural regulation* authorities: How an organization engages with risk-taking, including its attitude to risk and reward (risk appetite); employees' conduct with customers and between internal businesses; and its transparency in acknowledging and remediating any problems of risk control and customer care.

risk engagement How you approach a present risk; perhaps to quash it, manage it, deflect it, ignore it, or cope with (hide from) it.

risk equity / inequity / fairness Whether the people benefiting from any risk-taking are also the people who are bearing the main load of the risk.

risk governance Institutions, processes and mechanisms, often at senior management level, that make and implement decisions on acceptable risk-taking.

risk mapping Drawing visual representations of a risk or group of risks as an aid to understanding their expected impact. Examples: risk matrix (cost-benefit analysis); distribution (scatter) chart; probability curves (risk profiles); 'heat maps'.

risk metrics Any numerical measure of the characteristics of a risk; commonly, *econometric* analysis.

risk perception – *see* **perception of risk**

Risk Society An influential theory proposing that we are all our own personal risk-managers[23]. In the modern 'me-first' era, everyone continuously makes personal decisions and value-judgements about whether to engage with or reject all kinds of risks and rules, or even whether to subvert them.

risk-aware working Encouraging everyone to use their intuition as a tool for everyday risk management; rewarding staff for reporting near-miss incidents and low-level customer dissatisfaction; promoting internal discussion about risk, rather than boxing risk into a technical 'silo'.

risk-risk trade-off Where suppressing one risk entails increasing another one; or where action taken to reduce one risk creates a new type of risk; trying to strike the best balance between such two (or more) associated risks.

rock-star defence Of a trader or salesperson, typically: excusing one's bad behaviour on the grounds that one is special and gifted, and so not subject to the same standards or controls as others.

rogue trader A single criminally misbehaving person who uses the company's marketing access and systems for money-making private dealings, and as a result puts the whole organization at risk.

routine nonconformity When misbehaviour goes unchallenged and so becomes part of everyday working practice.

rules-of-thumb / heuristics A way of simplifying a decision process, often unconsciously, by substituting an easy question for a difficult one.

(see example overleaf)

('Both these cars have lots of useful features. So, do I fancy owning the blue car more, or the red one?')

sanctions Regulatory 'punishments' against wrongdoers, such as fines or suspension of trading licences.

satisficing Doing the bare minimum of activity, just enough to qualify (as compliant, or whatever).

scalar – *see* **binary**

self-regulating Where a sector is responsible for policing its own standards of provision and customer care, as when historically the financial services industry was deregulated in various countries. As a system, no longer politically fashionable since the financial crisis.

self-reporting Sending in to the regulator your own reports on how well you're complying with the rules. Common practice before the advent of conduct regulation.

Senior Managers [and Certification] Regime (SMR / SMCR) Regulatory initiative making individual senior managers personally responsible for defined business functions, and having to regularly attest their fitness and competence to do so.

sense-making Mentally 'filling in the gaps' where information is incomplete; making your own sense of information you don't fully understand, or drawing your own conclusion where there are mixed signals.

signal value Of one initial incident, implying that it means we should expect more, similar and more severe incidents to follow.

situational awareness Being intuitively familiar with the range of likely threats in a given setting (business or public). Much improved by having a high level of intuitive skill in *dynamic sensing*.

skilled and competent Regulator's expected characteristics of providers' managers in general, and senior managers in particular.

Skilled Persons Review (Section 166 notice) UK regulator's formal demand for an organization to open its records and senior personnel to close scrutiny, on suspicion that an offence may have been committed.

slippery slope Emotive argument that the event of one incident suggests that more will follow (see also *signal value*).

social contract Understanding between employees and their employer, or voters and their elected government, that their interests will be looked after by those in authority. Only implicit, and all too often broken where trust is lost between the two sides.

social cues Hints, or informal suggestions as a result of how other people are behaving, that something needs to change.

social labelling How as a society we decide at any given time whether a certain activity is acceptable or unacceptable; the unacceptable activities are labelled (for example, 'deviant')[24]. These labels shift from generation to generation, as with major recent generational changes in social attitudes towards divorce, sexuality and debt.

social licence / 'licence to operate' The extent to which stakeholders are willing not to criticize an organization, so allowing the organization to exist and flourish. Social licence is not about a wider public *supporting* the organization – they're simply withholding their criticism.

social proof / 'informational social influence' Noting and copying what other people do; such as because we want to avoid having to make a decision for ourselves, or as a quick way to confirm that our own behaviour is acceptable. *See also* **mirroring behaviour** and **reciprocity**.

social purpose (of banking) / socially useful banking Historically, a core function of banks was to lend to businesses to help them build value and create employment; in the mid-2000s, many banks allegedly lost sight of this aim. Central bankers reminded them about it, using these phrases.

socially defined Other people's opinion influencing yours; whether people think that something's acceptable. *See also* **social labelling, social licence**.

sociopath Person lacking normal social *reciprocity* or empathy, possibly as a sign of mental illness, or simply an abusive approach to the workplace. *See also* **empathy-deficient**.

speech perception Physical and mental processes by which we hear and interpret what others are saying to us.

spotlight effect (bias) Our tendency to believe that we are noticed by others more than we really are.

stakeholders Anyone with an interest in, and affected by, how an organization is getting on – owners, customers, staff, suppliers, regulators, local communities, governments, and so on.

steady-state assumption Most regulation is designed to function optimally when the regulatee group is behaving itself. Of course, the time that most of us want regulation to work best is when the regulatees are *mis*behaving, but that's not how the assumption operates.

sticky bias / inertia 'Playing it safe', sticking with what you know. Passing up good opportunities; buying only on a clear recommendation.

Streisand effect When by making a formal attempt to stop something happening, such as by seeking legal restraint, one ends up drawing more attention to (and possibly sympathy for) the thing one is trying to prevent, so making an uncomfortable situation worse for oneself. *See also* **perverse effects**.

stress tests, stress-testing Formally testing how certain sources of stress will affect an organization or business sector; repeated tests to assess the limits of resilience, against expected possible situations.

symbolic enforcement The regulatory enforcer making a big show of punishing one organization as a way of signalling to others to be more careful.

System I / System II thinking (*see* **reason v intuition**). Not to be confused with *systems thinking* (see below).

systems thinking A basic mistake among rule-makers of all kinds, who assume that humans make decisions in a fully rational way and so will 'follow instructions' as long as these are sufficiently rational. In fact, as behavioural science now knows, people react to such well-meant 'instructions' in a wide variety of contrary, emotional and biased ways. Historically many governments around the world have relied on systems thinking to support a 'big state' idea that citizens need governments to tell them what is best for them.

tells / tell signs Involuntary signals that we may give off, when under stress, that reveal the presence of an underlying anxiety, uncertainty as to a decision, or abusive situation. A word borrowed from the world of professional poker-playing, where an uncontrolled 'tell' may lose a player the match.

three lines of defence A regulatory model for preventing harm. The first line is a firm's operational management, the second the firm's risk and compliance specialists, the third its internal audit and board risk governance.

tipping point The point at which a series of small changes or incidents becomes significant enough to trigger a larger, more fundamental change.

tragedy of the commons Where a limited public resource is overwhelmed by demand as many individuals push forward, each trying to get the greatest benefit from it. Eventually, the resource is lost, so that nobody benefits. Term originally coined by US ecologist Garrett Hardin in 1968, to warn of the dangers of overpopulation. Hardin noted that when medieval farmers allowed their livestock to 'over-graze' on public grassland (the 'commons'), this killed the grass, leading to the animals starving. Modern examples of over-exploited commons include 'tourist erosion' of cultural heritage; depletion by over-fishing of fish stocks in oceans; traffic congestion; anthropogenic climate change; and many market 'bubble-bursts' including the 2008 housing crisis.

transparency Allowing people, including colleagues and regulators, to see clearly into your operations and control systems; not hiding or obfuscating your systems and activities.

treating customers fairly ('TCF') A historic initiative by an earlier UK financial regulator, to try to force providers to keep their customers' best interests in mind at all times.

tribes / tribal network culture Of staff, being loyal to informal close groups of associates (such as one's sales team, or 'mates' at work) rather than to the employer brand.

untouchables Typically, middle and senior managers within a financial firm who believe that their high earnings for the firm exempt them from criticism or the need to comply with regulations.

vested interest Having a strong personal or corporate interest in keeping an activity going, because you stand to benefit directly from it; such as when 'dirty industries' resist new environmental controls.

volatility A measure of how much (and how rapidly) a trading price has varied over time.

watchdogs Informal name for regulators and other institutions guarding the public interest, such as ombudsman services, consumer advocacy groups, and even public prosecutors.

'what actually happens' Examining why people behaved as they did, looking for explanations not from economic models but by directly asking any *normal people* who were involved for their perceptions. Behavioural studies show that, for example, asking a wrongdoer to explain their misbehaviour to someone they care about – a so-called 'friends and family test' – is a much tougher ethical challenge than to account for the same behaviour on a corporate compliance form. British public hospitals (NHS) now commonly use a 'friends and family test' to debrief nurses on whether surgeons' conduct towards patients is acceptable. Also: the study of how groups of regulated people *actually* responded to the introduction of new rules – rather than what the regulator or politicians *hoped* would happen when they originally formulated the controls.

whistleblowing Where a current or recently departed employee raises concerns about wrongdoing in their workplace. Historically seen by many employers as 'disloyal', whistleblowing is now regarded by many legislators as an essential safeguard to the public interest. The rights of whistleblowers are now widely protected by laws governing 'public interest disclosures'.

wilful ignorance Persisting in taking a course of action without gathering available and relevant information that would lead to a decision taking better account of topical risk factors, including good conduct and public acceptability. Behaviour characteristic of boards trying to justify keeping 'traditional' practices, and to resist disclosing an ethical dimension that would reveal moral compromise.

yield The return on an investment, usually expressed as a percentage. If I buy a share for $1.00 and the share pays a dividend of 10 cents after a year, the yield on my investment is 10 per cent.

Reference and source notes

See Recommended Reading (p 271) for further citations of authors and titles

1   Phrases used by Prof Mike Power (LSE) in *Organizational Encounters with Risk*

2   (Posthumously) by Rev Thomas Bayes in *A Method of Calculating Exact Probability*

3   *See* Tenner, *Why Things Bite Back*

4   *See* Sykes and Matza's *Techniques of neutralization* (1957)

5   Prof Herbert Simon

6   Latane and Darley's *Bystander Apathy* (1969)

7   Profs Cass Sunstein and Richard Thaler, *Nudge* (2009)

8   Saul Alinsky: *Rules for Radicals* (1971)

9   Phrase coined by Dr Linsey McGoey in *On the will to ignorance in bureaucracy* (2007)

10 Prof Sidney Dekker: *The Field Guide to Understanding Human Error* (2006)

11 Prof Colin Camerer: *The Business Challenge to Economics: Understanding normal people* (2003)

12 Prof Simon Baron-Cohen: *Zero Degrees of Empathy* (2012)

13 A field of risk management research pioneered by Prof Lee Clarke: see *Mission Improbable* (1999)

14 Sarah Kaplan: *Framing Contests: Strategy making under uncertainty* (2008)

15 D Kahneman and A Tversky: *Prospect Theory: An analysis of decision under risk* (1979) and *Advances in Prospect Theory* (1992)

16 Kahneman and Tversky, as above

17 Pioneered by Profs Ron Howard (Stanford University) and David Spiegelhalter (Cambridge University)

18 Daniel Bernoulli: *New Theory on the Measurement of Risk* (1738)

19 Camerer, as above

20 Kahneman and Tversky, as above

21 Daniel Kahneman: *Thinking, Fast and Slow* (2011)

22 L Snider: *The Regulatory Dance: Understanding reform processes in corporate crime* (1991)

23 Ulrich Beck: *World Risk Society* (1999)

24 *See* Howard Becker: *Outsiders* (1963)

RECOMMENDED READING
With author's comments

This is just a personal selection, not an exhaustive list. It is for any reader new to the subject, or at an intermediate level, who wants to develop an understanding of behavioural research and regulatory design. All of these titles have proved themselves to me over the years (and to many hundreds of course attendees) as the most accessible and enduring insights.

Under each one I've added a comment or two about why it is worth a read. Again, this is my own opinion, not an objective critique. Although most of these titles are readable for general interest, a few of them stand out as both good science and a really 'good read' – these get two stars. There is only one that's a hard read, though it is an important piece of theory; you'll find it in the list, soon enough, under 'B'.

(If you already know your way around the core topics and would like to explore the field at a higher level, there are plenty of specialist citations at the end of each chapter in the main body of the book.)

Key, subject focus [ ]

**	– highly recommended
BE	– behavioural economics
DR	– design of regulations, policies and controls
F	– financial crises and their aftermath
OB	– organizational behaviour
P	– psychology (social and cognitive) of risk, biases and risk perception
RM	– risk modelling (theory and social history)

Ariely, Dan (2009) *Predictably Irrational*, Harper Collins
- [BE]: In our daily lives we tend to assume that we make choices that are rational; reality shows that they aren't. But our 'irrational' choices are not random. They're systematic and predictable. Find out why and how.

Arnell, N W, Tompkins, E L and Adger, W N (2005) **Eliciting information from experts on the likelihood of rapid climate change**, *Risk Analysis*, **25** (6)
- [P, DR]: How safe is it to assume that 'experts' know what they're talking about? Not as much as we'd like to think, as it turns out.

Beck, Ulrich (1999) *World Risk Society*, Polity Press, Cambridge
- [RM]: Why and how we're all our own personal risk managers now, in 'post-modern' society. (Caution: This is the one that's hard to read.)

Becker, Howard S (1963) *Outsiders: Studies in the sociology of deviance*, Simon & Schuster, New York
- [**, P]: When does 'eccentric' behaviour become 'deviant'? Why don't some people do as they're told? – and why don't we care so much, when certain people misbehave? A one-off, ultra clear account of this complex field, with an unusually diverse cast of case study characters: jazz musicians, marijuana smokers, violent cops, rapists and politicians on the make. (Its challenging central idea: Deviance is not defined by how someone behaves, but by how other people respond to and 'label' the behaviour.)

Berne, Eric (1970) *Games People Play: The psychology of human relationships*, Penguin
- [P]: The 'Parent-Adult-Child' model of engagement, and how various mind-games ensue. Useful, often unnerving, if a little dated now.

Bernstein, Peter L (1996) *Against the Gods: The remarkable story of risk*, John Wiley & Sons, New York
- [RM]: A good social history of commercial attempts to control risk.

Bevan, Gwyn and Hood, Christopher (2006) **What's measured is what matters: Targets and gaming in the English public healthcare system**, The Public Services Programme, ESRC in *Public Administration*, **84** (3)
- [**, DR]: Academically sharp (and highly entertaining) attack on the perverse effects of introducing commercial target culture into public service settings.

Brighton, Paul and Foy, Dennis (2007) *News Values*, Sage, London
- [P]: What makes 'news' news? Two journalist-academics take a fresh look at where news comes from – why we care, or don't care, about the various different kinds of stuff that happens out there. Very readable.

Camerer, Colin (2003) *The Business Challenge to Economics: Understanding normal people*, Caltech, Pasadena, CA: Proceedings of the Federal Reserve Conference
- [BE]: From its title line onwards, here's a professor who is happily spoiling for a fight with the profession of classical economics. As a behavioural scientist, he calls economists' bluff for failing to acknowledge basic truths of human behaviour. The date is significant here – five years before the banking crash. Presciently, Camerer lays into a heap of old-school economic assumptions, and finds many of them unfit for purpose.

Cialdini, Robert (2014 [5th edition]) *Influence: Science and practice*, Pearson
- [P]: People use various forms of bias and social proof in daily life. Often it's intuitive, sometimes knowingly. Once you recognize our underlying human needs – for reciprocity, reassurance, common good and other factors – all sorts of situations begin to make more sense. Full of refreshing advice on how to avoid being too easily influenced. (Example: Don't watch TV shows that use 'canned laughter'.)

Clarke, Lee (1999) *Mission Improbable: Using fantasy documents to tame disaster*, University of Chicago Press
- [OB, P]: Why you shouldn't delude yourself that your risk controls, or crisis response plan, will actually withstand a crisis. Some of the toughest crises have been successfully dealt with despite, not because of, such plans. Just allow room for intuition; here's how.

Cohen, Stanley (2001) *States of Denial*, Polity Press, Cambridge
- [**, P]: Brilliant, but scary, primer on how powerful people evade censure for misbehaviour; the many ways that authorities may redefine 'the public interest' to protect their private machinations.

Cox, Louis Anthony (Tony) (2008) **What's wrong with risk matrices?**, *Risk Analysis*, **28** (2)
- [DR, F, RM]: Why users of conventional, econometric risk tools (including HM Government) missed warning signs of an approaching financial crisis.

De Becker, Gavin (2000) *The Gift of Fear: Survival signals that protect us from violence*, Bloomsbury
- [P]: How our intuition gives us the best early warnings of misbehaviour, in many forms – if we know how to recognize them.

Dobelli, Rolf (2014) *The Art of Thinking Clearly: Better thinking, better decisions*, Sceptre
- [**, P]: A million-seller, for a good reason: it's hugely readable, and a fine primer on bias effects. Hundreds of real-life examples; many cheerful, some hair-raising.

Financial Conduct Authority (Annual, 2013 onwards) *Risk Outlook* (www.fca.org)
- [BE, DR]: Once a year, the British conduct regulator digests the research material they think will inform their future enforcement agenda, and shares this thinking with the rest of us. Not necessarily a sound predictor of the regulator's future focus (independent 'global taxonomy' research is more precise), but a good general steer as to what they're thinking about, at least.

Fischhoff, Baruch, Slovic, Paul, Lichtenstein, Sarah, Read, Stephen and Combs, Barbara (1978)
How safe is safe enough? A psychometric study of attitudes towards technological risks and benefits, *Policy Sciences*, **9**
- [P, DR]: How ordinary people make up their minds about whether to tolerate a risk. What makes the public expect the authorities to protect them from any given risk?

Gladwell, Malcolm (2000) *The Tipping Point*, Little, Brown, New York
- [P]: Where does public opinion come from, accepting or rejecting various forms of behaviour? How come certain 'outlier' ideas suddenly go mainstream? Many anecdotes.

Gray, J L and Starke, F A (1998) *Organizational Behavior: Concepts and applications*, MacMillan, London
- [OB]: Why do such different cultures prevail in public and private sectors? What accounts for the difference between the published version of the management structure and 'what actually happens'?

Hutter, Bridget (2005) *'Ways of Seeing': Understandings of risk in organizational settings* in Hutter and Power (ed) *Organizational Encounters with Risk*, Cambridge University Press
- [RM]: How the professions love to cut risk management up into mutually exclusive territories (silos).

Janis, Irving L (1972/1982) *Groupthink: Psychological studies of policy decisions and fiascoes*, Houghton Mifflin, New York
- [OB, P]: Why elite groups delude themselves that 'they know best what's good for the rest of us'; various catastrophes following from this belief.

Kahneman, Daniel H (2011) *Thinking, Fast and Slow*, Allen Lane
- [**, BE, P]: Nobel laureate originator of modern behavioural economics considers why we often don't judge risky situations well, as we 'overestimate how much we understand'. By acknowledging the 'two selves' within our brains, we can compensate for the flaws in our cognition of risk.

Kasperson, Jeanne X and Kasperson, Roger E (2005) **Social amplification of risk theory – a retrospective**, *The Social Contours of Risk*, **1**, Earthscan, London
- [P, RM]: A learned review of scientific progress in understanding how news and social media, and others, induce an exaggerated public view of actual risks.

Kasperson, R, Renn, O, Slovic, P, and others (1988) **The social amplification of risk: A conceptual framework**, *Risk Analysis*, **8**
- [P]: Why do people overreact to information about minor risks and ignore other more significant ones?

King, Anthony and Crewe, Ivor (2014) *The Blunders of Our Governments*, Oneworld
- [DR]: Two veteran political scientists take apart the major public policy misfires of the past generation – by all different shades of government – and the catastrophic cost of these to taxpayers. A serious warning about how bias in policymaking leads to dogmatic, expensive mistakes. Explains one origin of the current stubbornly low levels of public trust in politicians.

Kletz, Trevor (1993/2001) *Learning from Accidents*, Institution of
Chemical Engineers, London and Rugby
- [**, DR]: A distinguished engineer reviews his career of troubleshooting,
  with many practical lessons for resilience. How trivial inputs may
  combine to produce catastrophic outcomes.

Lanchester, John (2010) *Whoops!: Why everyone owes everyone and
no one can pay*, Penguin
- [**, F]: The most readable, humane and thoughtful account of what
  actually happened in the banking crash of 2008.

Lewis, Michael (2011) *Boomerang: The disaster tour*, Allen Lane
Lewis, Michael (2012) *The Big Short*, Penguin
- [**, F]: Two pacy and highly informed accounts of mid-2000s financial
  crashes: the euro currency crisis, and the market collapse brought on by
  over-selling of mortgage derivatives.

March, James G, Cohen, M and Olsen, J (1972) **A garbage can model of
organizational choice**, *Administrative Science Quarterly*, **17** (1)
- [OB]: What are organizations trying to do? High-end academic analysis
  suggests, cynically, that many of them seem to exist only to 'pass the
  time'.

Margolis, Howard (1996) *Dealing with Risk: Why the public and experts
disagree*, University of Chicago Press
- [DR, P]: Why experts and the public disagree about the severity of risks;
  how policymakers (and regulators) should set about dealing with this
  conflict of viewpoints.

McCormick, Roger, Stears, Christopher and Duarte, Tania (2016) *The
Conduct Costs Project*, LSE-Cambridge University-CCP Research
(conductcosts.ccpresearchfoundation.com)
- [DR, F]: An unsparing study of the catastrophic (and often self-inflicted)
  cost impact of conduct enforcements in the financial sector, since the
  arrival of behaviour-based regulation in 2013. For example: for three
  years (2013–16), *all* of the capital raised by major banks in the UK was
  expended on costs relating to conduct enforcements. It's a tragic tale of
  wasted resources that could have been far better directed, such as into
  the pro-social activity of lending to support growing businesses.

McGoey, Linsey (2007) **On the will to ignorance in bureaucracy,** *Economy and Society*, **36** (2)
- [OB, DR]: Challenging study of risk control strategies and political 'spin'. How senior managers and regulators evade blame for failure by designing deniability ('ignorant spaces') into their own processes for risk control and reporting.

McKay, Charles (1841, republished 1996) *Extraordinary Popular Delusions and the Madness of Crowds*, Harvard University/John Wiley & Sons, New York
- [F, P]: The Victorian editor of the *Illustrated London News* looks at the history of mass hysteria, including market bubbles, alchemy, witch-hunting, railway mania and other outbreaks of public craziness. It's not a scientific analysis, but a shrewd social study of behaviour. Fun to read – and nearly two centuries ahead of its time.

McRaney, David (2012) *You Are Not So Smart*, Oneworld
- [**, P]: Cheerful blog-sized tour of biases and other faultlines in human understanding. How to recognize and overcome delusions, in yourself and others. Accessible, grounded in good science, and often funny – a great place to start if you were finding the whole idea of behavioural science just a bit daunting. Cognitive psychology, without any boring bits.

Merton, Robert K (1936) **The unanticipated consequences of purposive social action,** *American Sociological Review*, **1** (6)
- [DR]: Why controls and policies often don't work according to plan.

National Audit Office, UK (2016) *Financial Services Mis-selling: Regulation and redress* (nao.org.uk)
- [DR, F]: The joy of democracy: One public body here questions the efficacy of another, as the British public auditor asks whether 'behavioural' regulation is really what conduct enforcement is all about. Do regulatees actually behave any better, since conduct regulation came in? Maybe not, it seems. Deflates some of the political hype over BE.

Perrow, Charles (1984, revised 1999) *Normal Accidents: Living with high-risk technologies*, Princeton University Press
- [DR]: Why it's impossible to design a failure-proof system. We should accept this and expect modern, close-coupled control systems to fail – sometimes catastrophically. Here's what we should then do, given that starting point.

Rolt, L T C (Tom) (1955, updated 1982) *Red for Danger*, David & Charles
- [DR]: A classic social history of how we make sense of risk arising from new technologies, using rail travel as an extended case study. Shows where new regulations come from; usually as a political knee-jerk response to disasters. Finely observed and still topical, with some pithy one-liners. (For example: beware the type of risk manager who 'regards the business of public protection as a mere formality' – one of these accidentally killed Charles Dickens.)

Samson, Alain (Ed), with Miles, Roger (Co-ed) (Annual, from 2014 onwards) *The Behavioral Economics Guide*, LSE (behavioraleconomics. com)
- [**, BE]: Annual digest of the latest thinking in behavioural economics, including a list of definitions of key terms and concepts.

Sandman, P (1987) **Risk communication: Facing public outrage**, *EPA Journal*, **13** (90)
- [P]: A (US) regulator's measured response to the angry mob, following toxic emission incidents.

Schlosser, Eric (2014) *Command and Control*, Penguin
- [DR]: What happens when you give fallible human beings the job of keeping safe a stockpile of weapons of mass destruction? Almost armageddon, as it turns out. A documentary that's also a thriller, this is 'among the most nightmarish books ever written', said the critics (as a compliment). Looking at the politics of nuclear weapons safety, and its history of accidents, sheds new light on the modern science of control design. Also maybe a sense of relief that the human race survives at all, after so many human-made catastrophes.

Seddon, John (2008) *Systems Thinking in the Public Sector*, Triarchy
- [RD]: A public servant questions whether pro-forma 'rational' rulemaking isn't always doomed to fail. Many examples of the demotivating, wasteful and sometimes tragic consequences of trying to regulate humans as if they were machines.

Sheedy, E and Griffin, B (2015) *Risk Governance, Cultures, Structures and Behaviour*, McQuarie University
- [RD]: A serious challenge to the new generation of financial regulators, opening up a fresh view of which behavioural factors really matter.

Explodes several lazy assumptions that financial regulators had come to rely on too heavily – such as the power of 'tone at the top'.

Slovic, Paul, with Finucane, S, Peters, E and MacGregor, D (2004) **Risk as analysis and risk as feelings: Some thoughts about affect, reason, risk and rationality**, *Risk Analysis*, **24** (2)
- [P, RM]: This paper marked a sea-change in the outlook of academic risk analysts. We now seek to include 'affect' (emotion, mood, intuitive) aspects of decision-making; we're less convinced now about the 'rational actor' analysis so beloved of public policymakers in days gone by.

Smith, Peter (1995) **On the unintended consequences of publishing performance data in the public sector**, *International Journal of Public Administration*, **18**
- [DR, OB]: Why and how groups respond perversely to target-based control interventions.

Sunstein, Cass and Thaler, Richard (2009) *Nudge: Improving decisions about health, wealth and happiness*, Penguin
- [**, BE, P]: Governments can cost-effectively get people to 'do the right thing', by redesigning how decisions are presented.

Sykes, G and Matza, D (1957) **Techniques of neutralization: A theory of delinquency**, *American Sociological Review*, **22** (6)
- [**, P]: Wrongdoers use various arguments to justify (to themselves) their bad behaviour towards other people. A classic, 'grandfather' paper that's still well worth reading.

Tenner, Edward (1997) *Why Things Bite Back: Technology and the revenge of unintended consequences*, Random House, New York
- [RM]: Be careful what technologies you wish for: check for the sting in the tail of every innovation.

Thaler, Richard H (2015) *Misbehaving: The making of behavioural economics*, Allen Lane
- [BE, OB, P]: A genial account of why 'BE' came to matter as the failings of classical economics were found to have contributed to catastrophic problems. One of the leading thinkers behind the new science, Thaler introduces the others – including the great Daniel Kahneman, who called him 'lazy', which turned out to be a compliment. Find out why.

Toft, Brian (1996) **Limits to the mathematical modelling of disasters** in Hood and Jones (Eds) *Accident and Design: Contemporary debates in risk management*, UCL/Routledge, London
- [RM]: Don't let statistics fool you into thinking you have a resilient system in place. Rather than rely on numbers and models, observe people's behaviour directly.

Vaughan, Diane (1996) *The Challenger Launch Decision: Risky technology, culture and deviance at NASA*, University of Chicago Press
- [DR, OB, P, RM]: How failures of culture and control destroyed a manned spaceship in flight. A masterful analysis, showing how a work ethic of 'normalizing' misbehaviour, including (here) the faking of risk reports, leads to a tragic outcome.

Vaughan, Diane (1999) **The dark side of organizations: Mistake, misconduct and disaster**, *Annual Review of Sociology*, **25**
- [DR, OB]: How misconduct 'trickles down' from management into the workforce, undermining value and resilience.

Viscusi, W Kip (1992) *Fatal Tradeoffs: Public and private responsibilities for risk*, Oxford University Press
- [OB, RM]: How staff tend to make up their own minds about whether to follow instructions.

Weick, Karl E (1993) **The collapse of sensemaking in organizations: The Mann Gulch disaster**, *Administrative Science Quarterly*, **38**
- [**, DR, OB, P]: How a few individuals' perception of a risk may disrupt a whole organization's plans for risk control, with terrible consequences: what happened when staff under stress fatally misinterpreted instructions.

Weick, Karl E (1995) *Sensemaking in Organizations*, Sage, London
- [DR, OB, P]: How control officers react to off-the-scale risk events: in times of crisis, the cognitive signals we're getting tend to conflict with rulebooks; what can we do about this? The value of acknowledging and working with front-line managers' intuition – and how this may go awry if it is not properly managed.

Zimbardo, Philip (2007) **Investigating social dynamics**, chapter in *The Lucifer Effect*, Random House, London
- [OB, P]: How a small group of 'gamers' can contaminate larger, well-behaved groups.

INDEX

Note: The index is filed in alphabetical, word-by-word order. Within main headings, numbers and the prefix 'Mc' are filed as spelt out in full and acronyms filed as presented. Page locators in *italics* denote information contained within a Figure or Table.

CPSIA information can be obtained
at www.ICGtesting.com
Printed in the USA
LVOW01s1438020317
525946LV00011B/81/P